ACCLAIM FOR

GOING DOWNTOWN

"*GOING DOWNT...* ...n the U.S. Air Force's ... Broughton's office ... ...of an F-105, and he saw the daily human cost. . . . He takes you downtown—to Hanoi, the most heavily defended city on the planet. He makes you watch as the flak and SAMs smash planes and kill your brothers. . . . Read this book. It's the Vietnam experience in 300 pages."

—Stephen Coonts, author of *Flight of the Intruder*

"Gripping reading. . . . Broughton's experiences were hair-raising."

—*Atlanta Journal & Constitution*

"His writing, like his flying, is aggressive and laced with devastating attacks. . . ."

—*Washington Times*

"Col. Jack Broughton is truly a hero. . . . Men asked to do the impossible and die valorously is the real tragedy of *GOING DOWNTOWN.*"

—*The Daily Oklahoman*

"Broughton's prose brings to life the courage, skill, and fear present in cockpits in wartime. . . . For its accurate depiction of combat, I recommend Colonel Broughton's book to those who flew in Vietnam and to those who never had the experience. . . . [*GOING DOWNTOWN* includes] timeless lessons on the conduct of war."

—John McCain, U.S. Senator, *Proceedings*

"*GOING DOWNTOWN* will join *Thud Ridge* as a military history classic."

—*Marine Corps Gazette*

A Dual Main Selection of the Military Book Club

GOING DOWNTOWN

THE WAR AGAINST HANOI AND WASHINGTON

JACK BROUGHTON

Foreword by TOM WOLFE

POCKET BOOKS

New York   London   Toronto   Sydney   Tokyo   Singapore

POCKET BOOKS, a division of Simon & Schuster Inc.
1230 Avenue of the Americas, New York, NY 10020

Copyright © 1988 by Jack Broughton
Cover art copyright © 1990 Drew Blair

Published by arrangement with Orion Books/Crown Publishers, Inc.
Library of Congress Catalog Card Number: 88-1250

ISBN 0-671-67862-0

First Pocket Books printing February 1990

10 9 8 7 6 5 4 3 2 1

POCKET and colophon are registered trademarks of
Simon & Schuster Inc.

Printed in the U.S.A.

To Our Comrades Up North

I regret to say that after twenty years I must still raise the fighter pilot's toast to those we lost and to those who have yet to be accounted for. I especially honor their families.

I also extend many thanks to my friend and coach Harold Livingston

CONTENTS

FOREWORD

by Tom Wolfe

It was in 1969, when the press was full of stories of poor morale among American combat forces in Vietnam, that I came across Jack Broughton's first book, *Thud Ridge*. It was the most astonishing account of the war I had ever read. Broughton had led a wing of Air Force F-105 fighter bombers that went "Downtown," to borrow the slang of the book before you. Operating out of bases in Thailand, they attacked Hanoi, Haiphong, and other North Vietnamese targets. Day after day they ran into surface-to-air missiles and concentrations of computer-aimed 37-, 57-, and 85-mm cannon fire as fierce as the flak around Berlin and Merseburg in World War II. American air losses over North Vietnam became, in Broughton's own words, "astronomical and unacceptable." Yet without being aware of it, Broughton and his fellow fighter jocks (as they called themselves) looked at the war like knights in the age of chivalry did half a millennium ago.

Everyone, friend or foe, was judged by four standards: courage, skill, coolness, and eagerness for combat. Contempt was rarely directed at the enemy. It was reserved for one's own comrades who funked it, ran for cover in combat, "crapped out," in the fighter-jock parlance Broughton uses in *Going Downtown*. The fighter jocks routinely upped the odds by volunteering for hazardous missions, even in the face

ix

of extraordinary restrictions imposed by the White House and the Defense Department, and by Lyndon and Robert, Broughton's names—contemptuous, you can be sure—for the president and the secretary of defense in the late 1960s. The pilots could bomb Haiphong harbor but not if a non-Vietnamese ship was in port. ("And they've got a neutral ship welded to the dock," quoth the jocks.) They could bomb a surface-to-air missile base, but only if it was operational (which it had to prove by firing at you).

The nation at large didn't have a look at the fighter-jock fraternity until the North Vietnamese began releasing prisoners of war in 1973. Practically all were pilots whose planes had been shot down over the North by ground fire. I vividly remember the scenes as they came down the stairs from the transports returning them to the United States. They saluted their welcomers and thanked the commander-in-chief, Richard Nixon, for the opportunity to serve their country in battle. The citizenry stared at them, nonplussed. The press was at that moment positively awash with stories of a veterans' neurasthenia, known as the Vietnam syndrome. The liberated fighter jocks seemed like creatures from out of a time warp, commissioned van Winkles waking up from a 1945 cryogenic freeze. Jack Broughton's literary talent is in his ability to make the jocks' mental atmosphere not only real but logical.

I have my own literary debt to Jack Broughton. His words were among the first to indicate to me the fact that such a fraternity did, indeed, exist and that it had an unspoken but rigid set of beliefs, which, by and by, I called the "code of the right stuff."

Toward the end of *Going Downtown*, one of Broughton's fellow pilots, Jerry Hoblit, says of his backseater: "We had matching personalities, we were both overly aggressive, both of us thought we were bulletproof, and we probably had the total maturity of a nineteen-year-old between the two of us. We were both dedicated to being soldiers who knew this was our one war, and we wanted to make the very best of it. As I reflect, if it had not been for the very excellent way we lived it, we both would have died trying." To which Broughton says: "The fighter pilot ranks are still full of people like that. Cultivate them well, America; you just might need them."

His angry charge in this book is that America wasted them shamefully in Vietnam by not letting them fight *hard enough*. He names names, from Lyndon and Robert on down the line. But I will let Jack Broughton go into that in his own words, which even now, two decades later, have the freshness, the vigor, the compelling candor of the young man who with such relish used to go Downtown.

INTRODUCTION: DOWNTOWN

This story is about the unique war of the Thuds versus Hanoi. Going Downtown we called it. Going Downtown against the fiercest array of defenses ever assembled in history. It is the story of the real air war of Southeast Asia, of the Republic F-105 Thunderchief, which we called the Thud, and the pilots, the Thud drivers I knew during the period from 1964 to 1967. They were there from the very start and, along with their navy fighter pilot buddies, they were there all the way, every day.

There were many wars going on in Southeast Asia. There were masses of dedicated people committed to each of those wars, and each of those wars was different. This is not about the will-o'-the-wisp war of the valiant ground soldier fighting the invisible determination of the North that took such a terrible toll of wasted lives. It is not about the air war of those who flew down South, nor is it about the logistics support war that stretched for endless miles. It is not about the spooky war in support of mysterious code names and ill-defined efforts that tried to do everything from changing the breeding habits of oriental animals and people to stripping the leaves and ferns from massive two-hundred-foot trees. It is very definitely not about the bureaucratic headquarters war of paper empires and obstructionists. It's about going Downtown, which was the mission that we lived for or died for.

One might assume that the objective of our effort in Southeast Asia was to hurt Ho Chi Minh, and thus make him responsive to our wishes; to force him to do or not do the things we considered to be in our national interest. One might assume that the most efficient manner to hurt Ho and curtail hostilities was to beat up his capital city and the few targets of significance and national pride that surrounded the heartland of North Vietnam. It didn't always come out that way, but that was the Thud's mission.

The Thuds took the war north to Hanoi. Thud drivers considered any other task or involvement to be of little stature. The Thuds were there for one reason and their crews were dedicated to one mission: to strike Hanoi and attempt to convince the North Vietnamese to cease fighting in the South.

At first we didn't know how tough the North would be if we let them run the show by their rules and if we played real war with less than real determination. Those of us who fought there learned in a hurry; those who controlled us from Washington never learned. The day-to-day diplomatic games between Saigon and Washington were a mere smokescreen. The only force that truly hurt Ho by striking repeatedly in his backyard, whenever the self-imposed limitations that were designed to put a choke hold on our effectiveness were temporarily relaxed, was the fighter force in general and the Thud in particular.

It was a common cliché that Southeast Asia was a living-room war. Results of carefully selected portions of the war could be reviewed on television nightly by the world, much as an instant replay in a sporting event—a brutal sporting event at best. It was not so with the war over Hanoi, and that facet of our Indochinese involvement was little known to the vast majority of the world's onlookers. There were no World War II massive bomber forays to allow camera and media access to the North. There were few pictures to show the intense environment that was Hanoi and its environs. True, there were gun camera films from the fighters, but gun camera film does not capture the ferocity or the intensity of battle from a wide view. Gun camera film is a tunnel-vision view of a single aircraft's attack against a particular target, and the camera is activated only in the event that the Thud driver is firing the Vulcan cannon mounted in the nose of his aircraft. It is a small field of view in isolation. Only those of us who were there, who went Downtown as regularly as we ate and slept, could describe the awesome display of the Hanoi environment.

This was a war of fatal oversupervision. President Lyndon Johnson said it all with, "Those boys can't hit an outhouse without my permission." The oversupervision was fatal because we repeatedly killed dedicated professional air officers and lost expensive and irreplaceable aircraft because of the maze of restrictions imposed upon those of us assigned the task of fighting in a nearly impossible situation. The entire effort was top-heavy with headquarters, supervisors, planners, and those who lived under the illusion that they were supervising and planning. The effort was run from the White House, through multiple layers of overlapping headquarters and staffs. They were in reality simply conduits of a no-win philosophy to the only action agencies physically striking Hanoi and the far north: two F-105 fighter wings, the navy strike forces, the F-4 fighter wings—and their commanders.

A normally accepted statistic is that in any combat operation, only 1 percent of the assembled forces are actually involved in the shooting. In Indochina, the excess of make-believe command functions drove that number well below 1 percent.

Fighter wing commanders and their key people were on the end of a ten-thousand mile sharpened stick. Their job was to lead and translate often conflicting directives into targets destroyed, while trying to preserve their aircraft and aircrews. The desired results should have been as simple to define as ordnance on target. It was, however, not a matter of simple definition. Everyone who had an opportunity to reach for that ten-thousand-mile stick seemed to feel an obligation to shake it, whether from good intent or from a desire for personal aggrandizement.

The good wing commanders went Downtown with their

troops. Politicians and generals didn't go Downtown. Their staff members didn't go Downtown, and the civilian bean counters with the shiny loafers didn't even know where Downtown was. They had no idea what Hanoi was all about. Lack of direct participation was a job-determined fact of life and in itself could not be considered an overriding flaw. But it was a tragic flaw that a majority of those tweaking the ten-thousand-mile stick, whether military or civilian, were ill informed. They were not knowledgeable of the area or the defenses, nor were they knowledgeable of our own equipment, tactics, and potential. The supreme flaw of the effort against Hanoi was that a large majority of those in control would not listen to those who were doing the fighting. They did not want to believe what those on the scene knew to be the life and death facts of aerial warfare and mission accomplishment.

Never in the history of warfare have so many high-level supervisors been so involved in a massive campaign of not making waves. Some meant well, but their efforts were often clumsy or overruled. Some thrived in an environment of outright disrespect and arrogance directed at those dedicated to the demanding chore of attacking Hanoi. Regardless of the personalities or intentions of the individuals involved, the result was that the men on the end of the stick were constantly harassed and bothered in their pursuit of successfully completing an already extremely difficult task. No credence was given to the premise that you give an operational commander a job to do and then allow him to do that job.

And did all of this matter to the Thud drivers when the boss rang the bell? No way. Dave Groark, who was one of the first ones to deploy down there from Japan with his Thud squadron and who flew on the first Barrel Roll mission into Laos, tells it like it was for the fighter jocks: "When they told us that our country needed us to go fight a war and do the things we had trained for many years to do, we didn't know how to complain, even if we had wanted to. You enjoyed the fact that you were getting out there and getting a combat mission and you didn't care what they hung on the airplane. You figured that you'd be smart enough to find some sort of target where you could do some good. There was a war on and we were eager to do our job.''

While the scenario was well known to even the most junior of the pilots, it all meant nothing when they and their commanders strapped that Thud to their backside and launched. It only took a couple of trips Downtown to realize that we had met the enemy and he was us. It only took one searing mental snapshot of a comrade and his aircraft turned to a golden blob of flame by missiles, flak, or Migs striking from a Washington-designated "sanctuary" to convince him that his ass really did belong to Uncle, and in this one, Uncle wasn't very concerned about it.

The realism of the demands of the mission and the fallacy of Washington's graduated response only served to drive the Thud drivers closer together and to increase their dedication to perform in a superior manner. The fighter jocks squabbled among themselves for a spot on the toughest missions. They reveled in being the elite knights of the airborne round table of Downtown Hanoi. This book is about who they were, how they got there, how they looked at the rest of the world, and how they did what nobody else could do.

1 | GETTING READY

What we knew as North and South Vietnam were once parts of the Indochinese Empire that the French had ruled for a hundred years before the start of World War II. The Japanese moved rapidly to take control of the entire Southeast Asian area, and they remained dominant until the conclusion of that war. The Japanese seizure of Southeast Asia coincided with the emergence of an individual known as Ho Chi Minh, who was to be one of the dominant figures in the scenes that would unfold in the decades ahead.

Our fighter pilot legend has the town of Yen Bai, located to the west of Hanoi, as the place where Ho grew up. Actually, he grew up and went to school in many places, so it may be fair to assume that Yen Bai was one of them. Throughout our air war, Yen Bai held little of military or economic significance, yet it was fiercely defended. As we herded our Thuds north to enter the Hanoi area we usually skirted just to the north of Yen Bai and the mere appearance of Thuds near the town's periphery brought forth intense antiaircraft fire. Though intense, the ground fire never appeared well directed or accurate. It seemed to be directed vertically upward over the center of the village. Thud drivers rationalized that the reason the gunners of Yen Bai were so mean was that they shot straight up in the air and were repeatedly showered by their own rounds. For sure, they made plenty of noise in honor of Ho.

When Ho was nine years old he was carrying messages for his father's network of anti-French conspirators. As a young man he went to Saigon in 1911 for a three-month crash course in pastry cooking, hopped a freighter, and parlayed his cooking skills into jobs as pastry chef in plush Paris and London hotels. He went to America and lived for a time in Harlem until 1917. Back in France, as a photo retouching expert, he became very impressed with President Wilson's Fourteen Point Program for peace and saw those points as a way to independence for colonial nations. Bernard Fall reported that Ho borrowed suitable clothes and haunted the halls of the Palace of Versailles in the hopes of speaking to Wilson or other dignitaries, but they didn't have time for him.

In 1920 he became a founding member of the French Communist Party, and by 1922 he was traveling to the Soviet Union and other parts of Europe, establishing himself as the colonial expert of the entire communist movement. Despite his travels and foreign affiliations, his main interests remained anti-imperialism and anticolonialism in Vietnam.

When he arrived back in the Orient he did not find a warm welcome, and he quickly managed to alienate the colonial authorities in China, Hong Kong, and Indochina, and in rapid succession found himself spending a lot of time in their respective jails. In 1940, though all U.S. sources denied it, the United States apparently exerted its influence with Generalissimo Chiang Kai-shek and had him released from jail, on the grounds that his services were of value in the war effort against the Japanese.

Ho linked up with the American intelligence forces working out of Southern China, and when his forces finally took over Hanoi he was highly regarded by American authorities and apparently their choice as a leader in the area. He had been effective against the Japanese, and the Americans involved were lavish in their praise for Ho's determination and leadership, but the praise was later lost in a wave of political expediency. The allies were willing to return Indochina to its former Western rulers, the French. The allies even reached back into the ancient chain of Indochinese royalty and formally established Bao-Dai as head of an inefficient state composed of rival feudal sects posing under the banners of religious entities. Leadership was nonexistent, which suited French purposes, and the arrangement was doomed from its inception.

If Washington had exerted the same degree of anticolonial pressure on France that it had on the Dutch in Indonesia, it could have resulted in a completely different situation. From a point of pure conjecture, Ho could well have become no more bothersome than an oriental Tito. But despite his frustrations, Ho was smart enough not to show the hand of a full belligerent at that early stage, as that would have forced him to confront what probably would have been a strong American and French combined stand.

The United States compounded its mistake in junking the warm relationships of 1945-46 that had existed with Ho Chi Minh's Democratic Republic of Vietnam by reversing a firm policy that forbade France to use U.S.-supplied military equipment in Indochina. Even before the Korean War was a reality, the United States had done a complete about-face and fully supported France against Ho. The result was easily predictable; the First Indochinese War was fully engaged.

Southeast Asia was changing, but so was American air power. The jet age had become reality. In late 1944 the first sightings of operational Luftwaffe Messerschmidt ME-262 twin-jet fighters over Europe had come as a surprise to American pilots, and the strange machines were viewed with both curiosity and respect. They were real jet fighters and they were in combat. The days of prop-driven dominance were on the decline, even though the emergence of the German jets proved to be too little and too late to be of significance in World War II.

The U.S. Bell P-59 Airacomet first flew at Edwards Air Force Base on October 2, 1942, with its underpowered jet engines heralding an initial American venture into the jet age. The Airacomet was far from a hot item. Perhaps all that could be expected was a learning process and a demonstration of basics, such as the fact that jets don't accelerate and take off like prop jobs and that if you jam the throttle forward you can expect to get that new sensation called flameout. That's about all we got, and the P-59 was never in the same league as the ME-262.

It remained for the Lockheed P-80 Shooting Star to make the initial meaningful breakthrough into the jet fighter business. In late 1943 that vehicle was only a drawing-board item. Perhaps spurred by intelligence reports on the German effort and most certainly spurred by the fanatical determination of the American aircraft industry of that period to accomplish the impossible immediately, that drawing-board image was a flying P-80 aircraft just 132 days later. Only the almost instantaneous creation of the North American Aircraft P-51 at the start of World War II could equal that accomplishment. Even a casual observer is qualified to note that they don't make 'em like that anymore. Coast-to-coast times shrunk as the 80 hummed along at an amazing 582 miles per hour, and a climb to 39,000 feet was not too much to expect from this new bird. The production line closed down in 1950 after six and a half years of successful effort that resulted in 1,732 real, live jet fighters.

I helped reopen the gunnery program at Nellis Air Force Base in Las Vegas, Nevada, during the 1949-50 period, and our fighter gunnery school had A, B, and C models of the 80. The Cs were the Cadillacs of the fleet with lots of good things to make the job easier, like more power, ejection seats, and improved fuel controls. They were the ones we were to use later in Korea. The B was a limited-edition hybrid but the A was the fun machine. If the C was a Cadillac, then the A was a 1934 Ford roadster with wire wheels and a rumble seat. She was small, the cockpit was tight, and when you manually cranked that canopy closed and locked yourself in, there was no doubt that you and that bird were one. She flew the same way, like she was part of your mind and body.

My favorite was 059, the shiniest 80 on the whole line.

Corporal Wilson was her crewchief and he was so proud of that bird he bubbled. The only time she was out of commission was when we had to put her down for something like a hundred-hour inspection and she would get through things like that in record time. I was instructing in gunnery and some days I'd make three trips to the range and back in 059 and I could shoot with the best of them. One of our mutually happiest days was when Wilson got his third stripe and became a buck sergeant. That was a big deal back in those days. Nowadays the titles have changed and it seems like everyone is at least a sergeant by the time they get out of basic training.

The A models were pretty tired before we ever went to Korea and I got to be part of one of their last rides. I was in the dive-bombing pattern with my three students as we went round and round making runs with out two-pound practice bombs with shotgun-type charges in them to spot our hits. We had lost some A models recently and nobody knew why— they just went uncontrollable and pranged. Since we didn't have ejection seats in the A, none of the pilots had managed to get out of their aircraft and the cause of the problems was bugging everyone.

I was just rolling in on my dive on the target, a wooden shack in the center of a big scratched-out circle on the Nevada desert floor, as Ron Bliss, my number-four man, dropped a bomb and started to pull off the target straight ahead. His nose didn't come up as it should have. He mumbled something on the radio that indicated big problems and started staggering across the desert, way too close to the ground. I aborted my pass and rammed the throttle forward, and since I had several thousand feet of altitude on him, it was not too much of a problem to get right on his tail. There was no doubt that his aircraft was about to become part of the cactus and I kept telling him to get out.

He had the same idea, but getting out was easier said than done. You were supposed to turn a crank to crack that manual canopy open an inch or two, then pull another handle to release it. He couldn't get the dumb thing to move. He had no choice but to unbuckle his harness and get his feet up underneath his seat so he could beat on the canopy with his head, shoulders, and back, while he kept pulling the release lever.

As I closed on him I had my doubts that he could stay airborne long enough to get out, but the thing that really caught my attention was his horizontal tail surface. The outboard three feet on each side were bent ninety degrees and were standing straight up instead of lying flat. His rear end looked like the triple vertical fin on a C-121 and there was no way that dude was going to fly right. Suddenly the canopy flew off from the internal beating he was giving it, roughing him up in the process, and I kept trying to calmly urge him to hurry up and crawl out. With his legs doubled up underneath him he finally kicked upward as hard as he could, banged against the canopy rail and windscreen, pulled the ripcord on his chute, and somersaulted through the slipstream to clear that triple fin by inches.

He was only a couple of hundred feet above the dry lake when he left, but since he had pulled the ripcord before he cleared the aircraft his chute started to blossom while he was still traveling forward with the velocity of the aircraft, parallel to the ground. The aircraft nose rolled left and down, hit the ground and exploded while he swung ninety degrees under the blossoming chute and hit the ground hard, knocked out. The wind was blowing about thirty miles an hour and it kept that chute canopy full as it pulled him face down along the rocks, sand, and cactus of the desert. He was out cold and he never wiggled; he just slid along that terrible abrasive surface for three full miles. The canopy finally snagged on a big Joshua tree and collapsed, but as he ground to a crumpled stop there was still no movement.

My number three man had been relaying the details on the radio to the range officer and he had the beat-up range truck and the old ambulance bouncing across the desert in Ron's direction. We didn't have very long legs on those A models and since I was hurting for fuel I had to head for the base with some real doubts about Ron's survival. By the time I landed and crawled out of my aircraft, the range troops had reached him, found him alive, and were headed for the hospital. Our Base Commander, Colonel Joe Mason, was there to meet me and we went to our base hospital to intercept Ron's wife, who was just about to have a baby. We assured her that he was busted up, sandpapered raw, but recoverable, then we headed back for the flight line to try and figure out what had caused that tail section to fail.

Ron made it okay and the last I heard of him he was back on flying status and in combat. The A models didn't make it. With my description of what I had seen and with what the Lockheed engineers could dig out of the aircraft debris, they realized the horizontal tail on all the A models needed major modifications to overcome structural fatigue if the A models were to stay in service. It wasn't worth it, and that was all for a series of real fun fighters.

While fighter pilots love to reminisce about good birds and cuss the poor ones, they never waste much time talking about old airplanes if there are some good new ones in the offing. The C model 80s were healthy and ready to fight in the budding Korean War, so we knew that there was good flying in store there. The newest additions to the inventory were also becoming available as the Republic F-84 Thunderjets and the North American F-86 Sabres joined the operational force. Republic and North American made their birds from different molds. It was simple, the 84 was like the World War II P-47 Jug—heavy, not a tight turner, but smooth and tough. The 86 was like the P-51 Mustang—light, easy to handle, and capable of excellent maneuverability.

The 86 was great from day one and I never met a pilot who had flown one who was not an immediate fan of our first swept-wing fighter. They were zippy, they did just what you wanted them to do, and they were ready to go to Antung and wax the Migs the day the first one rolled off the assembly line. Their capabilities increased as the newer models appeared, and if the fighter jock of the day had any lingering regrets about the 86, they were that the later models didn't arrive sooner and that the budget didn't allow for more of them.

I was in Chicago, getting ready to fly an F-80 back to our base in Las Vegas, when I heard the news that the North

Koreans had invaded South Korea. I spent most of that flight spinning the dial on my radio compass from station to station in search of more detailed news. It was clear that the F-80 squadrons in the Pacific were already involved in jet combat, and I was anxious. I wanted to be part of that combat.

By the time I got back to the base things were already starting to happen, and the transition that took place in our fighter program during the last half of 1950 was sensational. The base had been home to our fighter gunnery instructor program as well as a P-51 training program. Within a few weeks those old programs exploded, as pilots of widely divergent levels of qualification poured in from both the active and reserve units. Additional aircraft showed up from all over the world, and we were in a rush program to train fighter pilots for deployment to Korea.

All of our military forces had been cut back too severely as economy dominated readiness after World War II. Suddenly we needed fighter pilots in Korea, but it was alarmingly clear that there were very few of us who were current and proficient in P-51 combat maneuvering and weapons delivery, fewer still who had a reasonable level of jet fighter experience, and only a small number of us who were well qualified in jet fighter bombing and gunnery.

Those of us who were instructing at Nellis were told in no uncertain terms that we were to turn those statistics around in a matter of a few weeks. At times the pace was awesome, but the sheer joy of fun flying produced a widespread high among us. The first replacements were on their way before the end of the year, and I managed to have my name included on the orders moving that group of pilots to Korea.

Even casual monitoring of the news during that frantic last half of 1950 told us that things were going poorly for the French in Vietnam and that President Truman, rationalizing that he was protecting Japan against communist aggression, had increased aid to the bogged-down French effort. But our job was to fly, sleep, and eat fighter tactics for Korea. Hanoi didn't mean much to us. We occasionally wondered what the French were doing in Vietnam and whether we as individuals would get involved in a shooting war down there, but we didn't know or care a lot about Ho Chi Minh or his long-term plans.

Most of 1951 was a glorious swirl of Korean jet fighter combat that completely captured and held all of us. It was ultimately demanding, and since we were still a relatively small group the losses hurt bitterly, but the challenges seemed very personal and they never slowed or paused. Then suddenly, almost without warning, I became aware that what had sometimes seemed like an insurmountable goal of one hundred missions was behind me. My F-80 Cs were now old, tired aircraft being phased out of combat. The euphoria of the past eighteen months of my kind of flying was fading.

I was a bit sweatier and a little more tired than usual when I touched down from what was officially the last combat mission of the F-80. I felt dejected by the time I taxied my trusty yellow-nosed bird off the pierced-plank runway onto the dirt in front of my home away from home. My crewchief guided me with hand signals as I moved slowly through the swirling dust in front of the tent city that was the maintenance and operations complex of our Eighth Fighter Squadron. He gave me the hand slash across the throat and I shut her down for the last time. The F-80's tour of duty was over.

Crewchiefs are usually gutsy guys. It had only been a couple of months ago that our crewchiefs and some unknown air police troop had saved my neck. The snow and mud were still there as they got our aircraft ready for a predawn takeoff. All of a sudden, in the black of 3:00 A.M. there was a North Korean infiltrator trying to stuff a handful of hacksaw blades down the engine intake scoop of my bird. Our guys chased him out into the open and the AP shot him dead. I'll never forget having to detour around the hulk with the maggots crawling out of his belly as I climbed aboard. That's guaranteed to get your attention as well as make you love the guys who help you get there and back.

As I pulled off my oxygen mask and helmet, the unattractive countryside surrounding Taegu came into focus and smell. It didn't look all that bad when you skimmed it at 30,000 feet but it was bad from close up. Matter of fact, the makeshift airfield known as K-2 looked just as bad as it had

101 missions ago, except that I was free to go if I wanted to. Everybody wanted to go, but I was bugged because I hadn't managed to do what I wanted to do. Way back when, when this forsaken piece of land was covered with dirty gray snow and mud, when the North Korean enemy was just across the river on the other end of the runway, I had set out to win this damned war, all by myself if necessary.

The hills were no longer covered with snow—they were brown. Once the snow left, everything was some shade of brown, and did it ever stink. Bob Hope stopped by to do his great thing for us one time and one of our shiny, nonflying public relations lieutenants was assigned to greet him. As Bob stepped off the aircraft he sniffed the air and asked what that horrible smell was. When the lieutenant explained that the Koreans use human fertilizer, Bob replied, "I know that, but what did they do to it?" It was pretty bad, but you sort of got used to it.

The enemy was not on the other side of the river now, but they were only a few hundred miles north on the other side of another river. They were still there and, along with their Russian and Chinese associates, were still giving our troops a bad time every day and every night. They were still there, but a lot of our ground troops weren't around anymore and a lot of our F-80s were gone and a lot of my good buddies weren't around either. We were in a political quagmire and no matter how hard those of us who were pulling the triggers tried, it was a military fiasco. And I had not won the war.

Now that I had earned a ticket home by passing the one hundred mission mark, the other guys were not overjoyed to see my name on the flying schedule. Everybody who had not yet earned their ticket home wanted those flights. Our fighter group was switching aircraft, from the F-80 to the F-84, and the mission I had just flown was the very last one for the F-80s. It had been sort of a courtesy: "Even if the old fart is only a junior captain, let him fly the last one if it's a big thing for him," and it was a big thing for me. I was parked, shut down, and with my previous F-84 experience, probably on my way to the replacement training depot in Itazuke, Japan, destined to check new guys out in the 84 and make them aware of the thrills they could expect upon visiting downtown Pyongyang. Big deal; I hated it.

My crewchief bounced up the ladder with a cheery "How is she, sir?" that jarred me out of that thought pattern. I was telling him that he had the best and prettiest F-80 in the business. We hated to see them go, but they were tired aircraft and we knew it. I scratched a quick "Flight number one okay" in the aircraft Form One, shared a good handshake with my crew, gathered up the other guys in my flight, and headed for debriefing.

You hang your hard hat on the same hook each time and your chute goes into the same bin each time. While much of the routine becomes habit, one thing is always different. Each time you debrief you seem to have found something different about the combat area where you just worked. There's always some new buildup to describe, some new movement of people or equipment to report. The chatter is rapid and full of the tones and excitement that only combat can produce as the returning pilots report: "There's got to be a bunch of troops, right about here . . . and those new tracks must have come from vehicles on this side of those hills." I always figured on getting them the next time I swung that way, but then came that empty feeling again. I didn't get them. I tried hard so many times, but there were still so many of them up there. Now I'm trying to pinpoint them for somebody else's next time. Will somebody remember that I said they were there? Will they get them next trip? Sure they will, but I'd rather do it myself.

That's that. The group's on stand down and the 80s are all through. Tomorrow starts the 84 program for some, but tonight the makeshift mud building that serves as the dining hall and club will ring to the songs and stories of a bunch of keyed-up fighter pilots. To an outsider it will look like mass confusion, but to us it's better than any fancy dress ball. We were always ready for a fight or a frolic and the first yell that "the Old Man's buying" was all it would take. So ends one era and begins another.

If you have never had the experience of waking up in Korea on a sickeningly hot and humid morning with a burning hangover, don't feel bad—it's awful. The air smells of human fertilizer, the flies stick like glue, and the entire world looks as bleak and grim as the barren rice paddies outside the hut window. It's especially grim when you're awakened by a smiling young face advising you that the Old Man, who in this case was the commander of the 49th Fighter Group, wants to see you in his office on the flight line, on the double.

I fought my way out of the ineffectual mosquito net and across the dirt alley to the community bath and washstand. We had rigged up a fifty-five-gallon drum on the ten-foot-high roof and had a small gas engine pump that forced water up and into the barrel, which had a steel trap door on a heavy spring in the bottom. When the barrel was full, the weight of the water would overcome the spring and, ready or not, it would dump fifty-five gallons of cascading water under the wooden eight holer that we shared. As the barrel emptied, the spring took over and slammed the steel trap door closed with a monstrous clang. Bob Hope had remarked that it was the only place where you could get shell shocked and slivers in your behind at the same time. After a tooth brushing in rancid water and a cup of the mess hall's finest acid coffee, I was wide awake and on my way to see what the boss wanted.

As I walked the dusty mile to the flight line I couldn't help staring at the old F-80 parking area. The birds looked proud, but they sure looked strange just sitting there as the troops prepared them for a flight out to who knows where. I knew that they were going to somebody's boneyard or melting pot. So be it, I thought. I wondered if the Old Man was sending me to the repl depl and I sweated it out a little bit more with each step.

The boss was ready to see me and after gritting my teeth and saluting I sat down and waited for I don't know what. We shot the breeze about what each of us had done on yesterday's missions, and he made some nice remarks about my flight doing good work. He knew what he was talking about since our leaders flew with us during that war and took the tough ones right along with the rest of us. Then he leaned forward and told me that he had a project that needed some attention. I figured here comes the replacement depot.

He said we had four brand-new 84s coming in here in a few days to be used on a combat test of a new rocket the Swiss were making. Now I was leaning forward with escalating interest. Washington wanted us to provide the combat test guys for this thing. He said he knew I had finished my regular tour, but he wondered if I would like to sign up for an extension and be the flight leader for that job.

My enthusiastic acceptance drew a knowing smile from the boss. He had a hot thing called Project Swatrock and he had picked me to run it for him and he knew I was happier than I had been in a while. He said that the job was mine and that he would cancel my orders to the repl depl and give me the details in a couple of days. This time my salute had a lot of pep in it and the air almost felt fresh and clean on the walk back. As I walked past the 80s my only thought was that I needed to get my crew moved so they could work on my new 84 for me; I was looking toward the other end of the ramp where the new aircraft would park.

This was a chance to get back on the mission list and bust some of those targets that were still up there taunting us. It was a chance to put a brand-new weapon and a brand-new aircraft to work.

A few days later the details began to trickle down through Far East Air Force Headquarters, then Fifth Air Force, and finally to us. All we had at the moment were pictures and pounds of operating instructions, technical orders, and previous test results, but you can learn a lot from that stuff before you ever put your hands on the hardware. The new rocket was made by a Swiss company called Oerlicon and it was designed as a high-velocity air-to-ground weapon. It was only a little over three inches in diameter and thirty inches long, with a weight of twenty-two pounds. Quite a change from the cumbersome, ineffective five-inch rockets we had dragged around in the past. It was next to impossible to hit anything with a five incher, and if you did, most times the explosive warhead never detonated. You never knew where they were going. I had a wingman who fired one that went straight up, completed a loop behind him, almost went up his tailpipe, then veered hard left and barely missed taking my nose off.

The new rocket came with a choice of detachable warheads, allowing you to preselect the one best suited for the planned mission. One head had a shaped charge that was optimized for attacking and penetrating heavy armor such as a tank. The high-explosive head was intended for larger and softer targets, where the force of the blast was the key to success. The entire operation reeked of class.

Preliminary testing had been done by the weapons center at Eglin Air Force Base in Florida and the results were outstanding. Washington was interested to the extent that they wanted to see them work for real in combat. The rest was up to us.

Our four F-84s had made the trip from the States to Japan by ship and were being unloaded and prepared for us to fly. They were brand-new and had been instrumented to record all the details of flight and weapons delivery that we would encounter. We were to carry twelve rockets under each wing and each aircraft had been equipped with twenty-four sets of stubby little posts in tandem, called zero-length launchers. They offered little drag in flight and the rockets snapped into position on the launchers with minimum effort from the armament crews.

The cockpit in the pictures did look a bit different from that of the 84s I had flown in the States. The cockpit was dominated by a sophisticated-looking pinball machine, called an intervalometer, that was mounted in front of the stick and below the instrument panel. The intervalometer allowed us to select ripples of one to twenty-four rockets to be fired when we planted our thumb on the bomb release button on the control stick. It would also monitor the circuits we selected, and providing we had set the switches up properly and the electrical circuits and the rockets were ready, it would wink back at us with a little white light that meant aim and fire. The operating instructions were complicated, as they usually are, and the fire control system schematic drawings looked complex, but we were sure that after a few hours working with the equipment we would feel completely at home with it.

Our outside assistance consisted of a project officer from Eglin and one from Washington, plus a gunsight technician and a gun camera technician. My first job was to pick the pilots and crewchiefs who would put Swatrock into action.

The boss wanted what he called a well-rounded flight, since a varied experience level within the flight would give us a more realistic evaluation of the new system. Most of the pilots in the group wanted to be in on the project and since we had a lot of talent, my problem became screening, evaluating, and picking a top-notch flight.

The first requirement was for another pilot who had about the same qualifications that I had. He and I could alternate flying lead and element lead on our missions. We should have good depth in flying and combat experience and it would provide a good chance for the two of us to nitpick each other. That should maximize good flight leadership and minimize the chance of overlooking something or doing something dumb.

The natural choice for the job was my fellow flight leader in the Eighth Fighter Squadron, Captain Lee Roy Stanley. Lee Roy and I had been together for some time now. We enjoyed flying with each other and we had a constant "anything you can do, I can do better" hassle going on. That type of competition between good friends in the fighter pilot ranks makes for better performance all the way around and also makes for excellent bar chatter. I had a few hours and a few missions on Stan but he had me one down for just plain stubbornness. He wanted the job and I wanted him in the flight.

Next we needed a pilot who had a relatively broad experience background, who knew something about the 84, but who was not particularly familiar with our Korean operations. I picked Robert G. Loomis, a thirty-year-old captain who had 1,150 total flying hours and 300 fighter hours, all in the F-84. He had been a gunner and a bombardier, and prior to coming to Korea he had been an armament officer for three years. He did not have any fighter combat missions when he joined the flight.

Our fourth man needed to be a new head. I wanted a pilot relatively fresh from flying school, but one who had shown outstanding potential. That slot went to Second Lieutenant Ronald W. Reed. He was twenty-two years old and about half of his five hundred hours of total flying time was in the 84. He always reminded me of a character out of *Terry and the Pirates* with his clean-cut and oh-so-eager expression. He flew wing like he was glued there and you knew he had what it takes to be a good one.

Reed and Loomis were to alternate on missions, while Stan and I were to go on all of them, alternating as leader. The fourth spot on each mission was to be filled by Major Thomas "Red" Hergert, the Eglin project officer from the states. Red gave us the necessary indoctrination on the rockets and the fire control system and monitored the previous test results against our combat results.

It was a good flight and a happy flight as we set about preparing ourselves and our equipment for our trips up north. Stan and I caught a ride in a C-47 gooney bird heading for Tokyo and picked up our first two birds. They were beauties, clean and fresh with brilliant black and yellow slashes on the vertical fins, but they looked huge compared to our F-80s. We each jumped into a bird and raced each other to remember where the old switches were and what the new ones were for. As usual, it was just about a tie and after fifteen minutes we gave each other a mutual thumbs-up, fired up the engines, and blasted off for Itazuke. By the time we got there, with some acrobatics and max performance maneuvers en route, we both felt quite comfortable with our new machines.

Within a few days we had all the birds at Itazuke and had checked everybody out in them. We had allowed time for a couple of training flights, so naturally Stan and I elected to meet for the acrobatic championship of the Swatrock flight. We scanned the map and picked out an abandoned airstrip south of Itazuke, then took off in formation and headed for the strip at 20,000 feet. As we crossed the runway going east to west, I rolled into a 270 degree turn to the left and Stan did the same to the right. Exactly ninety seconds later I was passing the center of the runway, full throttle, heading north, and Stan was in the same configuration heading south. We played a good game of head-on chicken and, as our wingtips passed, school was out. We used up all the airspace between 20,000 and the rice paddies several times over, but neither one of us could get on the other's tail and stick there. Both our arm muscles and fuel tanks gave out at about the same time, so we joined up and headed home. When we climbed out of the birds our beige flying suits were black with sweat but we were both smiling; we knew we were ready. As soon as we were satisfied that the others were comfortable with their aircraft, we packed everything up and headed back for Korea.

At Taegu we had our first face-to-face meeting with the Oerlicon rockets and to say the least, we were amazed. They were sitting in neat little boxes that looked like overgrown sardine cans. An airman pulled a wire around the top of one of the boxes and it flipped open like a pack of smokes. There they were, small and mean-looking, polished like a new car. We got a demonstration of how twenty-four rockets could be mated to one of our aircraft and checked out in five minutes. We thought we were ready to go.

It didn't move quite that fast, since Red Hergert insisted on a complete practice phase. He wanted camera missions first, where you go through all the motions but you fire gun camera film instead of rockets. The purpose is to evaluate the pilot's target tracking, range estimation for firing, and the probability of hits. I thought this was for the birds until I struggled with my intervalometer a couple of times in flight and then assessed my film to find that I probably would have done no more than waste rockets on my first few flights. Once we realized we had not yet mastered all the techniques, we meekly spent several days making dry runs against some captured Russian T-34 tanks in the river-bed right off the end of our runway at K-2.

We couldn't have picked a tougher spot to practice. We didn't realize it then, but the workouts we got there made a lot of difference when we took the rockets into combat. Our practice range was described in the final report: "The combination of debris, turbulence from thermals and ground effect, a prevailing 90 degree crosswind and the natural obstructions made air-to-ground rocketry problems at this location extremely complex." That was an understatement, it was rough as hell.

When all of us had managed to advance to the point where we could handle all the selectors and indicators in flight and when we could keep the supersensitive gunsight pip on the target, we started firing the different types of warheads at the tanks. Red had done some firing on the early tests at Eglin and was most anxious to set up a pool on high number of hits. We were all for it. I think Stan would have run into those tanks rather than let Red beat him. I sneaked through and won the pot on the last day. Red had mentally pocketed that money when he suggested the pool, but he finished way out of the money and paid off with a few unintelligible sounds.

During our practice sessions we had managed to chew up three Russian tanks with our shaped-charge heads and felt we could guarantee a tank kill with a ripple of four rockets and had a good chance of getting the kill with two rockets. We were confident because the intervalometer had become friendly, we were tracking smoothly, and our range estimation was consistently on the money. Our hits on the T-34s averaged nine inches of penetration through armor and we had one super hit on a tank gun barrel that made eleven inches of armored steel disappear completely. When the rockets hit they would drill a neat round hole as their torch bored through the plate. When they emerged into the interior of the tank they were preceded by a nine-inch-long slug of flame and molten metal that exploded into the tank's interior. Having had the opportunity to drive a tank for two weeks of maneuvers while I was a West Point Cadet, I understood what that would do to the crew, ammunition, and fuel within a tank.

Once all concerned were confident that the people and equipment were ready, all we had to do was set up the ground rules. We came up with an ideal arrangement with Fifth Air Force on scheduling and control of our missions. The first step was a meeting at Fifth's advanced headquarters detachment in the city of Taegu. They were all okay folks, but they didn't look at war in the same manner that Stan and I did. Lee Roy thought they were stuffy and they thought Lee Roy was uncouth. Both assumptions were probably well grounded. Joint Operations Center, JOC to us, was made up of a bunch of senior officers wanting to be more senior. Stan, Red, and I were able to dominate the meeting, and we wound up with a blank check to roam the peninsula and hunt for targets.

They accepted the responsibility of planning missions that could provide potentially good targets for us and our rockets. More importantly, if they found something that looked like it could be a hot one, they would scramble us and let us do whatever we thought was best. If they had nothing special to offer, we could take off at our discretion and fly an armed reconnaisance, or recce, to an area of our choice. They set up some potential target folders and we used them for reference if we couldn't come up with something better from past missions or from real-time mission debriefings from other flights.

We had finished our homework and were hot to trot. All we had to do was wait for the first scramble. We didn't have long to wait before Swatrock changed from a test program of a new weapon, with nobody shooting back, to a deadly serious battle for life and property in the desolate wastes of North Korea.

Next morning JOC had nothing special for us, so Stan and I picked an area about fifty miles south of Wonsan where I had managed to get five live locomotives on a good mission a few months back. We hit the deck about fifty miles north of the area and started searching for some action. When you recce on the deck you strain so hard that it feels like your eyeballs are about to pop out of your head. We did the bob and weave along the general course of the railroad tracks, in unison with two elements of two, but never with any two aircraft at the same altitude or on the same heading. We spotted several loaded railroad cars backed into a siding and were having at them with various combinations of our new rockets when Reed called out what we all saw at the same time, "Flak!"

Unless you're on something really big or unless you lose your walking around sense, that call will make you change your plans right away. The cars were all burning merrily, we had seen our rockets do the job, and the red tracers and white puffs from the ground guns were getting disturbingly close, so we broke hard to the left and swung north, still on the deck. The terrain was pretty open and flat under us and it was no trick to see just where those guns were located. We had burned enough fuel while we were down at low altitude so that it was not practical to do too much more hunting; we were all pumped up from the way our rockets had clobbered those cars, so why not? I decided that we would indulge in a bit of that not so smart pastime of dueling with the flak guns.

Flushed with confidence about our new aircraft and new weapons, I swung us around to the south, picked up the gun pits from way out, and lined us up for one high-speed pass. We were in an ideal position to hit them and they obviously didn't expect us back. We had a total of twenty-three Oerlicon rockets left between us and, all firing within seconds of each other, we introduced the North Korean gunners to a new threat. Heading home we all agreed that the pass had looked good and our gun camera film backed us up. Each of our ripples had struck home within a few feet of dead center. Four direct hits on the guns for four attempts; we wiped those pits out. All we wanted to do was reload, refuel, and have at it again.

Our shiny new aircraft got their baptism of fire on our second mission. The weather was turning sour and it was tough to find an area to work in. We poked and probed through the rainstorms until we got down to just about the altitude where the mountain tops were supposed to be, then when we hadn't broken out of the clouds we climbed a bit and tried it again on a different heading. We finally broke into a hole south of Wonsan. The best ceiling in the bowl we found ourselves in was 3,000 feet and it dropped to 500 feet as the clouds met the hills. That's not comfortable working space since you don't have much freedom of maneuver and since the ground gunners know just how high the clouds are and have a much better chance of zapping you as you move about under the base of the clouds.

We found a road leading into a little valley that looked promising, so we started working it. Sure enough, we spotted a string of fat, loaded trucks resting along the roadside in the rain and not expecting a call from us. The Oerlicons fired, the trucks settled in a heap like a string of sick elephants, and the mobile flak guns and the automatic weapons accompanying the trucks barked out at us and followed us right up to the base of the clouds.

Getting hit by flak is bound to shake you up. If it's small stuff you may not even notice it until you look around and get a sickening feeling from the torn metal or the neat little hole staring back at you. If you get tagged by the big stuff it often hits you so hard you feel like you've been slugged and you may have trouble holding onto your mount and getting her to do your bidding. Three of the four of us got hit on that run and while we all limped home okay, our new machines were out for various degrees of patchwork. We were so enthused about our results that our main concern was the delay we had encountered. Our crews worked for seventy-two hours straight and we were ready to go again.

Korean weather can stay bad for days and even weeks and it got worse while our birds got better. We pored over our maps and the weather charts and decided to take a crack at an area up in the northwest of the peninsula. Usually that section had nothing to offer but railroad tracks, concrete bridges, and Migs from just across the river, but the weather told us we didn't have to worry about Migs that day. Fifth Headquarters was starting to get some pressure from Washington about increasing our effort to cut railroad tracks and knock out rail bridges and reinforced-concrete structures. They were anxious to see if our rockets would fit into their future rail-cutting plans. During our planning meeting we had accepted the task of trying some rail cuts and this looked like it might be a chance to get on with that test.

We went in under the weather and got some good hits along the main tracks, but we didn't hurt them badly. Our weapons had too much direct concentrated power and not enough area or blast power to hack the rail-cutting job. We managed to tear down the side of a small bridge but we were not impressed with the results. We had to wait until our next mission to go against reinforced concrete, and again we were unimpressed with the results. We put the rockets flush against the sides of the reinforced-concrete surface of a bridge and got good hits but minimal damage. That was not the job the weapons had been designed to accomplish. It had been worth a try, but we were glad we had knocked those two requirements off the list so we could again have freedom to attack targets we knew we could kill.

Next day the weather went from bad to horrible, and as we sat in our mud alert shack we wondered if the belting rain would wash the shack away or if the wind would blow it away. As any fighter pilot can tell you, that's the kind of a day someone finds a hot target. The red JOC phone jangled and some faraway-sounding controller said, "We got vehicles and tanks in the Chorwon area. One of the Mosquitos has 'em spotted and he wants fighters for the kill, you take it?"

Six eyeballs were splitting their time between me and the downpour as I replied, "Sure we'll take it. What's the word?" He gave me, "Contact Mosquito Oarsman Able, Channel George, coordinates CT 632532; good luck."

We all scribbled a few notes and calculations on the plastic covers we had over our maps to protect them from the rain and grabbed our flight gear. We hit the door as if the sun was shining, but as we slopped through the mud and slime of the flight line I know the four of us had mixed emotions about an all-weather ground attack force.

The runway at K-2 was a flat spot in the normally dry river bed that snaked around the city of Taegu and past Mount Bustyourass. The runway and Mount Bustyourass were perfectly lined up, which was no big problem when the sun was out, since all you did after takeoff was slide around it on one side or the other. When neither you nor anybody else could see that knob it was a bit of a concern, since fighter bases did not have ground radar nor did fighters have airborne radar at that time. We bounced off the pierced plank, sucked up the gear, made a quick turn toward where Mount Bustyourass should not be, and lost sight of everything but each other's wingtip lights and the rain inside the bumpy clouds for the next hour. It was all time, distance, and dead reckoning, and an old, outdated map in that operation. The map was even stamped: ELEVATIONS INACCURATE. But most of us had done it many times before, and this time we broke out into surprisingly good visibility and a few thousand feet of ceiling near Chorwon.

We came up on G for George and contacted our gutsy Mosquito pilot whose understandably tense voice indicated he was glad we could make it. He was driving his unarmed AT-6 trainer around under the clouds, dodging the hills and the fire from the ground troops who knew full well that his mere presence in their area indicated that fighters were on the way.

All of us had nothing but admiration for those forward air control pilots, and I remember feeling especially proud of that unknown troop as he pointed his little machine right into the middle of all the ammo they could throw at him and put a smoke rocket right on the target for us. You have a special incentive not to miss when you get a show like that for openers.

The targets were in the trees on a hillside and the outline looked like a couple of tanks and a great deal of neatly packaged and stacked supplies. We quickly set up a very tight attack pattern because you had to keep your eyes on that spot on the hillside all the time or it would blend in with the rest of the countryside. That was one of the times when you ignored the ground fire and got on with the job at hand. We had set up our intervalometers to fire ripples of four rockets and we each got in three quick passes before that spot on the hillside went boom for the last time and disappeared.

Once I took my eyes off that spot I could see that the entire hillside looked like an anthill swarming with enemy soldiers and equipment, all obviously headed south toward our ground troops. We still had bags of fuel and full loads of ammo for our 50 caliber machine guns, and we used it well. We raked them from all angles until we had all called "balls out," indicating that we were out of ammunition. One of the best feelings a fighter pilot could get in Korea was to know that he had shortstopped a bunch of the enemy before they could even come close to our grunts and we all felt good about that mission.

My mental exercise of patting myself on the back was interrupted by a loud smack and a wrenching bump and I was upside down. I'd taken a hit from something relatively large, and reflex action guided me through the routine of righting my bird and checking everything quickly to be sure she was still flyable, which she was. About the same time, two of the other three fighters checked in hit. Obviously, once again, we had not knocked out everything down there. We were already getting the hell out of there, having hung it out over the target for quite a while, but we hastened our exit even a bit more.

We were all flying okay, so we re-entered the clouds, reached for some altitude, and started to think about the requirement to find a parking place before too long. As soon as we got farther south we established radio contact with JOC and found that the weather at our home base had gone from horrible to impossible; the base was shut down. They said there was one F-86 strip still open just south of Seoul, but it was going down and we had better hurry. You don't particularly like to hurry when you don't know the details of your battle damage, but we hurried anyway. The weather was still up when we got there, and since we were about the only people dumb enough to be airborne in all of Korea, we had no traffic problems as we let down through the clouds, spotted the strip, and put our aircraft down.

We found some unused parking slots and I leaped out to see what had happened to my machine. The entire underside of the fuselage and the left wing were burned black. I had evidently taken a fair-sized hit in the left underwing pylon rack that we used to carry external fuel tanks or bombs. Fortunately all the shrapnel had gone into the pylon itself and the rest of the damage was mostly a scorch job. The other two aircraft had only taken light hits and I figured we would be able to fly all four back home as soon as the weather broke, but they would have to go back into the repair cycle and that meant another slowdown.

The F-86 base was loaded with old buddies from Europe and Nellis, and we had a small reunion right there on the flight line. There were lots of war stories to tell and we had to explain our new aircraft and rockets. It had been a long day, so the flight line tent that served as their club seemed like the right place to take care of all of that. After several fun hours of fighter pilot comradeship, accompanied by appropriate doses of medicinal booze and a normal flight line gourmet meal of gravy-covered something, we flopped into some spare sacks and rested up for the trip back to the home base in the morning.

As we flew our damaged birds back the next day I found myself reviewing our progress to date. With five missions under our belts we had knocked out some good targets and we had confidence in our rockets and aircraft. But we had yet to find the targets we really needed to show our stuff—locomotives and tanks out in the open. JOC hadn't come up with anything like that and it was doubtful that they would unless it was day-old info and the targets were long gone. The only answer was to take advantage of our freedom to search for targets on our own, go as far north as we could, and recce until we found what we needed.

Our pilots were all doing nicely and young Reed was very impressive, especially considering his experience level. He was doing everything just right and as was often the case with a new pilot who was good, he was paying more attention to the exact firing ranges and speeds than the rest of us were. Loomis hadn't had quite his fair share of the action yet but was okay. Stan bothered me a bit. If possible, he was more stubborn than ever and he wouldn't back off on anything. As for me, I had scared myself pretty good on our second mission and my inner smarts had convinced me that I had better blend some common sense in with my enthusiasm or else I was in for trouble.

It's funny how a near miss such as the one I had on that second Oerlicon mission will stick with you: not up in front where it bothers you, but way back in your head so you can recognize the trouble symptoms earlier and avoid the trouble itself. The turbulence was really bad and I couldn't get lined up on that truck the way I wanted to. I kept bouncing around, overcontrolling my machine, and despite the fact that I knew I should have aborted the pass, I didn't. Instead I pressed in a lot closer than I should have and fired the rockets sloppily and off target. Instantly I knew I'd goofed. The ground was coming up like crazy so that I could make out the details of leaves and bushes. Despite having bottomed out in the dive with my nose coming up, the aircraft was still sinking. I was way too close to the ground, but all you can do when it gets like that is pull back on the stick a little harder, but not too hard. It all went by sort of like a slow motion fight scene. There was no sense of panic as the terrifying panorama filled my eyes and my muscles worked smoothly and automatically. As I eased in that little extra pull that makes so much difference when you're sinking at 450 miles per hour, earth, rocks, and rocket debris hit my canopy and wings. Next came a spray of mud and rice paddy slop over my left wing and left canopy. I had flown through my own rocket blast. The nose struggled up and I had not only missed my target, I had only avoided augering in by a few feet. I backed off and began paying more attention to the rules of the game I knew so well. While it had been a bad few seconds, it had reminded me of my responsibilities in the only way that would have made any real impression on me.

I wished that there was some way to make Stan back off a bit, but at the moment I had the runway at Taegu in sight, and it was back to reality.

As soon as we landed, our crewchiefs took control of our damaged birds and two days later we had a total of three aircraft ready to go for mission number six. As soon as I picked up the phone and relayed that information to JOC we got a scramble for some vehicles in convoy. Three of us started for the runway but I snagged an upturned corner of razor-sharp pierced plank, blew a tire, and had to abort. Stan and Hergert got airborne only to have JOC advise them that they had lost the target. Nobody would talk to them on the radio when they got in the supposed target area and they couldn't find anything on their own, so the entire mission was a waste. They returned to base with their rockets and we all pouted for the rest of the day.

The next day we flew our seventh mission and got our rockets into the iron-busting business for real when JOC sent us after an oil storage tank in Pyongyang, the flak capital of North Korea. Ping-Pong, as we called it, was always good for excitement. We set up for one high-speed run on the oil tank from an angle where we could immediately hit the deck heading out of town, which was the only way to avoid taking up permanent residence there. Red and I split about twenty degrees on either side of the run-in line and hit the tank with big ripples of twelve rockets each, while Stan followed two seconds behind us for a strike on the pump station off to the side of the tank. Our gun camera film showed that Red and I torched twenty separate explosions, and JOC later got a photo recce bird in there to confirm that the tank looked like a sieve. Stan goofed and you could hardly talk to him for days. He forgot to recheck his intervalometer and fired only one rocket instead of a ripple of twelve. While that one rocket went right into the middle of the pump station, it was not enough. No way do you try Ping-Pong twice on the same mission, so we kept going east and found a good deal.

Stan spotted a fair-sized storage area of some type on the side of a small mountain. The sides were reinforced with heavy logs and the top was covered with corrugated steel sheets. He rolled in immediately, redeemed himself by re-membering to check his switches, and put a ripple of eight rockets right through the metal roof. The entire thing let go with one big bang. There were logs, steel, fire, and junk all over the hillside, and the only evidence that remained was a black spot.

As we pulled up, what should we see about a mile down the road in a wooded area but a group of T-34 tanks. They were tough to spot unless you were looking right at a little break in the woods but there was no doubt that we had four nice fat tanks. We fanned up into steep firing runs to keep the clearing and the tanks in sight and our rockets bored into them and blew all four of them, just as advertised. Elation turned to frustration after our last rocket ripped the fourth tank: We were out of rockets when we spotted two more T-34s just over the next knoll.

We broke the world's record for returning to base, taking on a load of fuel and rockets, and heading back to look for those other two tanks. To our complete surprise they were still there, stuck or out of fuel or dumb. We demolished them and just for good measure we knocked out a truck we found heading in their direction. We had done good work and once we crossed the bomb line heading south we did acrobatics all the way home. We knew the Old Man had left for a trip to Japan, so we beat up the strip and ruffled the flaps on a few tents to close out the day.

We were still flushed with success the next morning as we loaded up a set of the high-explosive warheads and headed for Sariwon, where we got skunked. We knew there were plenty of locomotive revetments up there but that didn't interest us much; we were hoping to find some live locos to go along with them. No luck. We battered the revetments and took another crack at a bridge but we didn't hurt anyone too badly.

The next trip, a late afternoon run to a marshalling yard in the Huichon area, turned up paydirt again in the form of a long string of new-looking railroad cars, covered with light-colored tarpaulins and pointed south. We set up for ripples of two and found that each ripple was good for at least one and most times two cars. There wasn't any flak and each loaded car we hit torched immediately.

It looked like they were getting set for a run south during the night so it seemed wise for each of us to save a couple of rockets and go hunting the locomotive that had to be close by. We didn't have to hunt more than a few miles to the north before we spotted a tunnel mouth in the side of a mountain with the telltale wisp of smoke and steam curling lazily out and up. They had fired the boilers and were building pressure for a night delivery to the front, but they never made the trip.

Red got the first crack at that black hole at the end of the tracks and it only took a ripple of two to do the job. One rocket hit the edge of the tunnel and the other one disappeared into the black spot. While Red was still breaking off his firing pass, it looked as if not only the tunnel but the entire mountainside shook with the intensity of the explosion. The force knocked him 90 degrees onto his side and he skidded past the front door at 450 miles per hour. Smoke, dirt, and flame continued to boil from the tunnel mouth, indicating that a string of ammo cars was probably already hooked behind what used to be the locomotive in that tunnel. That was a lot of ammo that our grunts would never have to dodge.

Stan led the next mission and it turned out to be another Korean weather drill. The only ground we saw was the runway on takeoff and landing. The rain was so heavy and the clouds so black that even with our wingtip lights on bright I could barely see that little spot of colored light to maintain my position, even though we were tucked in so close that our wingtips were practically touching. My canopy seal popped, evidently from a microswitch that didn't like the wet weather, and opened up a slit that allowed the downpour outside to come inside. I didn't have the time or free hand to try and recycle it until we rolled out on the runway and all I got that day was wet.

We tried again the next day and got in to work over some loaded railroad cars and some stored fuel and oil drums, but we were hungry for more locomotives and tanks, especially Stan. The next evening was better, probably the best all-around shoot of the tests, and though we didn't know it, our next to last mission; and Stan got his locomotives. We had been amazed at the casual way they were building up trains in the Huichon area and decided we might as well give that spot another try about twilight when they would be getting ready for the night dash.

We hit the deck along the river and started to recce a long, straight stretch of track when *wow,* there they were, about one hundred bulging cars and three big, black locomotives, all in the open. The flak was only moderate and we ignored it as we had a ball ripping up the engines and then burning as many of the cars as we could. When we ran out of ammunition and had to leave, we knew that despite their obvious and careless desire to get that stuff south to the bombline they were not going anyplace with what was still usable until they cleaned up that mess. We had also managed to zap a sizable group of their crewmen, who seemed to be standing unconcerned along the tracks, so we figured morale was not too sharp on that stretch of the Peiping to Ping-Pong railroad that particular evening.

It was too late to try again that night and I was nervous as a cat during the restless hours that we waited for a predawn takeoff. The birds were ready, the weather was good, and we had wheels in the well by 0400. It was Stan's turn to lead but since I had led us there the previous afternoon, he wanted me to lead us back to the same spot. We didn't even get to that spot before it started.

You could see for miles in the cool, gray predawn, and while we were still 60 miles out of Huichon at 30,000 feet Stan called out the white streamer of a locomotive running hard in the open. We popped the speed boards, yanked the throttles back, and screamed for the deck, but in the short time it took us to get there the train had beaten us to a tunnel and ground to a halt inside.

Steam was pouring from the tunnel and we were about to throw a rocket in there, when Stan spotted another train heading for a tunnel farther south. The place was alive with engines, cars, and people.

We cranked it hard left and tried to get on the second one which had two very short tunnels in front of it and then farther south, a long tunnel that was evidently supposed to be its sanctuary for the day. With Loomis on my wing I lined up on the fleeing train, but just as I got in firing range it passed through the first short tunnel and I couldn't get a clear shot. The flak came quickly, heavily, and accurately, indicating that the short tunnel marked the defense perimeter for the tunnel complex ahead. I called, "Breaking hard left, flak bad!" as I pulled on the stick as hard as I could and skidded left.

The last thing I ever heard Stan say was, "I'm on it," as he approached firing range. He never wiggled, never evaded never paid the slightest attention to the intense flak that now surrounded him; and he never got that train. I strained to look over my shoulder and keep track of who was where, and I saw the horribly bright orange ball of his exploding aircraft as he took a 40mm right down the scoop and disintegrated. Just like that.

The sensation of watching your buddy get blown up defies description and throws you into a state where only animal sense and passion rule. I was sick and I was mad and I wanted the gun crew that got my friend.

I was still cocked up on my left wing as I raced along at a hundred feet above a slender island in the middle of a small river that ran at a right angle to the tracks. There were five gun pits in a straight line on the island, and I could see the dirty gray jackets on the puppetlike creatures straining back in their gun belts as they tried to bring their guns to bear on me. I had a mad desire to roll the canopy back and yell at them; crazy but clear as a bell. I felt like I could reach out and grab them with my hands and I wanted to. Everything was in slow motion again.

I didn't know where the rest of the flight was and I didn't care, since this was a private matter. I kicked hard left again and amid a shower of red tracers and white puffs I made a complete 180 degree turn, never raising my nose above 100 feet. As I rolled out they were right in front of me and still firing. Beyond them the river curved to the left and flowed between a small knoll on the left with a big gun pit on top of it and the tunnel on the right. That was the gun pit I wanted; the one filled with the guns and gunners who had hammered Stan. They were right in front of me.

I made a quick swipe at my intervalometer and twisted the selector to twelve rockets, half of my load, just in case. I was almost over the first of the five pits on the island in the river and I swung my 50 caliber gunsight down onto them. I was saving the rockets. I pulled hard on the trigger and just held it for the length of the island, and while those 50s aren't like rockets, they scattered people and equipment all along the line. As I passed the last one there was the hilltop pit, right in the sight. Mustn't miss—a little closer—NOW! I pressed the rocket button on the stick and off they flew, twelve of our little beauties and all true as they could be. I kicked right rudder and slid down the side of the hill past the tunnel, watching over my shoulder until I saw the top of that hill vanish in a blaze of fire and dust. Poor consolation, but I got 'em.

You can't quit in the middle and there were still three birds to fly and the war hadn't stopped, just a small part of it. I regrouped, headed north, found another string of rail cars, and dispatched all of them. We headed home with a familiar empty feeling.

After landing we found that one of our birds had swallowed something and was out for a new engine and another bird needed a mandatory inspection, which left us with only one rocket bird for several days. Reed hadn't flown with us that morning and wanted to know if he could fly with his squadron that afternoon. Of course, I told him to scrounge as many flights as he could until our birds were back in shape. He got himself an air-to-ground mission and took a direct hit at low altitude. He tried to belly the aircraft in far to the north in enemy territory but the left wing and the tail burned off; the aircraft crashed and exploded and he never got out. That was the end of the short but illustrious career of a fine young fighter pilot and the end of our tests.

Red had received a call from the States; they wanted him back there with our results for evaluation. Once we got that news, the Old Man decided again that he really wanted me back at the repl depl since we were getting a big batch of replacements who needed checking out in a hurry. Our combat test had shown that the Oerlicons were supergood and it was time to move on.

I still hadn't won the war, but I felt better about leaving because I had finished up doing something different and had posted some decisive results. I gave myself a big attitude lecture as I threw my limited belongings into my B-4 bag and turned my cot, sleeping bag, and mosquito net over to a bright-eyed second lieutenant who was saturated with enthusiasm and war stories. Then, just like in the movies, I went down to the flight line about sunset, jumped into a T-33, made a low-level pass over the strip, and pulled up into a beautiful roll as I headed for Japan.

You know what? We never bought those rockets, but one of the big generals we sent all our combat reports to must have agreed with our view that they were supergood. Despite our decision not to buy the rockets, Oerlicon went into full production on them and the general retired and went to work for them. It's not too hard to figure out who the customer was and I hated the thought that we went through all that to combat test the rockets for those bastards.

I kept thinking we could use those rockets if there was another war. A wing of fighters carrying them could knock out a bunch of fuel tanks or a thermal power plant in a hurry. Hell, you could probably cripple a fair-sized industrial complex in one or two good strikes.

2 | ON YOUR MARK, GET SET—

When I got back from Korea I was assigned to Luke Air Force Base in Arizona. Since I had flown the latest model F-84s at Nellis and on Project Swatrock in Korea, I was not too thrilled to find that we had a lot of the older models of the 84 to work with at Luke. The early 84s were dogs. I don't think I ever knew anyone who flew an A model of the 84, in fact I don't know if there was such an animal. But I was among those who flew the 84B, C, and D, and they every bit deserved their monikers, such as the Lead Sled and the Hog. They were underpowered, sluggish, and uncomfortable, and except for the fact that you were getting some time in fighters, they were a pain to fly.

There weren't too many of those early models of the 84 but somehow we managed to put them at Luke in the Arizona heat, where we tried to run a training program for our new people going to Korea and for the Military Defense Assistance Pact nations who were with us in NATO. On a hot day at Luke, there wasn't a runway built that was suitable for the beasts. We would get up at 1:00 A.M. and hold 2:00 A.M. morning flight briefings in hopes that we could get the first missions off by dawn and the last ones off before noon. It was extremely difficult to coax those aircraft to be ready to fly and the schedule always slipped. Exhausted crewchiefs and pilots wound up trying to nurse recalcitrant 84s through the sizzling afternoon temperatures when their ground-loving tendencies were at their worst. Our accident record was abominable, in fact, unacceptable if common sense had prevailed, and we killed more pilots and lost more aircraft than made good sense.

The first time I flew an 84B was on a hot afternoon and I almost aborted on takeoff. I planted my feet on the brakes, ran her up to faltering full power, and released the brakes. Nothing happened; I mean absolutely nothing. I just sat there, dead still, without the wheels even turning, and I figured I'd flamed out and the instruments had just not had time to unwind. I was actually starting to push the mike button and announce an abort when she inched forward ever so reluctantly. I picked up a few knots, then I rolled and rolled and rolled and the controls felt like a broom in a bucket of slop, but I determined not to panic.

A lot of the pilots we lost at Luke were killed because of panic or because they never made up their minds. To stay alive, you either went or you quit. I watched one NATO student change his mind four times in a few seconds one afternoon after the throttle went full on for takeoff, then off, then full on, then off as he elected to try a panic stop when the end of the runway approached and the barbed wire fences and cotton patches beyond began to look real. He ground the wheels flat and they torched the aircraft and he just sat there, still strapped in, and died in the cockpit.

I was committed on that takeoff and, since she showed minimal signs of performance, I reverted to the bounce. To bounce, you pulled the stick back and lifted the nosewheel a foot or so, then you rammed the stick forward so the nosewheel bounced off the concrete and threw the nose a bit higher on the next cycle, eventually forcing the goat into the air. If you didn't choose that technique, the only alternative was the dirt sniffer. The wags had it that all 84s had a dirt sniffer installed at the factory; we called it the foundry. The dirt sniffer remained passive until it smelled the dirt off the end of the runway, then, if it was in commission that particular day, it would hurl the hulk into the air. I blew dirt off the end of the runway that day and I sat motionless for several seconds, afraid to even wiggle the controls as I staggered along barely above a stall and barely fifty feet above the cotton patches. I just shook my head and wondered what I was doing flying that hunk of junk. The only fun we ever had with the early models was flying them to the boneyard when we finally got the E and G models.

The Es and Gs were still straight-wings; the first swept-wing 84Fs were hung up on delivery while the foundry tried to get them to fly well enough to sell them to the Air Force. The E and G models were very similar to each other; they both did a good job in Korea as well as in other spots around the world. One of their selling points as far as the government was concerned was that they were remotely nuclear capable, but those of us involved in fighting the war in Korea had a frank indifference to nuke weapon potentials. The 84Es and Gs earned their keep with us by virtue of their iron bomb and bullet capability. They had reasonable power, good controls, and gave us a stable platform for bombing and strafing. Air-to-air combat was something else, and you simply fell out of the sky if you tried it with an 84 at any reasonable altitude.

I only saw the 84 as an air-to-air threat one time. We were training all nationalities at Luke and our accident record had some of the NATO pilots petrified, especially the French pilots. Many of them were youngsters who were flat afraid of the aircraft and that fear caused additional accidents and often ran us very short of available aircraft. When faced with anything resembling an aircraft malfunction, many NATO students would just as soon eject from an 84 as they would go to dinner.

My friend Aron J. Bowman was well aware of that tendency, having had a couple of his previous students eject for no real reason, and having received appropriate guidance from the group commander on his responsibilities to keep students and their aircraft together. Bo was herding three of his French students around the gunnery range one day when one of them experienced a minor malfunction that had absolutely no effect on the aircraft's capability to complete the mission safely. He came on the radio and announced that he was stepping out. Bo advised him to stand by while he pulled in behind him to take a look at his aircraft. Once in close trail Bo advised the French pilot to look out over his right front toward the gunnery range, then Bo fired a burst from his 50 caliber guns over the Frenchman's nose. Ever the cool and calm one, Bo then hit the mike button and said, "Now, you son of a bitch, if I see the canopy come off that airplane I'll blow you up and even if you get out I'll gun you down in your chute. Get that machine back to Luke and on the ground." The Frenchman returned, made an uneventful safe landing, and the rash of NATO bailouts came to an abrupt end.

Republic produced 4,457 F-84E and G aircraft over seven years before they shut the line down in 1953. We formed the Thunderbird acrobatic team using the Es and they were exceptionally good performers for audiences all over the world. I got to lead the Birds for three years flying the straight-wing 84Es first, then switching to the swept-wing 84Fs, and then to the F-100s. The Tbirds have always been great but the duty was different in those early days of the team. We only had five fighters, a two-place T-33 for our narrator, five demonstration pilots, and fifteen crewchiefs, but we did it all ourselves. We showed the flag, the people and the machinery were tops, we had a ball, and we were as close knit as the acrobatic formations we flew. Things always seem to get more complex, more sophisticated, and more subject to higher-level management, so I can say with confidence that you'll never see another outfit like that. It was the greatest.

The evolving American jet fighter program, which would eventually lead to the Thud, was going through some rough times. When the 84Fs finally got out of impound and into action there were plenty of people who were displeased with Republic's first swept-wing effort. Actually it was not the swept wings that were the problem; it was the tail. The newer swept-wing fighters needed one-piece horizontal stabilizers, or slab tails. The slab tail provided a larger control surface that moved as a single unit with the pilot's fore and aft control stick pressures. The result was a smooth-flying aircraft all the way up to the higher maximum speeds. The 84F had a split tail like older and slower aircraft, and once again we had a dog on our hands. The first batch came to Luke and by the time the guys who ferried them in had landed and made it to the bar at the club, we had christened the split-tail F model the Super Hog.

You could tell a Super Hog driver by his bulging right biceps. If you wanted your nose to come up you pulled back on the stick, then you pulled some more, and sometime thereafter the nose moved. Going down was equally exciting, but in straight and level flight and maneuvering around the roll axis, it performed well. Maintenance was awful and if anyone had told us the truth it would have been that the split tails were a dreadful mistake that the Air Force chose to swallow, or was directed to swallow. We pranged them here and there about the desert and their maintainability got worse instead of better. We all knew they were short timers but we did have a bit of fun with them when we won the last of the Bendix Trophy coast-to-coast races. Lucky Palmgren, my Thunderbird slot pilot, and I tried them on the acrobatic bit and had high hopes for the upcoming slab-tail model. The split-tails got so bad that we quit flying them at Luke and sent part of them to the weapons lab at Eglin and the rest to the army armament proving grounds in Maryland, on flatbed railroad cars, to be shot up during testing and weapons demonstration airshows.

Like everyone else, Air Defense Command (ADC) had long since gone the jet route. The F-94 had been a logical and relatively easy step in the early days since it was sort of a funny-nosed two-place F-80 without much to brag about in the way of air-defense capability. Except for the aircrews who flew it, and even for some of them, it was sort of a who cares airplane.

The rest of the 86s had done so well that much was expected from the 86-D when it came to ADC. It was full of nice ideas but it would be tough to say it was ahead of its time. When you started it the fuel system played its own pinball machine of cockpit lights and it often went tilt and locked up in a configuration where you couldn't make it go and you couldn't shut it off. The radar was okay if you had a canned situation and a radar ground controller to steer you close to the target, but I was never overwhelmed with the results when I pulled the trigger. There was a traylike pod on the bottom of the aircraft, under the seat, that popped down and fired twenty-four Mighty Mouse two-inch rockets that raced forward in a scattergun pattern. I chased a lot of little red drones around gunnery ranges, and when I think 86-D, the immediate mental image that comes up is of a red drone continuing to fly merrily along while surrounded by a loose matrix of rocket smoke trails. I never did knock one of those little red turkeys down.

But the system did work, at least once, and tragically at that. Art DeBolt was scheduled to demonstrate a blind-flying, live shootdown of a ground-controlled drone B-17 over the water range at Eglin. Another B-17 was on the range with a load of observers who were there to see, evaluate, and hopefully buy more 86Ds. The ground controllers set Art up for the intercept and when he called contact they confirmed the tiny sliver on his radar scope as the target. When Art locked onto the sliver and called "Judy," signifying that he was locked on and taking control of the intercept, he was cleared again. The onboard aircraft system guided him and he flew to keep the white dot in the center of the shrinking circle that counted him down to five seconds to go. Another call from Art—five seconds to go; another clearance—clear to fire. He pulled the trigger when the circle popped full open and again quickly compressed to nothing in five seconds to be replaced by a big X on the scope. The rockets swooshed on their way and the B-17 full of observers exploded. Anytime you heard about that fiasco, you heard an account of how Art shot the B-17 down. That's not fair.

The other early ADC jet was the Northrop F-89 Scorpion, which reminded me of an airborne locomotive. It was a twin-engined, two-place heavyweight that carried two huge wing-tip pods of the same Mighty Mouse rockets as well as six

20-mm cannons. I did my F-89 flying out of Yuma, Arizona, and again heat was a factor. On my checkout ride I walked around in the normal preflight ritual and was flat amazed at the wheels on the 89. They actually looked like they belonged on a railroad car and they made their tires look skinny and little. They were surrounded by landing gear doors that were of battleship construction and they were even painted battleship gray. My flight was set for 4:00 P.M. takeoff. Even if you didn't touch the brakes while you taxied out to the end of the runway, the wheels became very hot just from rolling friction. There were a couple of airmen at the end of the runway with a water hose connected to a big tank and they had to hose the wheels down to try and cool them off before I was cleared for takeoff. I'll admit it; I was adversely prejudiced before I even pushed the throttles forward.

The pods and cannons on the 89 were later discarded for Falcon missiles on the tips and Geenie nuclear rockets. Those Geenies were something else. They were connected to the aircraft with a nylon rope lanyard and when the ejection squibs forced the rockets down and away from the aircraft and stretched the lanyard all the way out, the lanyard pulled the firing pin in the rocket and off it went. You would have had the same thing going for you if you had gone hunting with a string tied to the trigger of your shotgun; then when you saw a bird you threw your shotgun down until the string stretched to pull the trigger. Results in both cases were predictable, but the theory with the Geenie was that the nuclear explosion would be big enough so that it didn't have to be too close to get the job done.

Two specific cases made me a non-Geenie fan. The first Geenie that was test-fired from an F-106 came right back up, blew the nose off the aircraft, and killed the pilot. Years later I got a chance to go to Tyndal with my F-106 squadron. ADC had saved their resources too well and wound up with a large number of Geenies that only had a few days to go before they would run out of shelf life and would have to be destroyed. The plan was to fire as many of them as fast as we could, so for a week straight we saturated the Gulf of Mexico with every Geenie that we could get to accept the fire signal and leave our aircraft. They took off in all directions, but very seldom toward the target drones. One particular Geenie turned hard left as I fired and I watched it do lazy concentric barrel rolls as it headed straight down to my left. I knew that if it was for real the boom only had to be close, but suppose straight down and to the left was the area I was supposed to be defending? Well, the other theory of the times was that we would intercept all the invading bombers way up north someplace, where I wouldn't know anybody living off to my lower left.

We got our slab-tail 84Fs for the Thunderbirds and we did a lot of good work with them. We also found out that they were typical tough Republic airframes when Lucky Palmgren tried to plow through a railroad track embankment with one of them in Montgomery, Alabama. We got there a day before our scheduled show and were flying a short practice routine while we also test hopped some maintenance that the crews had done on each of our birds. Just as we were coming across the top of a loop, Lucky called from the slot that he had flamed out. There was no problem on separation between the aircraft since we just kept going while Lucky hung there minus engine and let his nose fall through.

Billy Ellis and Bob Anderson rolled off to their respective sides and started calling the emergency folks while I did a split S and picked up on Lucky. There was nothing much under us but Montgomery so I advised Lucky to glide away from town and find the most remote area he could and then eject. He didn't have much spare time since the glide angle of any Republic product without power is exactly the same as a large rock. Lucky was always stubborn and this time he had a small cultivated field in sight that was simply not large enough for a jet fighter, wheels or no wheels, and besides it was not considered wise to belly in jet fighters. I couldn't fly his aircraft and he had his mind made up, so he made a big deadstick turn and damned if he didn't slither that huge hulk in at 200 miles an hour on its belly, right on the edge of that field.

That was the end of the pretty part as he plowed two thousand feet of wet sod like it wasn't even there. There was a ten-foot-high embankment and railroad track at the end of the field and he hit that at about a hundred miles per hour. It looked like that was all for Lucky. It didn't burn, but as I made several passes over him at about fifty feet all I could see was Lucky slumped over in the cockpit with his helmet and head jammed up toward the windscreen. I saw the fire engines and rescue people headed down the road in his direction and since I was about out of fuel I had to return to the base and land. I was really sweating old Lucky out.

He was conscious by the time they got there and he flew the show the next day in our spare bird. He was the only guy I ever met who could say, "Aw, pshaw," and make it sound real. He wouldn't believe any of us when we told him that he had been knocked out for ten minutes. To the day he augered in down in Southeast Asia, he swore that he was never knocked out and that he just slid gently to a stop against the tracks, unstrapped, and climbed out as the fire trucks drove up. I hope his crunch in the jungle didn't hurt either.

The Thunderbird schedule was demanding of both men and machines, but our supercrews pampered the aircraft. We took better care of them than we did ourselves, but after about a year our 84F Thunderstreaks weren't streaking as well as they should have been. That's not the kind of longevity you expect from a high-priced fighter, but in retrospect the F was a gap filler for what Republic and the Air Force thought they had in mind for the future. Driven by the party line of the times, which relegated the iron bomb and machine gun to insignificance, they both wanted an all-weather, fast-moving, low-level, nuclear-capable penetration fighter. There was no way the F could fill that bill, but the Thunderbird acrobatic team sure gave them a year's worth of maximum-performance test time that money couldn't buy elsewhere.

We really didn't care that our 84Fs were pooping out since Century Series fighters had become a reality and the F-100 was a production item. We flew the 100A a few times and, even though it had some rough edges, we knew we wanted Super Sabres for the team. We got the first six 100Cs off the production line and became the world's first supersonic acrobatic team. With air-to-air refueling and the new Tactical Air Command (TAC) mobility concept, the 100 quickly picked up a global mission. Talk about longevity, the Thunderbirds were still flying the 100 twenty years later and the 100 was also a sound combat warrior in Southeast Asia.

We got some new Century Series aircraft when McDonnell Douglas came along with the F-101 series. The A model was designed as a tactical fighter; the RF model was a photo reconnaissance version that was later to fly in Southeast Asia until replaced by RF-4s; and the two-place ADC version was known as the F-101B. All of them fought the pitch-up problem. The position and shape of the wing and tail surfaces on the 101s caused the aircraft to pitch up or toss you up and out of control. When you pulled the nose up to the spot where the wings blanked out the tail, off she went, out of control.

The 101B was my only venture into the two-place business and while guys in the back seat, or Gibs, have their place, I preferred to do it myself. I got six of the first production Bs in my squadron at Tyndal and while those two engines let you know that you had a bag of power, the rest of the aircraft never gave me the sense of confidence I liked to have in my flying equipment. For instance, it had a very small nosegear hydraulic retraction system that had trouble overcoming the force generated by the increase in airspeed after takeoff. If you didn't yank the gear handle up smartly on takeoff before your airspeed built up, you had a hung nosegear. But if you pulled the nose up too sharply to hold your airspeed down so the nosegear would come up, you were on your way into pitch up. Throughout the flight envelope it always felt like you were flying on the top of a pencil point, wobbling back and forth, looking for the right place to stop the stick, without ever finding that spot.

When they stretched the original 101 airframe to accommodate the larger canopy on the two-place version they came up with a new meeting place for lots of wires. That electrical junction was buried someplace under the canopy and looked like a small pineapple. Seems like the pineapple was not well protected and was always picking up stray bits of wire, washers, or other hardware that would short all sorts of circuits. One circuit that was often shorted caused the canopy to fly off in flight. As I turned on approach for landing one night I was concerned because my wingman wasn't answering my radio calls. When I looked out at him to give him a backup visual signal for a frequency change I could see why. There he was, tucked right in there, but minus the canopy. The two of them were hunched over and hanging on to a 300 knot open cockpit Stearman in the black night. I had 101s, 102s, and 104s in that hybrid squadron, and while I flew all three of them because my people were flying them, I frankly admit that any time I had a choice, I let someone else have my 101 ride and the Gib that went with it.

The Convair F-102 was our first production venture into delta wing technology, and despite the fact that the Deuce had significant drag problems at the start, it turned into an ADC workhorse. Its original fuselage lines simply would not allow it to reach the performance specifications and speeds that had been established for the aircraft. The problem was also inherent to the developing F-105 and it was obvious that more work on the drawing board and in the wind tunnel were mandatory for both airframes. Solving the problem resulted in the design philosophy known as the area rule, or more popularly, the Coke-bottle effect. Contouring the fuselage to look like a Coke bottle did the job and except for the two-place training version, the 102 was a smooth, good flying aircraft. The two pilots flying the trainer for checkouts and instrument checks sat side by side and were housed in a big bulbous cockpit pasted behind the needle nose. No design study or wind tunnel testing could overcome such a flagrant disregard for sleek lines. We called the two-place version the Pig and it performed like a completely different aircraft. Like the F-100, the Deuce was around for a long time and even did a tour in the air defense role over Saigon.

As early as 1951, Alexander "Stasha" Kartveli, Republic's emigrant Russian genius, was giving his all for his last conceptual dream, the F-103. That was his parting shot in the aircraft design business, since he restricted himself to giving guidance to his helpers who were working on Republic's next endeavor, the budding F-105. The 103 was a radical departure in almost every way, but the man who had been creating aircraft since the days of the P-30 believed in it as much as he had believed in his most resounding success, the P-47 Jug. The F-103 performance specifications were astounding for the times, even exceeding many of the capabilities our first-line fighters of today.

His fuselage was rocket shaped and you entered by means of a ground-level elevator that also served as an ejection capsule. He provided pilot vision by means of a periscope rather than a canopy. That was not too surprising coming from him. Most of us considered the fighter canopies of the day to be quite smooth and sleek. Stasha said they looked like pickles. His wing surface and flight control concepts were unheard of and his propulsion schemes combined jet and rocket principles that were far beyond the capabilities of available engine hardware. He talked in terms of decreasing weight while increasing strength by fabrication with titanium and new materials called composites. He had the kind of track record that made people listen, but the 103 concept was too far advanced for a country mired in an expensive, no-win mud war in Korea.

I was somewhat of a favorite son at Farmingdale when I was leading the Thunderbirds in 84s, and one of my cherished rewards was an uncommon trip through the 103 conceptual mockup. I was impressed. It was a heady glimpse of the future and of genius in action, and even today I enjoy reruns of things I saw that day, now billed as ''new'' ideas for futuristic air vehicles surfacing under other sponsors. Mundane things like money and current military requirements turned Kartveli's 103 into little more than the world's most impressive mockup; but I repeat, it was impressive.

On the other side of the country, Lockheed was producing the F-104 Starfighter, and fighter pilots loved it. You put it on like a glove and it was even fun to taxi. I used to lay the canopy over on its left side in the full open position and run the seat full up to put my shoulders and head above the top

45

of the windscreen and out in the breeze while I taxied. When you jazzed the throttle out of idle and pulled it right back the engine gave out an eerie *woooh,* like a strange train whistle. Even at idle it taxied pretty fast, and I loved to cruise down the flight line on the way to the runway and look for a group of airmen bent over some attention-consuming task and oblivious to the passing world. They never heard me coming and I'd give them a big *woooh* and laugh like crazy as they jumped straight up. Who says fighter pilots are weird?

The 104 fought a tough reputation all the way and perhaps never gained the universal acceptance it deserved. None of us cared for the downward ejection seat, and Ivan Kinchloe was probably the best-known fighter pilot to buy the farm because of it. He lost his engine just as he broke ground at Edwards and was too low to eject downward, so he tried to roll to inverted and fire the seat but he never made it around and out. They finally changed the seat. There were some details that were not too neat, like the fuel gauges. I once flamed out as I turned into the chocks to park when I was showing better than an eighth of a tank on my cockpit gauges. The backup flight instruments weren't operationally adequate and when I lost my artificial horizon on a maximum burner climb through an overcast, going straight up, I had to try to make the transition to a small standby gauge about the size of a half dollar that was tucked way up in the far left corner of the instrument panel. The task was just more than a guy could handle in that position, and a break in the clouds over the ocean was all that saved me on that one.

The 104's boundary layer control system also gave some people a lot of trouble. The wing was so small that you had to blow engine bypass air over it at low speeds to make the wing think that it was going fast enough to support you. It could get sticky on final for landing if you didn't have yourself set up for a smooth approach. If you got too low and had to add power, the boundary layer air came on and the wing gave you too much lift and forced you almost straight up. Then when you cut the power, you lost all the boundary layer air, and the wing let you down like a high-speed elevator. If you repeated the process a few times you wound up approaching the runway in square-cornered altitude oscillations and you never caught up. The solution was either to set up a perfect approach or, if you got in trouble, to go around and try again. Operationally, it doesn't always work out so that you have those choices.

We gave a bunch of 104s to NATO and their operational record was pretty grim, so the aircraft's reputation suffered again. But we set all sorts of speed and altitude records with the aircraft and when it came to pure performance, not to mention fun, she was right at the top. We sent a small squadron to Southeast Asia but that was a horrible mismatch. The fallacy of trying to strafe the jungle in Laos with the world's top-performing air-to-air vehicle should have been obvious, but it wasn't until Tom Finney augered in on a worthless mission against the trees that the war planners realized that the 104 was not designed to duel oriental flak gunners.

Our Century Series aircraft closed out with Convair's F-106 and she was a beauty. If I could ever fulfill my fighter pilot's dream of having my favorite bird parked in the garage for weekend use, I'd take a 106. She was a big delta wing, as long as an old C-47 Gooney Bird and able to gross over 40,000 pounds for takeoff, but was as light and responsive as anything I've flown. You could beat her up and do all sorts of things the book said were no-no and she would come through like a true champ. Just for fun, you could set up on final for landing and keep pulling that nose up until she was in a full stall. Then you could ride that stall through a thousand-foot drop, still with full lateral control, then lower the nose a tad and touch down within a few feet of where you wanted to. Fast or slow, tight turn or cruising in comfort, she was hard to beat.

The radar and fire control functions on the 106 worked great, but one of the best gadgets was the Tactical Situation Display Indicator that sat between your knees like a little round television set. You could put in any number of film strip combinations of maps and navigate all over the world with a complete picture of the terrain, landmarks, airfields, and navigation aids constantly unfolding and updating in front of you. For air-to-air combat situations there was even a nice-looking little moving bug that was you and an ugly little moving bug that was your adversary. What a natural for every mission we flew in Southeast Asia.

I carried on a one-commander campaign to try and get the "gears" to become interested in getting the 106s over there. We could have had the best possible machine for everything from flak suppression to self-contained Mig killing support. An infrared sight, air-to-air refueling, and 20-mm cannon pods would have converted her to the perfect vehicle for the job. I made that recommendation to the Pacific Air Force planning officer, who told me that since I was a tactical commander and not a requirements staff officer, I had better shut up and go away before I irritated the general and his staff any further. The 106 got all those modifications a few years later, but of course we never got the 106 over there. I don't know what good the modifications did in the States after the war was over, but the 106 sure could have saved a lot of guys and a lot of grief in Southeast Asia.

The aircraft that was to eventually become the star of our show down south was an unlikely candidate for the role. During the 1950s and the early 1960s, anybody who bet on the reluctant dragon known as the Republic F-105 Thunderchief was due for a skeptical glance at best. If ever an aircraft had an up-and-down career it had to be the Thud.

Before we even got out of Korea both the air force and industry people were squabbling about what we should have for a nuclear-capable fighter, with some wanting to extend the fuselage on the F-84F and some wanting a new machine with internal weapons-carrying capabilities. Despite the fact that it had drawbacks, the 84F did have some potential for answering the nuclear requirements, which were created by the strategic pressures of the early fifties. But a new machine turned out to be the more practical approach and many of the strong points of the F-84F wound up going into the Thud.

While the F-105 struggled through its drawing-board phase, the 84F showed up in all sorts of strange test-bed configurations. There was an F-84 with wings that were fatter and wider outboard than they were inboard and there was even a turboprop contraption that truly never looked real. There was activity on the zero launch or Zel concept, where a fighter was blasted aloft by a rocket without benefit of a runway, but we only spent enough to do that to a few 100s and straight-wing 84s. Government and industry finally settled on a new F-105 design, but during building of the prototypes the contracts went through a constant on-again/off-again process. In the resulting procurement confusion the air force and the manufacturer constantly bickered and blamed each other for the Thud's slow development. When the initial contracts were signed, the plan was to have one F-105 wing fully equipped and capable of fighting a war by 1955. As it turned out, the first experimental YF-105 prototype didn't even get airborne until 1955.

That experimental 105 was as woefully underpowered as some of the earlier 84s had been. Despite claims that she went supersonic on her first flight, those on the scene bet that if she did, it had to be going straight down. That YF only lasted for twenty-two flight hours before one main gear refused to come back down and she got ripped up on a dry lake-bed belly landing at Edwards. She flew long enough to establish one fact: Like the early F-102, she needed major design changes to come close to the performance demanded of her.

The air force insisted on aid from the National Aeronautics and Space Administration for both the 102 and 105 airframes. Over five thousand hours of wind tunnel time resulted in a fuselage that was shaped like a Coke bottle to reduce drag, higher and larger tail sections, and variable-inlet technologies that allowed Century Series progress to continue for both aircraft. It should be noted that Republic's Alexander Kartveli immediately condemned the bumps on the Coke-bottle fuselage as ugly, but conceded that the solution was indeed one that seemed to work.

For the Thud the immediate result was the first 105B, which flew in May of 1956, one year after the fleet was supposed to be ready to go to war. The initial B flights went well but serious consideration was still given to completely dumping the F-105 concept, and the air force tried out a possible replacement in the North American experimental YF-107.

Based on past performance of the P-51, the F-86, and the F-100, there were plenty of supporters in the 107's corner when she tried out at Edwards from September of 1956 until March of 1957, but she didn't get selected. The decision was made that, based upon past development efforts and the NASA Coke-bottle design changes, the 105 airframe had a greater potential and the 107 contract was canceled.

The 105B was a step forward, but still not the machine that filled future requirements. Planning for the F-105D, the aircraft that would fill those requirements and be the all-weather, nuclear-capable fighter of the future, started in mid-1957. By 1958 there were already over five million engineering hours tied up in the Thud, yet the first B model was not accepted by the air force at the foundry until May of 1958. The Fourth Tactical Fighter Wing accepted that same aircraft as the first of sixty operational B models in August of 1958, but the list of required changes and modifications that still had to be accomplished was as long as the flight line.

The B flew like a charm, but you had to overcome an unworkable 150 maintenance hours for every flight hour to keep her going, and there were precious few spare parts available. The foundry was not even close to keeping up with its contractual schedule and blamed the air force because of its vacillating requirements. The air force blamed the foundry for not planning properly. Some may think that this type of bickering was unique or is outmoded in the aircraft business, but such a conclusion is wishful thinking.

The Fourth Tactical Fighter Wing struggled with scheduled modifications and unscheduled groundings throughout the time they flew the Bs, but somehow, despite being in the midst of a major modification when the Cuban missile crisis hit, they managed to accept the Cuban alert commitment with distinction. The first of the new D models were arriving about that time and the Fourth eagerly switched to the newer aircraft and peddled their old B models.

The woes of the early B models were not over, and unfortunately the Thunderbirds took them public when the air force decided it could bolster the sagging reputation of the 105 and modernize the acrobatic team at the same time. There was a big goof when the participating aircraft were picked and run through an upgrade before they went to the team. The depot doing the modifications failed to screen the records well enough to pick up the fact that one of the birds had been involved in an aerial refueling incident where the refueling hose and basket extending from an old KB-50 tanker snapped wildly and wrapped around the 105's wing. Before the 105 pilot could back off hard enough to rip the hose and basket loose, the heavy metal couplings and the basket set up a high-frequency whip that beat the main wing spar with a hammer force. That beating weakened the F-105's wing spar to the point that catastrophic wing failure was only a matter of time and additional stress. Nobody caught it and that almost dead bird came out with a gorgeous Thunderbird paint job, supposedly ready to go.

Lucky Palmgren was back leading the Thunderbirds and he and the other demonstration pilots worked their tails off getting the show ready. The stripped-down red, white, and blue spangled aircraft, with no armament to haul around, performed like champs, and the show was just super. They were on an early road trip when they streaked over the runway at Hamilton Air Force Base near San Francisco in a hello pass and pitched up for landing. Gene Devlin's wing fractured, fell off, and Gene, one of the best, augered in in front of a bunch of shocked people. That was it for the Ultra Hog as far as the team was concerned, and the machine became a tough item to defend.

But the Fourth and the new D models got along well, and by April 1963 they were winging their way to an initial overseas deployment in Spain. The production line and the D models assumed a semblance of orderly flow and Thuds moved into semipermanent homes in Europe and the Far East, and the recently reactivated 355th Wing in Kansas picked up their D models to fill the TAC outline for worldwide readiness and deployment of the F-105.

About that time a funny thing happened in the Gulf of Tonkin.

3 | GOING TO WORK DOWN SOUTH

During the night preceding the dawn of August 2, 1964, South Vietnamese commandos raided the North's patrol boat base at Loc Chao, a fact that went unnoticed by Commander Jim Stockdale aboard the carrier *Ticonderoga* cruising in international waters off Vietnam. On the second of August, as Jim led a flight of F-8 Crusader fighters from the squadron he commanded on a routine training mission, he was well aware that the destroyer *Turner Joy* was in the area and that the destroyer *Maddox* was steaming up the Vietnamese coast to reaffirm our right of passage in neutral waters. Jim's training mission quickly became a combat mission when three high-speed North Vietnamese patrol boats approached the *Maddox* from the shelter of Hon Ne Island and fired ineffectual torpedos. While the patrol boats had broken off their attack as Jim arrived with his flight, he pursued them and his navy fighters left one of them sinking and the other two limping and badly damaged. Jim's detailed accounts in his book *In Love and War* leave no doubt about what transpired that day, what happened two days later, or how the Johnson administration reacted.

Alert postures went up throughout the worldwide U.S. military network and F-105 units in particular started to move. President Johnson put his election campaign aside long enough to consult with the Departments of State and Defense, but they decided not to press the issue and only responded with a warning. Politically this bolstered Barry Goldwater's projection of Johnson as "soft on communism," and must have triggered an almost immediate requirement within the Johnson camp for some action to counter that impression. They did not have to wait long.

By August 4, the destroyer *Turner Joy* had joined with the *Maddox* and Jim was back in combat that night as both destroyers reported that they were again under torpedo attack by North Vietnamese patrol boats. The facts and conclusions are clear. There was no torpedo attack on the *Maddox* and *Turner Joy* on the night of August 4, 1964. Uncoded flash precedence messages from the destroyers supposedly under attack were put out in the open to Washington and the entire world describing an engagement that did not happen. Denials of the contents of those messages by the commodore on the scene, a skeptical appraisal of the performance of detection equipment and technicians, a complete lack of visual sightings from the air or on the surface, and finally doubt that there had been any boats out there at all—coupled with a request for evaluation of the mixup by the senior commodore involved—went unheeded. A decision came quickly from the very top and we launched what the bureaucracy in Washington thought would be a small war under false pretenses and in the face of the on-scene military commander's advice to the contrary.

In the Harris poll on the presidential race that was taken the following week, Johnson's rating shot up fourteen points. Three and a half years later, under oath before the Senate, Robert McNamara would debate the rationale he and Johnson used immediately after the Gulf of Tonkin incident. That testimony strikes at the heart of McNamara's veracity.

Within hours after the events of the night of the fourth of August, President Johnson directed that navy carrier-based forces that were close by be brought into limited action against coastal targets of the North and that air force units move toward Southeast Asia from both the Far East and U.S. bases. The Thud drivers from Yokota, Japan, were at the head of the pack since they had been alerted after the first *Maddox* encounter, and their first deployment flight had landed at Korat, Thailand, during the day of the fourth and was waiting, combat ready.

The F-105 units were not strangers to world travel, since the mobility concept was well established within American tactical forces. The fighter squadrons, with their integral supporting elements, were routinely rotated between the States and overseas locations. When a squadron deployed it usually took its 105s, about 32 officers, about 330 airmen, and all its maintenance and housekeeping gear. C-130 cargo aircraft were assigned to move the bulk of the support personnel and material.

The Thud squadrons had two main bases in the States. The 355th Tactical Fighter Wing had moved to McConnell Air Force Base, Kansas, in April 1964, and they were in the process of being certified as operationally ready in the F-105s. The Fourth Tactical Fighter Wing was still working out of Seymour Johnson Air Force Base in South Carolina. In Europe the main base activity was at Bitburg, Germany. In the Pacific, the 6441st Air Division had three F-105 squadrons at Yokota, located just outside Tokyo, while the Eighteenth Wing was located at Kadena on Okinawa.

The overall mobility plan can be simplified by saying that the stateside units rotated squadrons to Germany, Spain, Italy, and Turkey in support of the NATO commitment. The weapons range near Tripoli, Libya, was utilized by the constantly rotating squadrons to establish and maintain their nuclear weapons qualifications, with some attention being paid to conventional weapons capabilities. On the other side of the world, both Thud units had a full nuclear weapons mission, with the Yokota squadrons standing alert out of Osan, Korea.

The Thuds were still undergoing continuing modification programs, so there was a constant flow of aircraft needing the latest change coming back to the States from various corners of the world, while those modified to the latest configuration left for the overseas stations. Thud drivers were always going someplace.

The first movement of Thuds into Southeast Asia came from Yokota and was quickly followed with deployments from Kadena. As early as August 9, 1964, the stateside units began deploying squadrons to the Pacific under the control of Pacific Air Force, or PACAF, and these units found themselves being juggled between Kadena, Yokota, and Thailand. The squadrons based at Yokota and Kadena had been fairly well extended to maintain their previous nuclear alert commitment and the added requirement for aircraft and pilots down south required constant shuffling of all available resources to cover both efforts. This helter-skelter pattern was to continue for over a year until fighter wings took up full-time residence in Thailand at Korat and Takhli. Even then, Yokota and Kadena were to serve as nurse stations for the Thai bases and the worldwide inventory of Thuds began a slow but steady one-way migration to Thailand.

Mike McNamara was one of the first to fly into Korat from Yokota. In August of 1964 Mike was a flight commander in the Thirty-sixth Tac Fighter Squadron stationed at Yokota and it was his turn to go down to Numazue to the water survival course we all had to go through. While he was jumping off the tower perched on top of the survival school's big, fast-moving speedboat, with his chute, helmet, and other flying gear on, then paddling around in the ocean in his seat dinghy, he got a message that his squadron was going on alert immediately. A chopper was en route to pick him up, and when the chopper arrived he was whisked back to Yokota. He kissed his wife hello and good-bye, packed a quick B-4 bag, and was on his way to Korat.

Some of our people who suddenly found themselves in Korat were a bit amazed at the conditions and lack of facilities there. Not Mike; he was one-up on everyone else since he was not a stranger to the area. In 1960 he had been transferred from the Air Force Academy, where he had been a coach and physical education instructor for four years, to the 356th Tac Fighter Squadron to fly F-100s at Myrtle Beach,

South Carolina. About that time General Sweeney decided that he wanted air force fighter pilots to direct air strikes rather than having army people directing our fighters. Mike volunteered to go through the army jump school at Fort Benning, Georgia. Since he had just come from the athletic program at the academy, he thought he was in pretty good shape.

He went to Benning as a captain and he almost came out as a private. Those army sergeants tried to eat him alive and they almost did. Being air force, and supposedly the ranking officer in a class of almost 800 grunts going through the program, he just had to keep telling himself that he wasn't going to let the army beat him. He was always the first one out of the practice tower and the first one out of the airplane, but he was very happy when graduation rolled around.

Graduation at Benning was funny. All during the course Mike had been handling the ranking officer's responsibilities. But at the graduation ceremony, two army colonels appeared from who knows where and were congratulated for having done a great job leading their class through the training. He never figured that out, but took his jump wings and headed back to Myrtle Beach just in time to be transferred to Itazuke, Japan, for duty with another F-100 squadron.

Mike wasn't at Itazuke too long before several of the pilots in the squadron got sent back to the States to check out in the F-105. Shortly thereafter their Eighth Tactical Fighter Wing became the first F-105 combat-ready wing in PACAF. Right after that his uncle, Robert McNamara, changed the Eighth Wing designation to the 6441st Air Division and moved them to Yokota. He's not Mike's uncle, but it was a sick joke that we forced him to live with.

In 1963 the army's 173rd Airborne was sent to Thailand for a big exercise, and since Mike was the only jump-qualified fighter pilot in PACAF, he got sent along with them as their forward air controller. He joined them at Kadena and since he hadn't jumped in several months, he asked them to set him up for a jump so he could get his jump legs going again. They told him that they had done all of their qualification jumps and the only thing that was available was a special forces night jump. He hadn't made a night jump before, but said okay and stepped out into the black night over Kadena with his parachute bag containing everything he would need down there strapped between his legs. It all went uneventfully but when the commander of the 173rd found out what Mike had done he was pretty upset, since there were no replacements qualified to take his spot if he got hurt.

They loaded the whole operation into a bunch of very tired, very slow C-124 cargo aircraft and the first stop was Clark in the Philippines. One side of that base is superplush, the country club of the Pacific. The other side is a mess. It's covered with old dilapidated buildings from World War II, minus windows and doors, but with plenty of rats running all around. Of course, that's the kind of a place the 173rd liked to live in since they loved to rough it. They spent a couple of days there, but Mike managed to get a Jeep and go over to the other side of the base where he could get cleaned up and have a good meal at the officer's club. The 173rd always considered him a rebel and thought he liked to live too high, as fighter pilots always like to do.

About 8:00 one night they loaded everybody and everything into those beat-up C-124s, including their tanks and trucks and Mike's forward air control Jeep with all the radios on it, and off they went to Thailand. They were on the aircraft all night, and at about 10:00 the next morning they were over a little village called Royet in the rice paddies just east of Ubon. They jumped out, Mike made it just fine, his Jeep landed okay, and he was ready to start playing the first phase of their war games, which lasted for three days.

The second phase was to go into Korat, and Mike worked his Jeep up the road until he discovered the place that would be his home as a fighter pilot a year in the future. There wasn't much there except a runway and a few run-down buildings on one side and the Army Corps of Engineers on the other. The marines had a forward air control team in the games and they were supposed to handle phase two, but their Jeep had been damaged in the landing at Royet and they didn't make the show. So Mike had to take their place, and that made him the only one who had the "privilege" of jumping twice in that whole exercise.

The second jump wound up being on the runway at Udorn. It wasn't supposed to be on the runway, but since the Thais had flooded all the surrounding rice paddies, that's where it wound up. Udorn was Mike's first exposure to the operations sponsored by the CIA, and who knows who else, that flew under the banner of Air America. Mike found some of the things that were going on, even at that stage of our involvement, to be most interesting.

They finished up the games and Mike headed back to Yokota by way of Bangkok. He was the first of many to come back with Thai silk, bronzeware, and all that good stuff. Everyone at Yokota considered him some sort of a mystical adventurer from Siam until we all went down there later and Mike became just another collector of oriental junk bargains.

As soon as Mike found out that the squadron's destination with the Thuds was Korat he briefed everyone in the squadron on what to expect. He told them not to look for anything like a decent latrine, mess hall, officer's club, or a comfortable place to sleep. They went prepared with their mess kits, lots of funny entries on their shot records, and their malaria pills.

The Thirty-sixth had a unique situation that was bound to change as the war went on. They had trained together, they went back to the States together to get their new aircraft, they all moved their families into Yokota together, and they all sat nuclear alert together in Korea, so they knew each other pretty well. All that made for a tightly knit fighter squadron. They had their own maintenance crews, their own food people, their own intelligence folks; they were a complete squadron able to take care of their own needs. As the tempo of the war increased, that concept became more and more absorbed into the wing concept. By the time the wings were permanently assigned down there, much of what had been the old individual squadron effort was merged into the big picture of a wing operation.

It was August 4, 1964, two days after the Gulf of Tonkin incident, when Mike and the first Thuds landed at Korat. The Thirty-sixth got great support from the Army Corps of Engineers and in a short time they managed to set up some teakwood huts, or hootches, on the flight line for their squadron operations, fairly decent living quarters, a mess hall, and one set of living quarters that the pilots appropriated for their personal use. Mike Cooper and Jack Rawlings went down into the little village and hired a couple of young Thai girls, dressed them up in red T-shirts with their squadron insignia on them, put them to work as waitresses, and bingo, they had an officer's club.

They started out with a flight of four sitting alert out on the end of the steaming runway and it was hot duty. They were supposed to be available to suppress any antiaircraft guns that showed up over in Laos in the Plaine des Jarres, which was a well-protected communist area at that time. They didn't get a whole lot of action at the start as everyone was sort of feeling their way around, but David Graben managed to get himself hit and that was recorded as the first official case of Southeast Asian "battle damage."

When those first flights that deployed to Thailand got back to Yokota, "John Black" had to give them a tactics lecture. Colonel Chester L. Van Etten, whose World War II radio call sign of John Black became a nickname that has stuck with him ever since, had to remind his charges of some old lessons. Dave Graben had earned that dubious distinction of first to be hit while flying as number two on a flight into Laos. The rules at that time were that you couldn't shoot at anything unless you were shot at first. The flight was fired on by an antiaircraft battery and they proceeded to make several passes, in trail, down the same chute, just like they were at the gunnery range. Dave almost got his tail blown off.

John Black had to take great pains to analyze the situation and tell them that they would have to learn all over again that the things we had learned in World War II and again in Korea were still facts of life. If you follow in the gun smoke trail of the guy in front of you, if you attack a ground gun in close trail formation, or if you make pass after pass at the same target in the same direction—they're going to blow your ass off.

Dave Groark was also on that first deployment. It amazed him to sit back and listen and wonder, "Why, when we've been training all this time, do we find ourselves in a spot where we have to lose aircraft and relearn things we should have learned a long time ago?'' The answer was simple: We had ignored the basics of tactical aviation ever since the end of Korea in favor of atomic weapons delivery. That was a mistake I hope we never repeat.

One of the first times we as fighter pilots began to question what kind of balls our top leadership had came on November 1, 1964, when the Viet Cong mortared the airbase at Bien Hoa and killed five Americans, wounded twenty-six, destroyed five B-57s, and damaged eight others—all at a supposedly safe base just twenty miles north of Saigon. Since the White House had announced to the world that we would strike back if any such thing occurred, our people deployed down south were anticipating some action.

The Joint Chiefs of Staff, JCS in our lingo, had a plan on file for just such a happening. There was to be a thirty-six-hour air strike effort in Laos coupled with reconnaissance into southern North Vietnam, while American security forces moved in to protect our installations in the South and all dependents were evacuated from Saigon. Then the B-52s and the fighters were to be turned loose on the North to hit Phuc Yen and the other airfields, the major fuel depots in Hanoi and Haiphong, transportation complexes, and other military and industrial targets in the North.

But it was election eve in the States and the administration professed concern over Chinese reaction should America do what it had said it would do. The president, ignoring the JCS and Ambassador Maxwell Taylor, decided to make absolutely no retaliatory move.

As early as 1962, scholars of Vietnam, such as Bernard Fall, had spoken of the North's genuine fear that American retaliation would destroy their emerging economy and cause Chinese intervention and occupation. Ho had cleverly extracted the maximum in assistance from both the Soviet Union and China, which resulted in an industrial complex that was the only real economic entity in Southeast Asia. In less than forty years, he and his followers had gained the freedom from

China that had eluded their ancestors for the preceding two thousand years. The leadership and the people of the North were fanatically proud of those symbols of accomplishment. Ho had spent enough time in Korea to know what air strikes had done to Korean factories, railroads, dams, and towns, and he was hesitant to equate the glory of conquering the South to sacrificing his national pride and economic potential to American bombs. The fact that the leadership in Hanoi was smart enough to fear a determined assault by U.S. air power was lost on our Washington leadership.

President Johnson frequently cited concern for large-scale Chinese intervention as a justification for constraints on the bombing campaign. This was one of the great fallacies of the war. There is no indication that anyone in the Johnson administration ever requested a National Intelligence Estimate or any other intelligence analysis to prove or disprove this contention.

The worry over Chinese intervention ignored the historical enmity between the Chinese and Vietnamese, which persists to this day. The frequently made analogy with the Korean War was seriously flawed. In the fall of 1950 U.S. forces were on the banks of the Yalu River and Douglas MacArthur was threatening to enter China. In the Vietnam War, U.S. ground units were never closer than four hundred miles of marching distance to the Chinese border and never threatened to enter North Vietnam, much less China. Had Chinese ground forces chosen to enter the ground war in South Vietnam, such action would not only have widened the war substantially, but the Chinese would have faced the costs U.S. airpower would have forced them to pay en route to South Vietnam. Finally, as the Cultural Revolution began in 1967, the Chinese were too bound up with their own internal difficulties to respond militarily except to a direct threat to their national security interests.

It is questionable whether the "China card" was a real concern of Johnson and McNamara or something offered up as a justification for their unwillingness to do more in the air war against North Vietnam. If it was a real concern, it would seem that not only would there have been a National Intelligence Estimate, but in fact a daily monitoring of the pulse of China to determine the likelihood of large-scale intervention. There was none of this.

Admiral Sharp was Commander in Chief Pacific and the senior officer in the entire area, reporting directly to the JCS. In his book *Strategy for Defeat,* he said it all in commenting on the president's refusal to act on the JCS attack plan after the Viet Cong mortared U.S. forces in Bien Hoa: "In my opinion, such attacks would have had a major effect upon North Vietnam and might well have been the very thing needed to stop North Vietnamese aggression in the south and to bring Southeast Asia back to a peaceful, stabilized situation. At this critical juncture, some eleven years before its end, we might have prevented the costly and drawn-out war that followed."

Barrel Roll was the name of a new and yet to be executed program where we would be sent to attack specific targets in Laos, without having to wait to see if they fired on us first and did us in with their initial volley. The limited actions of phase one of Barrel Roll got partial approval on December 14, 1964, but Secretary McNamara cut the requested number of sorties to the ridiculously low figure of two four-ship flights per week. Admiral Sharp described one of these initial missions as "a small strike against rather insignificant targets . . . and generally ineffective as a reprisal action."

Dave Groark got a firsthand look at what Admiral Sharp meant when he got picked to be part of that small strike. Dave figured John Black was right when he said we had to learn all over again, but he didn't appreciate how broadly that statement applied until after that small strike. In 1964, General Moore was the ranking air commander in Vietnam, and initially his command was called Second Advon. The acronym Advon meant absolutely nothing, except that we were scared to tell the world that we had an air force down there. Later we changed the title to Second Air Force; then as things grew the organization became the huge entity known as Seventh Air Force.

They sent a flight of four—Dave, Jack Redmond, Art

Mearns, and Gordie Walcott—to Da Nang. It was the first time that anyone had staged a Thud mission out of Da Nang and it was the very first mission under the Barrel Roll program—Barrel Roll 001. General Moore personally briefed the flight and emphasized that they were the first flight with the authority to expend ordnance as a preplanned effort. They had two targets to hit: One was a small bridge and the other was a nondescript "village."

General Moore's headquarters dictated the weapons load and it was weird. Dave had six 750-pound bombs on his centerline rack, as did Gordie, and they each had two rocket pods on the outboard pylons. Art and Jack had useless Bullpup missiles outboard and two rocket pods inboard. They had a flight of four F-100s, which couldn't go as fast as they could, assigned as top cover.

The general's mission plan was that the flight was to go to the little bridge first. Gordie was to drop his 750s on the bridge and if he knocked it out they were to head for the village. If he missed, Dave was to hit the bridge with his 750s, then they would recce the road en route to the mysterious village.

They were supposed to run that thing at five thousand feet, and as it turned out, there were clouds at six thousand feet. When they found the bridge, Gordie was able to get up high enough to make something like a dive-bomb run and he knocked out the bridge. Then they started down the road toward the village. The F-100s weren't any good because the Thuds were trying to recce under the clouds and the F-100s were on top of the clouds, someplace.

It was the first time anyone had ever tried to carry an ordnance load as screwed up as that one. Sitting there with a heavy load like that, trying to road recce, and looking for a native village was a disaster. The machines were just not built for it. The four aircraft were superheavy with all those munitions on board, and they were falling out of the sky as they tried to weave back and forth on a road recce. They had to keep popping in and out of afterburner just to avoid stalling out and they were gulping fuel at full throttle. Dave sat back and thought, "This is the stupidest thing I have ever done."

They had no maneuverability and the fuel on all four airplanes was going like crazy as they snaked down the road, giving it the old college try to find that village. The villages all look the same over there: nothing more than a few thatched shacks. If the villages are connected by anything it's no more than a dirt footpath or a bicycle trail. There was no real way to tell where that village was. They finally got to the point where their fuel was so low that they found, or told each other that they had found, the village. Mearns and Redmond went in there with high-altitude, stand-off, fly-by-wire, pilot-guided Bullpups and made believe they were making a legitimate attack on a legitimate target. Under the best of practice conditions, few pilots had managed to hit much more than somewhere within the gunnery range with a Bullpup.

Meanwhile, Dave was struggling to keep his beast in the air with 6,000 pounds of bombs, bomb racks, and a bunch of rockets and rocket pods dragging him down. Gordie at least had shed his bombs back at the bridge, but Dave was hurting. He was running out of fuel and he couldn't get high enough to put the bombs anyplace worthwhile, even if he had found something worthwhile. He realized that he couldn't do any good with the bombs and that if he tried to haul them back to Da Nang he would run out of fuel before he got back, so he had to dump them on a hillside just to get rid of them.

They struggled back into Da Nang, without benefit of a tanker. Dave was one torqued-off captain and he didn't bother to disguise that fact when he said that the stupidity of the way that mission had been planned was unbelievable. The commanding general and his brass at the debriefing were too much. It took all Dave had not to get up and tell the general that it was the most stupid display of how to use airpower imaginable: Bullpups on grass shacks; road recce with six 750s dragging you down, while you try to find a tiny village in Laos under an overcast. Dave couldn't believe it. But he believed that John Black called it right; too many people over there simply did not know what they were up to and they had to learn all over again, if they could get that lucky.

* * *

Mike McNamara observed the same lack of planning the first time he ran into a rescue situation. He and Mike Cooper were up in Laos one day when an F-101 recce pilot got shot down and they found him sitting on top of a mountain peak. One of the strongest fighter principles is that if an airman goes down, you do everything within your power to divert your mission to Combat Air Patrol, which in our language is cap. Your priority becomes flying cover, or cap, and getting rescue forces on the scene. They capped that recce pilot for hours and called everybody they could contact on the radio to get a chopper up there to get him out. Mike knew what Air America had available from his old jump days and he knew they could get him out of there. But nobody would come to the rescue, and they finally ran so low on fuel that they had to leave. The next day Mike Cooper took another flight back up there but the 101 guy was gone. That first group of pilots suddenly realized that at that time there was no rescue capability in existence and that their radio frequencies were completely unorganized and overloaded. Even though Mike only got hit once in those early days, he found it very frustrating to know that if you got knocked down, that was it.

Toward the end of their first tour the pilots from Yokota noted some improvement in the rescue effort, but it was apparent that the 101 recce guys didn't have the benefit of John Black's advice. Chuck McLaren and Neal Jones were flying escort on a recce mission for an RF-101 pilot whose name was Walls. Walls was taking photos up around the Mugia Pass and all that Chuck and Neal had for ordnance was rockets. Walls made a pass on a gun site during a low-level recce run and he saw some people and some guns, but he didn't get any action out of them. He made a wide turn, with Chuck and Neal flying behind him, and said, "Let's just circle around and go back there and rattle their cage a bit."

Walls came in low with the other two above and behind him. About the time Walls got within firing range the ground guns opened up and his right wing burst into flame and disintegrated. He punched out and Chuck and Neal made a couple of passes with their rockets at the gun site to shut them up, which they did. They managed to get an Air America chopper in there and the chopper picked Walls up and brought him back to the Camp Friendship Army hospital at Korat. Dave Groark got the whole squadron together and painted up a sign to deliver to Walls, who was pretty beat up. It was a sketch of Walls rolling in on the guns, captioned, "Let's just go rattle their cage." He rattled it okay, but he gave the ground gunners a second chance, and their first shot took him out of it.

Rescue efficiency continued to improve with the assignment of more people and equipment dedicated to that particular task. In one early case, Takhli lost five Thuds in rapid succession, with two of the pilots judged to have been dead before they ever reached the ground. The pilots of the other three aircraft were recovered by rescue choppers. This was indicative of the fact that in the earlier stages of the war the North's defenses were not massive or supersophisticated. They were good, but nothing like they were going to be. The ground forces and ground fire were permissive enough to allow the choppers to move in and recover three out of three.

Mike McNamara was embarrassed by his Uncle Bob McNamara's confusion. Just when they were getting going, Uncle Bob had one of his many changes of heart. They were the only fighters down there, but Bob said they had to get out and go back to Yokota. He changed his mind again in early 1965 and Robbie Risner took his squadron from Kadena and launched for Korat. Those in the Thirty-sixth who had been on the first deployment didn't mind a bit that somebody else got to go to their old stomping grounds and utilize the limited facilities they had established, until a couple of weeks later when they got alerted to go back down there themselves. That didn't bother them too much either until they found out that they were headed for Takhli this time. Takhli was only slightly better than what they had encountered at Korat the fall before, so the squadron from Kadena at least got a livable setup, while the Thirty-sixth had to start all over from scratch. The one good thing they could say was that the Thirty-sixth had the distinction of opening up both Korat and Takhli.

Mike and the others were all pumped up when they got to

Takhli on March 6, 1965, and there was every indication that they were going to really go get 'em this time. The whole squadron was up for the first two days and two nights doing their planning on how they were going to hit them hard up North and get this thing over with, since they were alerted to go after the runways and the fuel dumps at Hanoi. They were excited. They had a sixteen-ship attack planned, and it would have been a good one against defenses that were minimal at that time. Colonel Don McCance was the squadron commander, and his plan was to have eight ships attacking from the east and eight hitting from the west. With a mixed load of bombs, napalm, and their Vulcan cannons, they were all set to do good work on both the airfield and the petroleum, oil, and lubricant facilities, which we called POL. Would you believe that it was two years later before anyone got up into that area and even then they were not after the good targets?

The largest mass effort the Thirty-sixth put up during that deployment was against Tiger Island, which was off the coast near Da Nang. It was probably a good warm-up for things that could have come, but they never came in those early days when the environment was relatively passive. They were supposed to drop their bombs, fire their rockets, and then strafe with their sixteen-ship force. Everyone who flew that one concluded that there wasn't a soul on that island. If there had been anyone there before, they obviously knew the Thuds were coming and had cleared out. Mike was so personally eager that he had dropped all his bombs, fired all his rockets, and strafed before most of the squadron got started.

While the PACAF squadrons continued to fly out of both Takhli and Korat, the stateside rotational, or rote, squadrons moved into position. The trip from one side of the world to the other didn't always go smoothly. As an example of the confusion of the times, the 354th was scheduled to deploy to Kadena on March 3, 1965, but on the first of March they were notified by Tactical Air Command, TAC to us, that the deployment had been indefinitely delayed. Since that meant they had to pick up their local flying commitment again, they started to unpack all their deployment gear. At 11:00 that night they were informed that the move would go as scheduled, so it was hurry up and repack. When the 354th was scheduled to return, MATS, which some called Military Airlift Transport Service but which we called Might Arrive Tomorrow, Sometime, claimed they knew nothing about it; thus there were no transport aircraft. That aspect of the war never changed. They were so bad they changed their name to Military Airlift Command, but MAC was no better than MATS.

Billy Ellis made his first trip over there as part of a rote squadron. He was over in Southeast Asia three different times, first in 1965 flying 105s, again in 1968-69 first flying 105s, then switching to F-4s, and then again in 1973 when he was running the big Strategic Air Command, or SAC, bomber and tanker operation down in Utapow, near Bangkok. In early 1965 Billy's stateside assignment was in the Standardization and Evaluation outfit working for Punchy Ferris, our old Thunderbird narrator, out of TAC headquarters. Things were heating up down south and Billy requested permission for his troops to go overseas and fly some missions. If the squadrons that they were responsible for evaluating were rotating back and forth to Southeast Asia and were flying combat on a temporary duty basis, it made sense that their evaluators ought to get some of that temporary duty with the rote squadrons. That concept was approved and was lying on the back burner in February of 1965 when Billy went out on McConnell Air Force Base to conduct an evaluation of the 355th Wing.

He arrived on a Monday and they asked him if he wanted to go with them on their upcoming deployment. He said sure, and since the 355th had a squadron leaving Wednesday, Billy got the job of leading the third cell across the Pacific. That was a bit faster than he had planned on, but he made a couple of phone calls and got the okay to go with them.

Later that night he tried to call home to tell his wife Barbara to throw some things in a B-4 bag for him and get it on the next courier aircraft, since he wouldn't be coming home right away. It's amazing how the big things seem to fall into place easily while the little details burn you up. The telephone operator at McConnell wouldn't let Billy make a call home through the government circuits and that really ticked him off. He wound up finding a pay phone and calling collect so he could tell Barbara to get that bag flown out to him in a hurry so he could go to the other side of the world for a few months to fight the war. But that was only a small part of many frustrations to come.

For a little while on Wednesday it didn't look like Billy was going to go because the Tacan and most of the rest of the navigation system on the Thud they gave him didn't want to go. But after a short delay they got her working, which meant Billy just sat in the cockpit with his engine running and didn't say anything more about the problems as the ground crew tweaked a screw here and there and changed a few black boxes, and he just kept nodding his head yes, to indicate he would take it as it was. After they blasted off, the first stop was Hawaii, where they Mai Taied a bit and turned the machines around for the morning trip to Anderson Air Force Base in Guam. From there they went all the way into Takhli. They had the usual problems with the lack of working radio navigation aids down in that part of the world, and there were the usual thunderstorms, but it was generally a good trip.

They had one day to get organized and then started flying missions. Originally they were mostly milk runs into Laos with a few into the southern part of North Vietnam around Vinh. There were some missions up to Dien Bien Phu, but for some unknown reason connected with the Chinese, our government kept putting that place off limits. There must have been something there that somebody in Washington didn't want hit.

Things were a little primitive when the Thuds got to Takhli. There were quite a few people and aircraft who showed up from various parts of the world at about the same time and, as usual, the facilities were not ready for them. The most available construction material in Thailand was teakwood, so the construction people and the Thai laborers were building teak hootches and teak sidewalks to keep people out of the mud, but it was a long way from being done. Seems like those construction folks always got told to build the wrong things first. They did have a post office and a library, and the pilots used them as places to sleep.

Billy was a major at the time and was supposed to be working for a squadron commander named Davis and his ops officer. He was surprised to find out that nobody in that particular squadron had ever flown any combat. His tour in Korea as a second lieutenant made him the only one there who had any combat and at least he knew some of the basic things. Each night he would check the operations order when it came in and figure out what everybody needed to know the most for the next day. Then he would put one-page memos on the bulletin board in the ops hut. He came up with one thing each day, like how to do a road recce, how to fly cover for your buddy if he gets shot down; the old "how to" approach on the basics that nobody in that outfit seemed to know. Billy found himself the de facto squadron commander even though he was almost a stranger on temporary duty from TAC headquarters. But it wasn't hard to figure out that most of them were youngsters and the older ones didn't have any experience and didn't much know what they were doing, so Billy moved in and did what needed to be done.

A hint of the confusion surrounding the real shooting war we were involved in was shown by the lingering peacetime approach to training requirements in some quarters. The air force had developed huge empires built upon the concept that people were not qualified to fly unless they had taken the appropriate number of exams, checks, and recertifications within some stated time period. Those flying and fighting had little use for those who worried that the training requirements, as defined by Air Force Manual 51-105, were being compromised by the war. Operational commanders waded through correspondence ad nauseum on the subject throughout our entire involvement over there, but we were more concerned with the real-life combat problems that faced our pilots. To quell the din we made sure that all of our more experienced heads were on orders as "examiners." When a combat pilot was due for some sort of check, one of the old heads would fly a combat mission with him. If the guy got back in one piece, the old head would sign him off and fill in the required squares on the training chart. If the guy didn't make it back, the squares didn't matter anyway.

Our real-life training concerns centered on things like the fact that navigation proved to be a bit of a problem for some of the pilots at the start of the war. Their recent involvement with the nuclear delivery mission had made them dependent upon dead reckoning, or more simply stated, they were used to getting from A to B by flying at high speeds, on the deck, steering a series of courses of X degrees for Y minutes. They also utilized their sophisticated on-board navigational systems to the maximum. In the shooting war of the North, a gun or a Sam or a Mig or a 50,000 foot thunderstorm often kept you from flying a straight line from A to B.

The Doppler position-indicating units in the aircraft were an integral part of that navigation system. These black boxes did not take kindly to getting tossed around the skies of Asia and were marginal at best. The more humidity and dirt they absorbed, the more *g*s they pulled, and the less time the harassed maintenance technicians had to try and get them working properly, the worse they got. The result was that the pilots had to go back to using their eyeballs to correlate between the ground and their maps, and in the early days those maps were French hand-me-downs that lacked detail. That kind of navigating is a basic pilot skill, but it takes some effort and practice when you're doing it under tough conditions in a strange place. You couldn't even use the old cadet trick of following a road or a railroad track. The roads were dirt trails leading to nowhere and if you could even find a railroad track, you would probably get shot at.

We were forced to put our pilots through weather drills that the training-manual people never even imagined. The worst of the weather in Southeast Asia is created by the northeast monsoon, which the Vietnamese call *Crachin*. The basic monsoon phenomenon is caused by winds that move inland from the South China Sea during the period from November to April. As these warmer winds collide with polar air that flows south from Siberia and China, a gigantic swirling air mass generates surface winds from the northeast that saturate the entire area. The mountainous terrain of Vietnam accentuates the condition, and the result is week after week of heavy rain, terrible visibility, and extensive cloud cover.

Even if you aren't fighting monsoon season, you often have severe visibility problems. They torch everything that will burn over there and the combination of smoke and wet air makes Los Angeles smog look like a clear day. If you're flying in L.A. smog you can usually at least see straight down. Not in Southeast Asia; it's like an all-enveloping blanket of gray that you know is filled with mountains. We lost people, especially in Laos, when they dived into that stuff thinking they knew where their target was, only to find a mountain or the ground before they ever found their target.

Then there are the thunderstorms. They are the tallest, blackest, and roughest storms that nature generates. They boil and bubble and bang into each other all day and all night, and produce absolutely spectacular lightning displays as they grow higher and broader. I've been pushing 40,000 feet in a clean Thud and been looking way up above me at the still-billowing tops. You can't go above them so you have to go through them, and they have bumps inside that are hard to believe. Even with your navigation lights on and tucked into the tightest possible formation, you often can see no more of your leader's aircraft than a pinpoint of red or green light on his wingtip, though that tip is only a few feet away. Penetrating a big one in a flight of four, loaded with bombs, stuffed with fuel, and covered with ice is a thrill for the leader. It gets even more thrilling when you're a wingman and it gets so thick that you watch that pinpoint of colored light fade to nothing. You've been flying only by visual reference on your leader and you have no idea where you are. You don't know if you're rightside up or upside down and you don't know where anyone else is, except that they're only a few feet away. You don't dare break out of formation and you can't get in any closer, so what can you do? Hang in there, baby, and breathe slowly.

Serious shortages of everything from pilots to munitions, and even proper flying equipment, were a fact of life. Nobody paid much attention to the calls for help from the operating units until the media finally discovered the problems and the *New York Times* had it on the front page on October 9, 1966. Congressional investigations followed immediately and Secretary McNamara did a lot of fancy talking. During the period that McNamara described as free of shortages, we had one fine young captain depart for the Hanoi Hilton as a result of his attempts to knock down a concrete and steel bridge with 20-mm cannon fire. Why attempt the ridiculous feat of attacking a bridge with a gun? The bridge was his assigned target, but we didn't have enough bombs to hang on his aircraft. As usual, much of what McNamara said was suspect at best.

Pilot morale was tops during the deployments, but then what else would you expect? The fighter pilots were flying combat, which is what it is all about. The initial losses were taken in stride and the twelve-hour days, seven days a week, were of little concern to the Thud drivers as long as they got to fly and fight. There was no running water. Sleeping hootches were hot and humid, but somebody managed to scrounge some fans from someplace and that stirred the wet air around. The maintenance troops didn't mind the flight line conditions. While they had only been able to coax twenty-six flying hours a month out of each bird back in the more comfortable areas, they were now cranking out fifty-one airborne hours per month.

While Billy Ellis recognized some early shortcomings, he and his rote squadron mates wasted little time getting to work. About the third day they were there, they were out after some trucks. Sam Woodward got a truck but flew right into a ridge after he hit the truck, and that was their first loss. When they got back to Takhli they went to their hootch, which was split into two sections. They used one part for sleeping, and they had a bar set up in the other. The sleeping part didn't work out too well since it was sort of a contest between the sleepers and the party troops. Billy wound up leading the wake for Sam into the early hours of the morning, and the fact that he had a first-light, early-morning mission didn't seem too important at that moment. They were supposed to fly over to

Da Nang and load up some leaflets and then go up North and bomb Vinh with paper.

A few hours after conducting the wake for Sam, Billy got up feeling pretty rocky and it was very dark. He got strapped in and just before he started his engine, the flight surgeon crawled up the ladder and wanted to know if he was okay. Billy told him he was fine, but he never knew if he had been that convincing or if his breath had just knocked the flight surgeon off the ladder. When they got to Da Nang there was a lot of sitting around while all the big gears were trying to decide if they were really going to bomb the North with those deadly leaflets. While that was going on, the Viet Cong zapped the base with one of their first real raids and they blew up a good part of the local bomb storage dump. Billy and his flight watched lots of explosions and scurrying around while they waited.

They finally got airborne again about 2:00 in the afternoon, went up north and did their leaflet thing, and went on home to Takhli. You had to wonder why they went through all the bother of going to Da Nang when they could have done the whole thing from Takhli to start with. The only thing at Da Nang that wasn't at Takhli was all those big gears who worried about the paper drop for most of the day. Seems like they could have gone through the exercise most anyplace, then given Billy a phone call and said "Go" or "Don't go." You learned early on not to bother trying to figure out things like that.

At first Billy used to wonder how come none of our ideas were ever any good. There were lots of us who were eager and somewhat smart, and we dreamed up several ways we could have done things better and easier. Before we got over there we had drilled for years on how to navigate and drop nuclear weapons using the systems we had in the 105. We wanted to use those systems to do some bombing up North. While we only had those old French maps, there were islands, rivers, and coastlines that would allow us to have a crack at it regardless of the weather. Billy began to bombard George Simler, an old associate who had made general and was in Saigon at what was then known as Second Air Division, with our ideas. After what seemed like about epistle number 34, George flew up to see Billy, just to tell him personally that, "We ain't gonna do it, so stop overloading the mail." Billy said he didn't ever remember anyone's ideas making the grade uphill from the cockpit.

Local conditions forced a lot of quick changes. The pilots had been trained for forty-five-degree dive-bomb runs, as this provides good accuracy and minimum exposure to ground fire. The weather always influenced the attacks, and when low clouds forced the pilots to use smaller angles of dive and longer, flatter approaches, accuracy went down and battle damage went up. Lots of quick homework went into devising and memorizing pilot solutions regarding flexible dive angles and quick computations for adjusting sight pictures to obtain proper releases under changing combat conditions. As the pilots learned to cope with local conditions accurately, Second Air Force made one of the first really dumb decisions of the war. They decided that the minimum pullout altitude on divebomb runs would be 10,000 feet. Accuracy really went to pot, since even the best of fighter pilots would be hard pressed to hit with any acceptable degree of accuracy dropping an iron bomb from that altitude. That was one of the few uneducated restrictions that didn't last long.

Secretary McNamara was determined that he would engineer a bombing pause in December 1965, even though Secretary Rusk was opposed to that course of action: a strange convolution of the commonly perceived roles of defense and state. Secretary Rusk opposed by memorandum, which apparently found its way to the repository for anti-McNamara papers, since it had no visible effect on the decision to stop bombing. All the military commanders, including the JCS who were chartered as part of the president's top team, were likewise ignored to the extent that they were not even made aware that the subject was under discussion. They were informed of the halt by a curt message received only hours before it was to take effect on December 25. They were never informed of the intended duration of the halt and their constant flow of messages requesting information and encouraging a resumption of action received little attention.

Why would McNamara act in that manner? Perhaps an answer to that question can be gleaned from his testimony in the 1984 Westmoreland v. CBS case. In his deposition Secretary McNamara testified that he and John McNaughton, who was assistant secretary of defense for international security affairs until late 1973, had concluded in December 1965 that the war could not be won militarily. They further concluded that Rolling Thunder, as McNamara conducted it, was not having any effect on North Vietnam. These conclusions led to McNamara's advocacy of an extended bombing pause.

The implications of that testimony are immense. The secretary of defense not only daily placed the lives of every single man who fought in Southeast Asia at risk, but he did so in a war he concluded could not be won through means he felt were not effective; and he would not permit those fighting the war to do more in order to be more effective. Now, as one of those doing that fighting, I can only wonder why McNamara remained in office for another two and one-half years. McNamara's continued and increasing restrictions were a classic example of a self-fulfilling prophecy. How many good men were lost so that McNamara could prove himself right?

Johnson and McNamara were hoping in vain that the North would petition to come to the conference table. The North had no such idea and used the truce time to effectively rebuild and restock their facilities to enable them to renew their struggle against the Americans. On January 31, the military was authorized to resume very limited armed reconnaissance, but it was not until March that it was allowed to resume even the general nature of operations that had been authorized in 1965, and then with even more restrictions than had been in effect before the pause.

The first phase of the fighter jocks' involvement ended with that cease-fire. Those doing the fighting were concerned, though still quietly, and the frustration was showing on the supereager ones like Dave Groark. Dave summed it up pretty well from the standpoint of a Thud driver getting shot at when he said that planning was absent and the people who were trying to do the planning had no idea of the capabilities of the equipment or of the realities of the situation. We didn't use the power we had and we were restricted from going after the targets we needed to hit to win the war right at the start. We screwed around until we had the bomb and ammunition shortages that McNamara said didn't exist, then we went out with rockets against bridges and tried to cut worthless dirt roads with napalm. Dirt doesn't burn very well.

Dave was right; it wasn't going like we wanted it to go and we were getting that feeling you get when your date doesn't show up or bother to call. But not to worry. We were getting more aircraft and more organizations and more command and control help. We built up a real strike potential and got over the initial pains of getting things set up. Things were bound to get better, weren't they? You had to believe that if you sat in the seat of a Hanoi-bound Thud, because you were betting your life on it everyday.

4 | IN SPITE OF COMMAND AND CONTROL

Those of us who were fighter pilots in Korea thought that we had more command and control than we needed. Little did we know that we had only witnessed the beginning of the intense amplification of command and control. During our time in Korea we were subject to direction that flowed from the offices of the secretary of defense and the secretary of the air force through the JCS, the air force staff complex, Pacific Forces in Honolulu, Far East Air Force in Tokyo, and then to Fifth Air Force, who had advance elements located in Korea itself. Our command and control was indeed tight, and while restrictions were ever obvious, they came nowhere close to the all-encompassing, smothering effect we experienced in Southeast Asia.

When I was flying F-80s and F-84s in Korea, our command relations were such that it was not uncommon for our unit commanders to be in close touch with our general officers and their staffs. Nor was it uncommon to find a general officer, be he air force or army, down among the troops, shooting the breeze with the fighter jocks along the dirt flight line of the operational squadrons. The visitors were generally constructive, eager, and anxious to talk with the people car-

78

rying on the combat operations. We all felt like we learned a bunch from those sessions and like we were fighting the same war. The proper mutual respect was always there, but so was the rapport.

In the interim between Korea and Southeast Asia the efficiency of communications channels improved vastly and their multiplicity increased dramatically, which was a mixed blessing. Since the ability to communicate was there, everyone in the chain of command seemed to feel they should be aware of minute details within units under their control. As a result, the instant transmission of information became paramount, thus saturating those communications channels. The channels were always inadequate because the more information they relayed, the more requirements they generated for even more detail. Enhanced communications made the highest commanders think they were in the cockpit or at the head of the platoon. Four-star generals, appointed secretaries of defense, and even presidents make poor combat pilots or riflemen.

Access to real-time information begat an increased desire for control, which justified more headquarters with larger staffs, who created new reports requiring further detailed analyses, which required additional information. I doubt that Arthur MacArthur would have made it to the top of the hill with the flag in the Philippines or that Eddie Rickenbacker would have shot down a single German aircraft if they had had the benefit of all the help we had in Southeast Asia.

Lyndon Baines Johnson called the shots in our league. He bowed almost exclusively to Robert McNamara. As a rule he ignored, or at best heeded lightly, the remainder of his cabinet, the JCS, and Admiral Ulysses S. Grant Sharp, Commander-in-Chief Pacific. If you were in the career military you suspected the dice were loaded from the first roll, but you didn't want to believe it.

I was going through the National War College in 1964 and early 1965 and it was not too difficult to sense the undercurrent of a lack of leadership and a sense of impotency at that early date. We had lectures from Southeast Asian specialists on things like strategic hamlets, pacification programs, and the ink blot theory, but they sounded empty even in the staid atmosphere of Fort McNair. We were briefed by a goodly number of the top policy people in Washington as well as several of the secretaries or their advisors. A lot of what I heard about the political situation and the ground war in Southeast Asia while I was there sounded a bit unreal, and I heard little about the air war.

We were made academically aware that the JCS were pushing for hard-hitting aerial attacks on a list of ninety-four prime targets without success. I was to learn later that the message traffic and briefings from the Pacific were endless, but the results were always the same. The senior military officers were forbidden to effectively fight the war they were directed to fight.

We had enough briefings to know that there was a constant series of plans, all with alternatives, with the weakest sometimes accepted and then usually canceled after acceptance. We knew that Secretary McNamara was the filtering agent for policy and that he always had an abundance of studies available so that he could pick the study that matched his already established conclusions and present it to President Johnson. For instance, McGeorge Bundy advocated influencing the course of the struggle in the South, while Ambassador Taylor advocated influencing the North. Take your choice.

I got to evaluate some things on my own when our war college class split into groups for month-long trips to various sections of the world and I got the Pacific circuit. We spent part of that time in Vietnam. It wasn't much fun but it sure was an eye-opener. Being an air force officer, I was oriented toward the air war, especially in the North, but I looked forward to the trip as an opportunity to learn more about how the political war and the ground war were being conducted out of Saigon.

We checked into the Caravelle Hotel in downtown Saigon late in the evening, and there was nothing in sight to suggest that we were in the city that was once called "the pearl of the Orient." I didn't need a wake-up call since sunrise was accompanied by the unmistakable rattle of semiautomatic weapons in the street right outside my window. It sounded like a full-fledged firefight and I expected to see at least a couple of opposing squads when I cautiously peeked out the window as the gunfire subsided. What I saw was a large number of heavily armed South Vietnamese soldiers emerging one by one from every visible doorway and alley on the street and one very dead oriental civilian in the middle of the street. There was little doubt that they had ventilated him from about every conceivable direction, and there was no doubt in my mind that the people of Vietnam were firing real bullets in anger.

This was obviously going to be an all embassy-army show, but I was anxious to be impressed that our overall national effort was one of strength and realism. Even at that early stage of the war, it didn't come across to me quite that way. According to the embassy people, the South Vietnamese were doing great and the Viet Cong and the North Vietnamese were little more than bothersome peasants. We got the standard tour all over town, with canned dog and pony shows at all of the military, state, and foreign aid sections. Without exception, the briefers were bored and tired of giving constant briefings to an endless flow of visitors. We spent about half of one day listening to statistics at General Westmoreland's headquarters and I felt like I was back at West Point going through Infantry Sand Table I, with lots of emphasis on the new buzz word of the day, "bodycount." I knew all over again how urgently I had awaited the day when I graduated from the Point, shucked the ground army image, and became part of the Army Air Corps.

The tour of the countryside was equally canned. The secured hamlet we inspected was surrounded by a board fence, complete with watchtower, and was presided over by a sharp West Point infantry captain in crisp khakis. He even gave us a make-believe attack by a VC complete with black pajamas and night makeup at 10:00 in the morning. The VC jumped up from the brush and charged across an open field to run straight into the ten-foot-high board fence, whereupon he was felled with blanks by the alert Vietnamese peasant in the watch tower.

Things were equally artificial at our next stop, a pacified village. Center stage was a manmade pond stocked with huge goldfish. A lone scrubbed pig, which looked to be of blue ribbon caliber, stood at incongruous attention next to the pond. The flimsy rolled barbed-wire fence strung loosely around the area would not have deterred the VC. The only thing that came across as real was the nervous fear radiating from the man, woman, and young girl, presented to us as pacified villagers and speaking to us through an interpreter. Their constant furtive glances to all quadrants to see who was watching them belied the glowing tale of well-being we were hearing in perfect English.

We got a few hours of free time one afternoon and a couple of my friends and I talked the army into giving us a car with a Vietnamese driver to take us about thirty kilometers out of town so we could look at a Vietnamese air force operation we had heard about. Driving through the city was bad. All the streets were jammed with tides of people, bicycles, South Vietnamese army trucks, soldiers, pushcarts, and a constant stream of out-of-control cars going all directions both on and off the road. It was complete disorder, but the worst was yet to come.

Once we cleared the city, that Vietnamese driver went bananas and full throttle at the same time. We were all over the highway and our own survival, as well as that of others, was in doubt. I have never been so terrified in a car. We were yelling in English, which he didn't understand, and he was literally screaming in Vietnamese. I was sitting up front and thought about grabbing him, but that would have crashed us for sure. The only thing I could understand from his screaming was "VC, VC," accompanied with a wild waving of one arm, which must have meant "all over."

I calmed down enough to take a good look at the driver and he was visibly shaking. We were on the open road, barely on the outskirts of Saigon, in broad daylight, and he was in complete panic because of uncontrolled fear of the VC. That driver gave me a different and far more succinct message than all the baloney briefings of the past few days. The VC owned the countryside; the VC controlled the people, and they didn't even have to show their face to make that control work. It took me a few years to fully assimilate what I learned that afternoon.

The trip was a bust all the way. When we arrived we weren't allowed to see anything and all we got was constant urging by an English-speaking South Vietnamese officer to get back to town. He couldn't or wouldn't help us with another driver, so it was hell on wheels back to the hotel.

I was so distressed at the obvious conflict I had just seen that I went for a walk on a relatively quiet street and stared into little shop windows. I'm attracted to bright colors in oil paintings and I pulled up short in front of a very plain, room-sized store that was more like a booth. Inside were about a dozen oils all done in fantastic shadings of bright orange that faded to small sections of yellow or brown and the artist was working, almost frantically, at his easel in the back of the booth.

The artist's name was Than and he spoke excellent English and I suspect fluent French. While he was eager to talk, he was subdued and obviously very nervous. The canvas on the easel focused on a small native wooden boat, very much alone, on a calm shoreline. The background was completely dominated by an all-surrounding, brilliant orange postsunset sky. That picture was for me. He wanted all of seven dollars worth of piasters, and as I paid him he explained that he would finish it immediately. Since it was wet I could not pick it up for a day and a half and then I must be sure to allow several more days for final drying.

As I prepared to leave, Than spoke to me softly, "Be sure you come back before noon on the day after tomorrow. My paintings and I may not be here much longer than that. These are troubled times, *Monsieur.*" Back on the street I reviewed my lessons as I walked back to the hotel. My afternoon ride indicated that the VC had a position of strength on the outskirts of the capital. My conversation with Than made me aware that the people and the shops in the city were getting some pretty firm directions, most probably from the VC. I wanted to believe the embassy and army people about secure hamlets and good government, but I was having trouble taking the bait. I shrugged and figured no sweat, the air force flying war up North is bound to be different from all this.

We were traveling in a big C-135, and when I got to the aircraft a few days later I scrounged some safety wire from the crewchief and hung Than's painting face down from the cabin ceiling where it swung and dried all the way back to Washington. It's quite striking in a broad black silk frame with gold trim, and often when I look at it I wonder what happened to Than. I call the painting, "Haiphong Harbor; H Hour plus 00:01."

By the time I arrived back at the hotel it was time to dress up and head for General Westmoreland's cocktail party and dinner. Everybody who was anybody in the American community was there. It was first class all the way and there was no doubt that Westy was to be the star of the show. About twenty minutes into the cocktail party an aide called for attention to relay the General's apology, but he would be delayed a bit since he was just returning from a "combat mission."

Our war college class was made up of people from all the services, the CIA, and budding future secretaries and undersecretaries of state, treasury, and other cabinet-level departments. The aide's announcement was obviously calculated to invoke visions of MacArthur wading ashore or Ridgeway inspecting Korean troops with bandoliers of grenades draped across his shoulders. It worked like a charm with my nonmilitary associates and, to my surprise, with the assembled embassy types from Saigon. The large room was buzzing with oohs and aahs of "go get 'em, Westy—that'll show 'em." Most of us in the military thought that was good time to locate the nearest bartender and wait for the next development.

At the proper moment the general strode in and there was no doubt that he was an impressive gentleman, in complete command of his domain. With everyone else in their fancy suits, his green cotton attire made him stand out even more as he doffed his combat baseball cap while his wavy silver hair and oversized silver stars accentuated his immaculate starched and pressed fatigues. It doesn't take too much imagination to figure out how the rest of the evening went.

The next morning the army took us on a helicopter combat strike. A long string of about twenty of those noisy beasts, full of grunts, was going to sneak up on a precleared open area that was surrounded by hostile VC. The grunts were to jump out as the choppers touched down and go get the bad guys. It seemed to me that if the VC were deaf and blind the choppers might surprise them in the broad daylight. It also seemed to me that if the VC were dumb enough to sit around a big landing area they had watched the Americans clear, then wait until the pilot in the lead chopper had fired his smoke rockets to check the wind and pinpoint his touchdown spot before they took off and melted into the countryside, they deserved to get chased and shot at.

The army did everything in alphabetical order when I was a cadet at West Point in 1942, in fact they had done it that way since the days of George Washington, so I got to ride in the first chopper, which was the command and control ship. It was horrible to sit there strapped into that flat-bottomed airborne barge knowing you have no control over what was going on. Two things made it even worse.

The choppers were flown by warrant officers who obviously enjoyed showing their proficiency. I learned later that they knew they had an ex-air force Thunderbird leader on board, and did they ever show me some tight formation flying. Personally, I was petrified as those choppers bounced and lurched, not in unison like close-formation fighters, but independently with each one doing its own little rock and roll, yet with the rotor blades sharing the same airspace. They kept it up all day, every place we went, and I'll admit I was suitably impressed, though not favorably. Throughout the war the army lost people and machinery playing that silly game.

Then some VC didn't read the script or ignored the fact that this was a daytime demonstration and our chopper picked up two hits, straight up through the bottom, and they lodged in an aluminum structure a couple of feet in front of where they had me locked in. One of the rips looked big enough to have been what was left of a 50 caliber round, while the other one was a neat round hole. When you get hit in a fighter you usually don't have reason to stare at the holes, because you're hanging on to the controls, jinking to avoid other hits, and getting on with your job. Just having to sit there caused my automatic pucker string to tighten up about four notches.

Having escaped the enemy during the landing assault, we were whirled about to see several selected outposts. Every Vietnamese officer we were introduced to spoke perfect English, had perfect teeth and a big grin, and looked like an oriental Jack Armstrong. They all had nicknames like Tiger or Cheetah or Night Eyes. I'd had enough of my guided tour of the Vietnamese ground war.

We departed the next day, March 29, 1965, but not before a debriefing at the embassy where they told us what we had seen and learned. The parting punch line was to the effect that we as Americans were here to see this thing through to victory. We were firmly committed to use whatever force was necessary to insure that South Vietnam be allowed to continue its successfully demonstrated progression to freedom and self-sustaining statehood. Our nation, and President Johnson in particular, was determined to act immediately and decisively to retaliate against North Vietnam and its forces in South Vietnam for any actions on their part that would interrupt this progress or that would threaten the American position.

We left the embassy shortly after 9:00 A.M., boarded our bus for Tan Son Nhut airfield, and hung on for another wild ride. Once again, the driver acted like an idiot possessed as we were engulfed in the confused, meandering masses that clogged every available street. Before we got to the airport the driver charged into a mass of humanity at an intersection, and with a sickening bump ran over and killed a small child. He stopped long enough to open the door and scream at the crowd, who screamed back as he slammed the door shut and lurched on.

By the time our C-135 landed in Tokyo the newspapers on the stands were bannered with the headlines that the VC had bombed and demolished the embassy in Saigon earlier that day. Dead and injured were still being sorted out. What had that embassy debriefer told us a few hours ago? "Our nation, and President Johnson in particular, was determined to act immediately and decisively to retaliate against North Vietnam and its forces in South Vietnam for any actions on their part that would interrupt this progress or that would threaten the American position."

President Johnson promptly announced that he had no intention of conducting any specific reprisal raids against North Vietnam in response to the attack on the embassy. Admiral Sharp summarized that "an opportunity to demonstrate American resolve and to rally the American people was lost; indeed, a fatal lack of will surfaced at the highest level of our government and our enemies were not slow to grasp this fact."

I played hooky most of the time we were in Tokyo and spent my time with John Black and his 6441st TAC Fighter Wing at Yokota. They were up to their ears in the shuffle of deployment down South and they were hurting for people, especially fighter pilot colonels about my size. He offered me the wing operations job and I jumped at it. But with the end of war college only a few weeks away and with the personnel people bent on making me a Washington staff weenie, we faced a battle with the impassive administrative system. I immediately shelved my remembrances of the ground war and the embassy-army effort of downtown Saigon. I flew comfortably back to Washington, pumped up with the prospects of flying and fighting in the F-105 in the real thing, the air war up North.

When we got back to Washington we learned that President Johnson had increased the role of the ground forces by authorizing them to become engaged offensively, while at the same time turning down all requests for meaningful aerial offensives. He did approve an expansion of the leaflet bombing campaign, so one must assume that somebody thought those leaflets were hitting them where it hurt.

In the war college you have people from all over Washington and the information grapevine works quite well. We learned early on that John A. McCone, who was directing the CIA, was making antiestablishment noises. Extracts from the *Pentagon Papers* cited him speaking out strongly in opposition to the president's latest decisions basically to do nothing but offensively engage a few ground troops. McCone observed that "[the decision] is correct only if our air strikes against the North are sufficiently heavy and damaging to really hurt the North Vietnamese. . . . It is my personal opinion that this program is not sufficiently severe or damaging to the North Vietnamese to cause them to compromise their present policy. . . . We must hit them harder and more frequently and inflict greater damage. Instead of avoiding Migs we must go in and take them out. A bridge here and there will not do the job. We must strike their airfields, their petroleum resources, their power stations and their military compounds. This in my opinion must be done promptly and with minimum restraint."

On April 28, John McCone was succeeded by Vice Admiral Raborn, whose far softer position suited Lyndon Johnson much better. Secretary of State Dean Rusk sought to be heard in July when he authored a paper slanted along the same lines as McCone's statements, but it also fell upon the deaf ears of McNamara and Johnson.

My battle with the personnel people went right down to the wire. The rules in the Colonels Assignment Section in the Pentagon say that when a colonel graduates from the nation's highest-ranked defense academic institution he should be placed in a relatively responsible spot on either the air staff or on a joint services staff. Early in the year I had accomplished my interviews with Bob Malloy, who ran that section. Despite my request for a spot connected with the operational fighter business, he dutifully reviewed his papers and computers and insisted that I should be assigned to the General Officers Assignment Section. I got a rundown on the job and while it looked like a ticket to a star, that was not my main goal in life. I couldn't warm up to being a super-aide for 435 general officers, especially when my buddies were flying combat. Bob and I thrusted and parried, and he finally said he would keep his eyes out for something else for me.

When I got back from the Pacific the something else turned

out to be Legislative Liaison, which involved getting answers for congressional staffers so they could tell Johnny's mother why he had not been allowed to go on leave last month, and arranging appointments and appearances for testimony by general officers at congressional levels.

I bounced over to the Pentagon to inform Bob that John Black had a "name request" on the way for me and that he and his generals were stating that I was needed for the war effort. Bob got all red-faced and told me that his job was making generals, not satisfying personal whims. I got all red-faced and said that my job was flying fighters and leading operational people and that I didn't care that much about his square-filling operation.

Bob's general backed him up and I went on orders to Legislative Liaison. A few days before graduation I even had to go to an L&L cocktail party that included a welcome aboard. Then just before graduation I got a call from Bob's office: "Damn you! You're going to Southeast Asia. Good luck."

In Southeast Asia our command ladder peaked at the White House and there was no doubt that the president ran the war. While our military commanders identified the targets they considered appropriate for attack, they did not execute attacks on those targets without precise and individual approval from the president. The group of ninety-four targets our military commanders had identified and recommended as appropriate for attack at the start of the war represented the industrial capability of North Vietnam, a symbol of North Vietnamese national pride. Our American political leaders never accurately evaluated the importance of that North Vietnamese national pride. In retrospect, it's interesting to ponder the possible long-range conduct of Ho and the North had those targets been hit forcefully and repeatedly until they were destroyed. Certainly there is a high probability that the entire course of American involvement in Southeast Asia would have been quite different.

When targets were recommended for attack by the military, they were presented to the president through the JCS for approval or disapproval. Review of those recommendations took place at a weekly working luncheon at the White House and a decision was made as to what targets were to be authorized, the number of sorties to be flown, and in many instances even the tactics to be used by the pilots.

The president gathered those whom he desired, including at least the secretary of state, the secretary of defense, and the presidential press secretary, and they reviewed the recommended targets in as much detail as their politically oriented personalities would allow. No military man, not even the chairman of the JCS, was present at those luncheons until late in 1967. It was Admiral Sharp's view that "This omission, whether by deliberate intent or with the indifferent acquiescence of Secretary McNamara, was a grave and flagrant example of his persistent refusal to accept the civilian-military partnership in the conduct of our military operations."

President Johnson was serious when he said that we couldn't even hit an outhouse without his permission. Mike McNamara saw that right from the first Thud deployments. Each time they went into Laos they had a little listing of what they could do, and that was it, nothing more. They would hit a bridge and right close by they could see where the North was building another bridge. But they couldn't touch that bridge; they had to leave it alone until it was completely built. Then maybe they would be sent back up after it. Irrational target control became a more significant problem as the effort eventually moved farther north with larger forces facing vastly improved defenses.

Johnson and McNamara never released that stranglehold and those of us boys driving Thuds, when we finally got up North and started going Downtown, knew it and resented it. We knew we were better qualified to sort out outhouses at five hundred knots than Johnson was, especially when those outhouses were shooting at us. He and McNamara lost a bunch of good people and good machinery all over Southeast Asia with their outhouse mentality on war.

When the president and his luncheon companions decided what could be released for a week's effort, those tidbits were transmitted through the Joint Chiefs of Staff to Admiral Sharp as Commander-in-Chief Pacific, or CINCPAC. In the case of the air force the details went down to the next level in the chain of command, which was Pacific Air Forces, or PACAF, in Honolulu, run by a four-star commander-in-chief referred to as CINCPACAF. He ruled the air force in the Pacific and he and his staff controlled all air operations to the most minute detail. The common complaint about PACAF headquarters was its detachment and lack of current professional knowledge. The majority of that staff were not familiar with the operational equipment or with the involvement of the pilots and the equipment during combat missions over the North.

Once PACAF was satisfied that it had become involved in adequate detail on a particular mission plan, the information would then flow down the line in a manner that must be described as cumbersome at best. Early in the war, Second Air Force was the next link in the command chain, but the effort rapidly outgrew it. Reorganization took place and the next stop along the line became Seventh Air Force, located at Tan Son Nhut air base in Saigon. This was our operational headquarters and it was commanded by a three-star general. Seventh translated what was already significantly detailed information into greater detail to be passed to the operating unit commanders.

At least twice daily, Seventh published a huge document that contained the operational orders for all units in Southeast Asia. Any one unit would be responsive to only a fragmentary portion of this huge document and the portion going to each unit was known as the frag. When we got ''fragged'' it meant we received our operational instructions for the next day. When a ground soldier got fragged, it meant someone on his own side had rolled a live grenade his way. Sometimes when we read our frag we felt the same way.

The frag contained not only our instructions but also those of other fighter units that would be on the same or associated targets. The details were also there for airborne refueling, search and rescue, airborne command and control, ordnance to be delivered, fuse settings, takeoff times, times on target, courses, altitudes, airspeeds, and most everything else we needed or didn't need to know. Much of this detail could better have been left to the unit commanders and those designated to plan and fly the particular mission. Those flying the missions then had to multiply this mass of detail by three as each and every fighter flight had a primary target plus a secondary target and an alternate target. Everyone had to prepare, all the way, for all three. Execution, or the specific go signal, was subject to the weather or the whim of higher command, right up to rolling in on the target. Even if it was only a fragmentary portion of the overall ops order, the frag still came out to be a sizable wad of paper.

To complicate the command structure even more, we also had to report to a unit known as Thirteenth Air Force, which was located at Clark Air Base just outside Manila in the Philippines. Theoretically, Thirteenth was responsible for the materiel and administrative support of tactical units in Southeast Asia, just as Seventh was responsible for operational support. It was very difficult for any of the operational commanders to rationalize the existence of Thirteenth. It contributed little or nothing to the overall effort, but in the manner of the times demanded multitudinous reports. While operational units felt that PACAF had an ill-informed staff, they were certain that Thirteenth was worse.

Staff personnel at Thirteenth, from the commander down, had absolutely no expertise and absolutely no interest in the war or in those who fought the war, other than to be sure that they concocted some excuse to set foot in either Vietnam or Thailand at least once a month and thus collect combat pay. They did not know what the war was all about and they very openly did not care.

Relationships were further hampered by the fact that Thirteenth was a country club. It was a neat place to go for a few days off. The golf course was superb, base facilities were number one, and Manila was close by. Nothing at Clark bore any resemblance to a combat-related atmosphere, yet Thirteenth imposed itself upon the combat units who fought from the bases light years to the west. The only justification for the existence of a military function is contribution to the accomplishment of the mission, in this case fighting a war. Thirteenth did not meet that criterion and thus there was no justification for its involvement in our mission.

Fighter units who were under the operational control of Seventh felt some affinity toward Seventh and those who were on the command staff there. They were operationally oriented, to some degree, and they were involved in getting the job done. While the flow of directives from Seventh was not always smooth nor void of mutual frustration, it was not unduly different from relationships between any large headquarters and subordinate units.

The fighter units felt no affinity toward Thirteenth Air Force, and the personality of Thirteenth closely mirrored that of its three-star commander, Major General James Wilson, a multiengine, Strategic Air Command type. Gentleman Jim Wilson had all the requirements for a personality clash with any operational fighter pilot in the world. He had the ability to grate on the nerves and conscience of anybody trying to fight the war. He delighted in abusing anyone subservient to him in rank, but he was big on details, details that meant nothing in the conduct of the war.

He was the author and executor of the notorious Southeast Asia Card File. He accumulated a hated file of Rolodex-type cards containing large amounts of unrelated detail on units under his purview. As an example, a card in General Wilson's file might state the fact that there were 573 two-and-a-half-inch number-five bolts in bin C 72-12 of the supply warehouse at Takhli. Unless one earned his keep by being intimately involved with maintaining the stock level of such bolts, this fact lacked overpowering impact. Nevertheless, he expected those in his chain of command to be aware of this and the other facts that he had collected in his card file.

Upon his at least monthly visits to Takhli, which coincidentally seemed to mesh with an afternoon departure and a subsequent overnight stay in the plush environs of Bangkok, he would besiege local commanders with his card file. While the natural response of a combat commander might well have been a haughty "Who cares?" that would not have been adequate for the general. If you were asked a card question and failed to answer promptly and correctly you were subject to immediate and abusive chastisement with a guarantee that such a lack of knowledge on your part would be noted on your performance report.

He fed his card file by openly and repeatedly inviting all enlisted, commissioned, or civilian personnel to communicate with him directly on any particular gripe they might have about their situation in life. Any outfit, whether it be military or civilian, with a strength of 5,500 people such as we had at Takhli, can depend on having some number of folks who do not particularly care for where they are or what they are doing. One particular disgruntled airman from Takhli wrote the general a personal letter, as invited, to complain that he was forced to put up with dents in the tin food trays used in the airman's dining hall. It made the card file and when the general arrived on his next stopover he demanded that his staff be taken to the airman's dining hall, where they proceeded to paw through stacks of tin trays in search of dents. It was not too difficult to find some dented trays, which provided a source of absolute satisfaction for the three star and his associates.

He had another habit of demanding meetings with those he called junior officers. These so-called junior officers were part of the fighter pilot parade who were daily busting their ass up North or signing in at the Hanoi Hilton for extended stays. We considered them to be part of our groups of senior heros, but General Wilson did not share our views: To him they were simply junior officers in need of his guidance.

We would usually be notified a day ahead of time that the general was on his way. When he wanted a meeting with the junior officers, it was his view that each and every captain and below on the base should be present in the base theater. The general was supposed to listen to their complaints. Then they were supposed to assimilate some of the general's wisdom, certainly not concerning tactical warfare up North.

He did not differentiate between junior officers who were combat pilots, those who were directly involved in supporting combat launches, or those who had other duties on the base. He never seemed to realize that we were not at the country club at Clark. While we were always fully committed as far as all of our people were concerned, and while we were often short in some of the nonpilot specialties, we were always short of pilots. We never had enough pilots to employ anything close to a realistic combat pilot workload, so the general's visits were a sure-fire bet to be a pain for all of us.

When I got the call prior to one of the general's visits telling me that he wanted the junior officers assembled the next day, I advised all the other commanders on the base and was told that nobody could afford to support the general's bitch session; besides none of the junior officers wanted to go or had anything to say. Our junior officers flat did not want anything to do with General Wilson. I told their commanders to suck it up and have as many people as possible show their face.

Next morning when the general arrived I drove him to the base theater. He didn't talk to me, but he never talked to us very much if he was not in a position where he could yell at us. I explained to him that we were working a pair of JCS targets that would involve going all the way Downtown and that the morning mission was about to return and we were hard-pressed to turn around enough hardware for the afternoon go. All of that made absolutely no impression on General Wilson; he did not care. So I dropped him off at the theater and he gave me instructions to pick him up in an hour. I backed up and started to drive away.

He stuck his head into the theater, looked around, and immediately came storming out, very red faced. He waved me to a stop, jumped into the car, and launched a profane verbal attack on me and everyone else west of the country club. There had been only seven junior officers there for him to talk to! Those guys were seven people who had worked all night. Their commanders had rousted them out after a couple of hours of sleep and forced them to attend, before going back to work for the next twelve-hour shift. All the other junior officers were involved in the day's double-barrel effort against Hanoi. That made no difference to General Wilson and after an hour of haranguing, cursing, and downgrading me and our fighter people, Gentleman Jim jumped into his executive aircraft and sped off to Bangkok.

The general was bad enough, but some of his staff started to mimic his way of doing things. On one particular evening we had just returned from an ass buster to Hanoi. Our aircraft were in miserable condition and we were trying to figure out how we could paste the battle-damaged Thuds back together for the upcoming predawn go. We had spent the last ten days fighting around the clock and all the troops were dragged out about as far as they could be dragged. Lo and behold, the chief of the air police for Thirteenth, showed up in our command center and announced to me that he was shutting the base down and that all of my people were to go on alert for a practice perimeter security evaluation. He wanted us to issue weapons to all of our maintenance and administrative people and have them charge out to the jungle-rimmed perimeter of our base and pretend that we were protecting our Thai home against an enemy invasion.

As politely as I could force myself to do so, I told him to go screw his hat. I explained, though I admit curtly, that we really did have some airborne missions of significance that needed to be attended to, since the Joint Chiefs had told us what they wanted us to do for the next twenty-four hours and they expected us to do it. That didn't get through to him and he demanded that I close down the base and play air police. When I again refused, he invoked the name of General Wilson and vowed that if I refused to play his game the wrath of the entire military world would be down around my head.

After a relaxing deep breath and muscle flex I said, "Hey we're going balls out for a hot Joint Chief's mission. If you or your three-star general want to send a message to the JCS or to Lyndon and Robert and tell them we can't make it 'cause you want to practice air police, I'll play your game." He spun on his heel, stomped out, and we got on with the business of getting ready to go Downtown.

To round out the complications in our command structure, we had two more supervising agencies. There was an outfit to the north of us at Udorn that was called the 329th Air Division. It was run by a two-star general and was a subordinate of Thirteenth Air Force in the Philippines. Nobody in the fighting end of the war knew what this unit did. I have not the slightest idea of what their function was as regards the overall effort in the air war over Southeast Asia. I know that the two star and his associates went to a lot of cocktail parties in Bangkok, thrown by the ambassador who headed the final facet of our command structure. But other than that, I frankly have no idea what they were there for. The ambassador and his staff communicated with us only occasionally and, other than receiving periodic reminders that we were under their authority, we had little to do with them.

Fighter people are often characterized as having a lack of admiration for bomber people. I would be the last one to say that there was no truth in that statement, and certainly nowhere in aviation history was that sentiment more prevalent than it was in Southeast Asia. But that premise is too general. It's the people who count, especially when it comes to commanders and how they view their command responsibilities and how they interface with their people.

When we first cranked up the Thud operation in Southeast Asia, CINCPACAF was a gentleman named General Hunter Harris. He was a bomber man from way back, but he was a very savvy type who was dedicated to and interested in the aircrews he directed into battle. On his departure from command he toured each and every base under his command, flying his giant C-135, to bid a personal farewell to the commanders and aircrews who were fighting for him. When he departed from Takhli, knowing that his departure would be viewed by a lot of fighter pilots, he honked that big C-135 off the ground after a minimum takeoff roll, wrapped it up in a tight turn around the control tower, and buzzed the runway. He had commanded fighter pilots in an atmosphere of mutual respect that resulted in our giving the best possible effort. He saluted us with something fighter pilots understand, a buzz job by the boss.

General Harris was succeeded by General John Ryan, better known as Three-Fingered Jack, since he had lost a finger in a bomber raid during World War II. His combat experience involved flying as part of a large bomber formation and holding his aircraft straight and level at high altitude as his bombardier toggled off the bombs. I salute the gallantry of a multitude of heroic aviators who accomplished that often horrifying task. However, it was a standard fighter pilot joke that he had probably lost the finger when someone stepped on it in his bomber as he reached for the coffee pot.

General Ryan had spent the majority of his career with bomber forces in Strategic Air Command, where everything was done by the numbers. As CINCSAC he had a numbered, ironclad solution for every problem, and nobody questioned or deviated from the system. He did not know the mechanics of flying and fighting our war and perhaps he felt lost without his SAC umbrella. He projected himself as the demonic, all-knowing, one and only personal ruler of all. His personality could be most kindly described as gruff and antagonistic. He was another general who enjoyed hollering and yelling obscenities as a method of leadership and he very definitely led by fear and intimidation.

Those of us in the fighter forces had difficulty with General Ryan not only because of the tone of directives he issued, but also because of his attitude and personal approach on his trips to the various operating locations. Nobody wanted to talk to General Ryan. That sentiment went all the way up the chain of command and everyone who worked for him seemed to feel the same way. We dreaded the thought of a visit from General Ryan and we felt that anything we accomplished was in spite of General Ryan and his immediate staff. In retrospect, that was probably a two-way street.

There was no doubt that SAC was running the air force. There was little if any doubt that General Ryan was slated to be the next chief of staff of the air force. To a casual observer, he had at least an intense desire for that position. Perhaps his desire approached obsession. Surrounded by immense political pressures, including what must have been incessant personal surveillance from the secretary and the president and all who purported to speak for them, it must have been imperative to him that his tenure as CINCPACAF reveal no flaw or conflict. As with General Wilson, what he had been doing was working for him. In the vernacular, he didn't want anyone to make waves.

Ryan and his staff abhorred the thought of a new idea and they forced that abhorrence on intervening commanders and their staffs, if such abhorrence was not already there to start with. I have been personally castigated in front of my own people by General Ryan for espousing combat theories we learned over Hanoi at the risk of our lives and in which we firmly believed. He was ignorant of what we were talking about. Rather than listen, learn, try to better the war effort and save lives, he publically called us ignorant and tried to run Southeast Asia like a SAC war game.

Billy Ellis hit it right on the head when he said he was always most frustrated with higher headquarters' lack of allowance for or appreciation of unit creativity, which is our American long suit. When we shut down that long suit we even further restricted ourselves, and we already had more restrictions than we could use. Billy thought it was awful enough to have all those operationally uneducated folks in Washington telling us which way to turn, but then we, our own air force, went and did it to ourselves by discouraging new ideas. Seems like nobody further up the line than the cockpit wanted to take too many chances or make too many waves.

Obviously General Ryan and General Wilson were far from fighter pilot favorites. On the other hand, we openly rejoiced when Major General Spike Momyer assumed command of Seventh Air Force. He was an operational general, he knew fighters, he knew fighter pilots, and he knew fighter tactics. On his first visit to Takhli we put on our normal dog and pony show, wherein we briefed him on what we did and how we did it. In General Momyer's case he knew most of it beforehand; thus he understood and appreciated what we were telling him.

At the conclusion of the briefing, General Momyer told his accompanying staff to get lost and requested that those of us on the wing staff plus a cross section of squadron commanders, flight commanders, and plain old GI fighter jocks gather with him for an additional exchange of ideas. When he entered the room we all snapped smartly to attention, whereupon he told us to drag up a chair, sit down, and relax, because he wanted to talk about tactics and operational procedures. The general pulled out a pencil and notebook and said, "Okay guys, how can we improve this operation and what should we do to fight the war better?" That was like a breath of fresh air and we unloaded on him. Our first target was the World War II, bomber-oriented viewpoint of General Ryan and his staff. They subscribed to the flawed routine of approaching Hanoi at the same time, same altitude, same heading and airspeed every day. They had no appreciation for the principle of surprise and no understanding of the maneuverability or flexibility of fighter aircraft. We were very frank and open in telling General Momyer that if anyone followed the letter of the law in General Ryan's frags, he could expect to miss a lot of targets and lose a lot of good pilots and good aircraft. We suggested specific alternatives, all of which were well thought out, based upon our experience over Hanoi, and which we had tried to surface in the past. General Momyer responded. Within a matter of days we saw commonsense changes in the manner in which we were fragged that reflected what we had told the boss. Unfortunately, it didn't last long.

Politics and personalities above wing level were important to a certain point. That point for a Thud driver was the end of the runway. If his commanders were trying to win the war as hard as he was, great; if they weren't, *c'est la vie*. Within the past hour or two his world had narrowed rapidly to his strike leader, then to his flight leader, and then to his cockpit. When he plugged in that burner he knew there was good work to be done and he knew that Hanoi was just up north a few hundred miles. To hell with them all—we're going Downtown.

5 | PACK SIX

We split the North into six numbered sections that we called Route Packages. Package One was the southernmost. While the defenses were lighter there, those who didn't properly respect them often paid with their lives for their carelessness. The significant targets and the tougher defenses were all to the north, and by the time you got to Pack Six, with Hanoi and Haiphong in the center, you were in the big leagues. About 80 percent of the North's war materials moved along two rail lines that ran south from China and converged in Hanoi, while about 80 percent of the material used to bolster the North's economy was shipped into the port of Haiphong. If you were an interdiction fighter pilot, Pack Six was what it was all about.

If we got fragged on one of the easy packs it was a letdown. It was even worse to get fragged on Pack Six, go through all the pre-mission preparations, get psyched up to go Downtown, then get skunked after you got airborne by the weather or a command hiccup from Washington or some other headquarters. When that happened, we had to paw through our cramped cockpits and sort out the piles of paper, maps, and target folders we always had to carry for each of our two alternate targets. Then we had to figure out how to get there from where we were. When we got there we usually found the alternate targets to be insignificant or nonexistent and far less stimulating than Downtown Hanoi.

The navy worked the same Route Package structures we did and they launched their strikes from carriers off the coast, while our air force fighter strikes came out of Thailand. The air force had about 40,000 men in Thailand, with 28,000 of them involved in some phase of combat mission support involving 300 strike aircraft and 250 support aircraft at six Thai bases. Between us we had a lot of hardware and a lot of dedicated people who are sure to this day that if we had been properly utilized, Vietnam would not have been the debacle that it was, and that many thousands of Americans would not have been lost needlessly in the mud down south.

In our wing we had a good exchange visit program going with our navy buddies. They would gather up four or five of their fighter types and launch from the carrier in their little Cod transport aircraft and recover at Takhli; then a few weeks later they would send the Cod back to pick up some of our troops and take them out to the carrier. Depending on the schedule, we would spend a couple of hours or days yakking about how we were fighting the war and we all learned from each other. The navy guys and my guys had long since agreed that neither of us had a corner on all the good tactical smarts or how a crazy war like this one should be fought. There was no friction at the operating level.

In April of 1966 Route Pack Six was split between the navy and the air force. It was far from a hard line and we constantly moved around in each other's area, with the navy choppers darting in to save a shot-down air force pilot or with us refueling in their area when we came up the water route to the northeast railroad. We always worked together to get the job done, and when we got together on the ground we always laughed at the big gears up the line arguing about who dropped the most bombs or flew the most sorties. Hell, there was plenty there for all of us if they had ever used us as they should have.

The navy was given the eastern portion of Pack Six, which was closest to the coast and included Haiphong, and which was where they had normally worked anyway. Downtown Hanoi and the areas to the west and south were given to the air force as their primary operating area. If we worked pretty much in the same area each time we were up there it gave us a better shot at knowing the terrain and targets. We also developed a better feel for the constantly moving defenses.

Those of us flying Thuds got to know Pack Six in great detail. If we didn't commit that geography to memory we simply increased our jeopardy on each trip. There was no time to sit around and cogitate or read maps when the action got heavy during a strike. We had to know where to expect the action and how to get there and how to get back out of there, but we also had to know where the off-limits lines were drawn.

If we wandered too far north while working in Pack Six we were violating our restriction against entering the Chinese border buffer zone. That sizable strip of the North, extending all the way from the desolate western border to the Gulf of Tonkin, was etched in Washington's mind and it contained many well-traveled roads and rail lines that stretched into China. It also provided sanctuary for the Migs when things didn't go their way. Our leaders wanted to be sure that we remembered where they had drawn that line, so they kept a bunch of big command and control aircraft flying around, to the south and out over the water. Those aircraft had radar eyes that allowed their crews to see from border to border and track us, then turn us in if we got a few feet offsides while we were being shot at.

Whether they were being catapulted off a carrier deck or struggling into the air from a jungle airstrip in Thailand, fighter pilots who worked Pack Six were sympathetic to the desires of Admiral Sharp, the senior commander of the entire Pacific operation. He was constantly involved in exchanges with the Johnson administration, and as the war dragged on ineffectively he became increasingly critical of the lack of action at the top. His proposal was that six basic systems in the North should be promptly and decisively destroyed: the electrical networks, the limited industries with war-making capabilities, the transportation net, the air bases and training centers, the petroleum, oil, and lubricant, or POL, facilities, and the constantly improving Russian- and Chinese-sponsored air defense network. His proposals were repeatedly rejected. Rather than attack and destroy those systems, Johnson and McNamara seemed to be determined to protect them, or at worst nibble at them bit by bit, in order to insure their no-win philosophy.

Rolling Thunder was the code name assigned to our strikes against the North. The project was on paper in 1965, but it took a long time to get it in motion and it never truly got rolling as it should have. The POL phase of Rolling Thunder finally opened on June 29, 1966. McNamara made the announcement in Washington, but before he talked to the press we had already been at work against the POL storage tanks that we had wanted to go after since the first days of the war. When we got there, still under all sorts of cumbersome rules as to where to go and how to get there and what we could hit, we found what we had expected—we were at least a year late. We did a lot of good work and had smoke billowing to 30,000 feet, but it was only a fraction of the good we could have done.

Recognizing the fact that McNamara and Johnson were afraid to move decisively, the Vietnamese had been busy for many months on a program to disperse and hide their POL all across the countryside. They used everything from large underground tanks to barrels in village backyards. The president and secretary had originally given permission to attack the POL sites in April, but in a real display of indecision they refused to allow us to attack. In effect we were told it was okay, but don't really do it until tomorrow, or someday. The military would say "Okay, we're ready," but Washington would say "Wait." Next day the process would be repeated with still another decree of "Not yet." Washington wanted more assurances of accuracy, more assurances that no civilians would be hurt, and more assurances that no third-country personnel or ships would be harmed. Finally, on June 29, the navy hit POL in the Haiphong area while a seventy-aircraft strike of Thuds hit POL in the Hanoi area. This pattern continued sporadically, at the whim of Washington, throughout the rest of 1966 and 1967. While the show was downright spectacular at times, it was a pale version of what could have been a real show.

Toward the end of 1966 we got all sorts of hush-hush briefings and indications that someone had sold Washington on letting us go right into the middle of Downtown. We rushed to prepare all the details and you would have thought we were going to a big party the way our pilots squabbled over who was on the schedule and who was flying whose wing in which flight. Nobody wanted to be left out. They all wanted to be part of the attacks against the hottest targets yet released to us, admittedly the most fiercely defended targets ever faced by any pilot in history. The adrenaline count was high throughout the wing. We were primed and ready to go. We got visits from generals telling us the importance of our tasks, as if we needed any extra pumping up, and we got lousy weather.

Once we had selected the lineup for those strikes we tried to keep it intact while we waited out the weather. I wound up leading the early morning crew for the night takeoff part of the effort. A 2:00 A.M. wake-up makes for short nights, and coupled with the other duties that kept us going until about eight in the evening, everything sort of ran together. But we just kept charging. Our little breakfast club was made up of the same group every day and after many days of the same thing it became difficult to work up a hearty smile or a strong appetite for greased eggs at 2:30 A.M. Normally we were not on the same schedule for too many days in a row and we could make up, to an extent, for lost sleep. But on this one, the weather in the target area would not break and the schedule would not change. We sat on this package for almost forty days before we got the job done properly. Some days we would get all the way through the briefing and be on our way to the aircraft before the no-go decision came in. Some mornings the word would be to divert to a lesser target;

sometimes it was slip the schedule for two hours, and everybody tried to find someplace to fall down and catch a restless nap. Some mornings when we got diverted to lesser targets we would substitute the newer heads and let them build experience while at other times the first team would go to keep in practice. Many times we would launch and go all the way to the target, bombs armed and ready, only to have to break it off at the base of Thud Ridge when we knew for sure that we were skunked with the target socked in by low clouds and rain.

During that run of bad weather, Seventh lost its cool. The pressure was on all the way from Washington for us to get in and get out. Seventh got so jumpy that it insisted that the mission leader fly directly over the cloud-covered target before canceling the mission. It didn't seem very wise to fly directly over the targets we wanted, day after day, if we wanted to retain any element of surprise, and it was plain dangerous. Why drag twenty-four of your best fighter pilots over the top of an undercast covering the hottest targets in history, especially when you're making all of them Sam bait because they couldn't hope to see a Sam heading their way through the clouds?

The decision on a mission like that rightly lies with the mission commander, the guy up front, and personally I never surrendered that authority despite Seventh's temporary whim. It's a tough decision to make and excited different sensations each time I faced it. I was usually the overall leader for both Thud wings and that meant forty-eight strike pilots and aircraft leaning on me. I didn't want to take my people into a situation where they couldn't see the target well enough to set up decently and bomb the way they should. You couldn't dive-bomb flying straight and level a few hundred feet above the ground in a rainstorm. It was not wise to hurl forty-eight fighters into the face of a spectacular defense, then expect the pilots to mill around at 500 miles an hour, on different attack headings in the clouds, where they couldn't see each other or anything else. I also knew that if Ho complained that any one of the 288 750-pound bombs that my strike force carried went a few hundred feet off target and hurt someone or something that Washington had not approved, McNamara and Lyndon would hold me personally responsible.

Regardless of whether it was a good mission that went all the way, a diversion, or a weather recce, we couldn't go much of anyplace without the support of the tankers and their crews. When refueling became the way to go for the worldwide mobility concept, we generally associated the tankers with something that had to happen to get across the ocean once in a while. We suddenly found out there was not a whole lot we could do without them in Southeast Asia and they became as much a part of our mission as the bombs we dropped. We were so heavy and overloaded that we could barely get off the ground and get organized before we needed fuel and we certainly couldn't get to Hanoi without fuel on the way in. Extremely important to the preservation of ourselves and our forces, we couldn't get back home from Hanoi without more fuel from the tankers.

For Mike McNamara, increasing fighter capability depended on the availability of tanker support. They didn't have any tankers when they were at Korat the first time because they didn't cover enough total miles to need them in those days. When Mike started flying the longer hauls out of Takhli he found out that we were still back in the dark ages of aerial refueling, but those tanker guys still did pretty good work for the Thuds. Those old KB-50 prop-driven tankers were slow, and when we started out with heavy fighters with a full load of bombs trying to poke that old-style refueling basket at 20,000 feet, those ancient tankers would have to keep diving from 20,000 feet to below 10,000 feet to transfer a load of fuel for a single fighter. Trying to hit those baskets on the end of a flapping rubber hose with a bunch of bombs on was a trick, but trying to stick there after finally catching it and fighting to keep from falling off or stalling out was some challenge. The entire operation improved dramatically when the jet-propelled KC-135 tankers arrived on the scene. They were far more compatible with the operating altitudes and airspeeds of the fighters. The fighter pilots could also depend on a stable refueling boom hanging there in space, as well as the skill of the refueling boom operator, or boomer, in the back end of the tanker. Those boomers saved lots of fighter pilot asses.

At first the 135s were not interested in coming up North when the fighters were hurting for fuel on the way out. That was because of the way those tanker crews had been trained, or brainwashed. They were completely SACumsized at that point in time and their rules, which had them orbiting on refueling tracks pretty far to the south, were all they knew. Gradually they got the big picture that all concerned were fighting for the same side, and that if the Thuds called for help they really needed help. The tanker crews decided they had to take some chances along with the fighters, except they were taking their chances more against their own authorities than the enemy. Nobody was going to shoot them down in the Mig-free neutral area where the fighters asked them to come. Eventually the problem went away as the individual tanker crews would come to get a fighter out of a jam whenever they could.

Dave Groark remembers the fighter-tanker duo as a soap opera. One day when he was headed north on a Hanoi strike, Ray Lewis was bringing his flight back from a strike up around Thai Nguyen. Some of the tankers serviced fighters both ways, going in and coming out, and on that day Ray and his guys were all really hurting for fuel and were heading for the same tanker Dave's flight was looking for on the way in. Ray had called that they were in bad shape and the tankers had moved as far north as they could. The thing Dave remembered most was being completely hypnotized by the radio drama that was being played out before him. The outbound flight was still looking for the tanker and it was a real emergency situation. They were very cool and very calm, but Dave could hear that they were hurting and got the feeling that they were just not going to get to the tanker and that we were going to lose four airplanes and four pilots. When they finally spotted the tanker the highest fuel gauge reading in the flight was four hundred pounds of fuel, which is something like fifty-nine gallons. The book says that if you're at full throttle, fifty-nine gallons will keep the engine turning for thirty seconds. The low man's gauges were on zero. It was like listening to one of those old radio suspense stories. Everyone on that radio channel could feel the tension as the wingman with his gauge showing zero plugged the tanker first and took a few hundred pounds of fuel, just enough to show on the gauges, then backed off so the second guy could get on before he flamed out. They rotated and juggled on and off the boom, calculating pounds of fuel versus survival for all four of them. But the tankers saved all four of them; they brought them all back. That was so exciting that Dave completely forgot about his own mission and the fact that he was going into the same fracas that the other flight was returning from.

The control of Pack Six targets from Washington was ridiculous, but so was the reaction down the chain right to the operating level. Nobody wanted to get Downtown as badly as the Thud drivers did. We were the ones who were humiliated by our own restrictions and we were the ones sharing in the loss of good people and Thuds. We were the ones going back time after time to nibble at what we wanted to eliminate and get it over with. If we had cleaned out what little there was up there that was worthwhile, that could well have stopped the foolishness down south. Then Downtown Hanoi would have been surrounded by tons of guns, Sams, and Migs protecting nothing but each other. Since we were the only ones who knew what the defenses of Hanoi were capable of and who realized what it took to make a successful strike, we felt that we should have been allowed to participate in the design and the detailed mechanics of our strikes. But damned few people listened to what those who went there had to say about how to do the job right.

What we wanted to do in an area like Pack Six is pick the day and the weather and the time that was best for us; utilize surprise and imagination; then take advantage of our capabilities and strong points to clobber them. What we didn't want to do was fly in, day after day, on make-believe dry runs over what we were going after in order to give the Migs, Sams, and radar tracking gunners lots of good practice until the day the weather would break and we really could roll in on the targets.

Swede Larson told of one particular mission that shows how the Pentagon got into the act. Early in the spring of 1967 the weather was really rotten up in Pack Six for a long time; it was just really socked in. The air force in Washington was nervous about trying to get some sorties going so they could have something to talk about. The navy had been very successful with its all-weather A-6 bombers, which were flying missions and getting all the publicity back in the States, while the 105s were all sitting on the ground. So in frustration, a frag order came in calling for two volunteers to fly a mission to hit a power plant up in Pack Six. The mission fell to Swede's squadron. His ops officer, who had more balls than sense, volunteered for it and took another young Turk with him. They went up there in impossible weather: They dead-reckoned to the target area, let down on the gauges, somehow found the power plant on the second pass while milling around fully loaded under an eight- to nine-hundred-foot ceiling, and damned if they didn't put a bomb right through the window of that power plant. The number-two man got a picture of it as he came in on his pass in staggered trail. It was one in a million that they would ever get in there, let alone get back out. Swede says that when they got back Willy Chairsell, his wing commander, who wore pilot wings but didn't fly, was so tickled that he could get the powers to be at Seventh off his back that they really played the mission up. Next thing they knew, Saigon sent over a Silver Star for the leader and a distinguished Flying Cross for the wingman. Swede's ops guy told them they could stick it. He told them that if it wasn't good enough for a Silver Star for both of them, he wasn't interested and that was the end of that. It was just another example of the fact that politics and publicity controlled much of what Swede and all of us did over there.

The raids against bridges, rail facilities, and other industrial structures proceeded in parallel with the POL strikes, and if an outside observer kept track of the claims for bridges blown up it would be easy to assume that the North was made up of nothing but bridges. Sometimes it seemed that way to us. Quite often when we would attack a bridge we could see the replacement pontoon bridges waiting along the river banks. The North had a construction force of 600,000 laborers to repair bomb damage, and they did their bridge work just like they did their rail work and their road work, quickly. As soon as we knocked a bridge down they dispatched masses of laborers and put in substitute facilities while they rebuilt the damaged bridge. It doesn't take much of a pontoon bridge to support bicycle and pedestrian traffic. If they needed to move something like a heavy truckload of supplies and the makeshift bridge would not support the truck, they used the people, bicycles, cattle, or whatever was available to haul the truckload, piece by piece, to the other side. There always seemed to be another truck, or another back, waiting on the other side to continue the journey. We did not match their sense of purpose and did not show the desire to do the interdiction job forcefully. If you go after a repairable target, then ignore it for a few months, you can bet the enemy will rebuild it if that suits his purpose. It's tough to win a war in Asia with an attack plan based on the whims and schedules of the Oval Office rather than a calculated interdiction plan.

During 1967 Admiral Sharp was still trying to convince Washington that if the six basic systems were released to him, he could execute a systematic plan of attack with a high probability of relatively speedy success. Admiral Sharp's requests were never honored. At the conclusion of one of McNamara's many press conferences in defense of his policies, the press dubbed him "a man looking down a long tunnel with no patch of light at the end." Those of us who did the fighting can only ask, "Who built that tunnel?"

One of the excuses that McNamara and his supporters made for not approving the entire JCS target list and for denying us authority to attack targets methodically was that bombing by itself could not win the war unless we attacked the civilian population of North Vietnam. Here is what McNamara said in his August 25, 1967, Senate testimony: "There is no basis to believe that any bombing campaign, short of one that has the population as its target, would itself force Ho Chi Minh into submission. Bombing the ports and mining the harbors would not be an effective means of stopping the infiltration of supplies into South Vietnam.''

McNamara's contention that the North could not be forced to submit does not correlate with authoritative views from inside Downtown Hanoi. John Colvin was consul general at the British mission in Hanoi during 1966 and 1967. In his book *Twice Around the World* he reports that Hanoi had been accustomed to spasmodic raids that came in clusters over the period of a week or so and at predictable times, usually about 2:30 P.M. But after April 1967 it was impossible for residents to continue their normal routines due to increased U.S. air strikes. Even if the strikes were directed at outlying areas, North Vietnamese officials would insist on declaring them as raids against Hanoi itself and the sirens wailed up to thirty times a day. Colvin rated the bombing as effective throughout the North Vietnamese countryside, pointing out that there was only one undamaged bridge between Hanoi and Than Hoa in the southeast of the country. While the damaged or destroyed bridges were repaired by teams on permanent standby or were replaced by pontoon bridges, travel was restricted and slow. Movement was at night in convoys, constantly monitored, halted, and respaced by girl wardens stationed along the way. Colvin states that many villages and agricultural cooperatives were wiped out by bomb damage with high casualties due to attacks against North Vietnamese gun emplacements sited in built-up areas on their perimeters. Schooling, repair work, and cultivation were inhibited as alert followed all clear incessantly. Fuel supplies had to be cached in five-foot-round, ten-foot-long drums at various points along the road, virtually inaccessible to U.S. aircraft. Bicycles often played a larger role in transportation than did motorized vehicles, each bicycle being modified to carry a load of 440 pounds. A major cause of delay was the time needed to reassemble the pontoon bridges at nightfall, since they were regularly disassembled at dawn.

Colvin recounts that on May 9, 1967, he and his vice-consul walked to their balcony as the air raid sirens sounded: "As we stood there, seven or eight United States F-105 Thunderchief fighter-bombers, flying at scarcely roof-top height and no more, it seemed, than one hundred yards away, shot across our vision at what appeared—so tight was the space in which the whole incident was framed between houses and sky—enormous speed. They had come on us suddenly out of nowhere, the hard, sleek aircraft, in superb formation at approximately six hundred mph, disappearing for an instant behind the trees and buildings that lay between us and the power station (thermal power plant) less than one mile to the south, and then quickly climbing clear and away. . . . Almost simultaneously, such lights as were on in the apartment went out, the fan stopped turning, and a column of dust, smoke, and flame rose from the direction of the power station. (As the planes had penetrated the city's defenses by coming in under the radar screen, the first antiaircraft batteries opened up only when the raiders had not only departed but were probably twenty miles away.) As we were shortly to observe, the performance of this squadron disposed of every Communist or other illusion about the laxity of American bombing or the imprecision of U.S. bombing techniques.''

When the all clear wailed and stillness descended, Colvin's apartment, without electrical power for the revolving fan and air conditioner, was crushingly hot. He and his assistant went to look at the power plant and found the antiaircraft guns, surrounded by their agitated crews, sited among the trees in the park. They noted an air of tense activity, almost hysteria, as orders were bellowed and the men ran around their positions as if further attack was imminent. Fists were shaken at the sky and little groups of civilians whispered apprehensively together. The war had come to Downtown Hanoi.

The power station was an oblong, gray, brick and concrete structure about six hundred by three hundred feet, one hundred feet high, topped by tall chimneys. Significantly, it was surrounded by terraced houses. The flames had died down as Colvin approached it, but the dust still rose from the effects of the high-explosive hits it had taken. The chimneys had collapsed and the entire structure, gaping with holes, seemed to be listing drunkenly to one side. Colvin wrote, ''There was, in our opinion, no hope at all for it. The accuracy of the attack had also been such that out of the complex of fifty or so small private houses around the power plant, only three had been at all damaged, and those from blast rather than direct hits.''

The next day the fans and the air conditioner in Colvin's apartment were still out and the inside temperature rose to 140 degrees. He estimated that there was no possibility of restoring the electric power, saying, ''Hanoi. . . . must now be finished as a functioning industrial and economic city.'' At that moment the lights went on and the fan and air conditioner came to life. Apparently mobile generators had been brought on line, as electrical power was not restored to the entire city, but only to the diplomatic area and to limited government buildings. For Colvin the lesson learned was ''the astonishing preparedness and resourcefulness of the DRV [Democratic Republic of Vietnam] only continual air attack of the kind that Rolling Thunder had not yet initiated would surmount those qualities. But Rolling Thunder did, thereafter, or so it appeared to us, begin to do precisely that, although without again striking the power plants or other targets in central Hanoi. The objectives, attacked without respite for the next two weeks, remained on the periphery of the city. The noise of bombing and gunfire was almost continual, and the damage to Vietnamese equipment was considerable, but . . . in early June, morale, health, and the flow of war material to Hanoi had not decisively diminished.''

However, by the end of July Colvin noted a growing sense of anxiety in Hanoi induced by the continued bombing. There was a belief that ''Hanoi was going to catch it again badly,'' but that perhaps the next step in escalation would be the mining of the port of Haiphong. A qualified medical observer told Colvin that he had seen the early signs of malnutrition among 60 to 90 percent of the children. Colvin summarized the changing situation by writing, ''For the first time, I was beginning to believe that in spite of the history of that extraordinary people over the past twenty-two years, of their proven ability to stand far worse suffering in other towns and villages of the DRV than they had to withstand in Hanoi, of their tenacity, of the implacable aims of their leadership, they must have a physical limit sometime. I could not predict when it would be reached, perhaps not in 1967, nor what form it would take—presumably slow collapse—but unless the war were further internationalized, I thought that the limit might come."

Colvin's next series of firsthand observations soundly refutes the first tenet of McNamara's August testimony before the Senate: "By September the evidence of malnutrition was clear among adults as well as children. . . . The population could barely get about their duties. . . . Food was not coming in from China. . . . American bombing of the entry points into Vietnam from China, as well as Sino-Soviet differences had their substantive effects. . . . For three days there was no water supply due to failed electrical pumps. . . . Mass epidemic, in the already unsanitary conditions of the capital, could not have been far away. . . . The economy was at last breaking down. . . . The country and its people were close to collapse which, for the first time, no amount of excited exhortation could correct. And every morning since I reached Hanoi, the streets of the quarter had been lined with war materiel brought in overnight from China across the Paul Doumer Bridge, amphibious vehicles, artillery, armored fighting vehicles, surface-to-air missiles on flatbeds, saucily parked even outside the British and Canadian missions. By June their numbers had somewhat decreased. By August and September there were none at all. . . . The trains were coming no longer. . . . The country's endurance had reached its limit. . . . If the Americans continued to cut the railway lines from China and Haiphong to Hanoi and succeeded in putting the ports out of action the DRV could not pursue the war in the south and keep the North running. . . . If the Viet Cong were really losing more men in the South than they could recruit locally or import from the DRV, then, failing Chinese intervention, the major war was over."

But we were not permitted by our own national leadership to attack the targets that would have made the difference. McNamara and his associates said they did all they could to win, and then implied they were forced to spend much of their time in office trying to restrain a bunch of crazy pilots who simply wanted to terrorize the Vietnamese population and kill babies. They implied that we as professional air soldiers belonged in the same category as those convicted of atrocities at My Lai, and that they had no alternative approaches. That is not true and that untruth and those who espoused it cost our country dearly.

Admiral Sharp was rebuffed, the Vietnamese defenses proliferated, and the North continued to march south. In complete disregard of Admiral Sharp's request, on May 23, 1967, the Washington leadership scribed yet another make-believe circle around Hanoi and advised Admiral Sharp that not a single bomb would be dropped within that circle. They further put him down by declaring that other specific areas, such as the port of Cam Pha, were completely off limits for any attacks if any foreign ships were in the harbor. That harbor was always full of foreign ships. We used to see them every day, waiting their turn to unload war supplies in the shadows of the surrounding Soviet and Chinese gun batteries. The ones flying Soviet flags were our own American-made Lend-Lease ships that we had given the Soviets back in World War II, but the flags of most of our allies were also there. This could really get to you, even in passing at five hundred knots, especially if you had just lost three or four guys and their aircraft only a few miles away.

6 | THERE WERE GUNS

The people we were fighting had been at war all their lives, and were constantly reminded that fighting for their cause was their only reason for existence. Their guns had done well for them against the Japanese during World War II, and their artillery had pulled off the supposedly impossible task of annihilating the French at Dien Bien Phu. So if the guns were working and if war had become your way of life, why not stick with what was working? Everyone was in the gun business and the guns came in all sizes and shapes. They were supplied, or captured, from all over the world, and they combined to form an impressive obstacle for us.

They didn't have to be big guns to give us a bad time. There were plenty of Russian AK-47 semiautomatic rifles in the hands of the local militia units, and that meant almost everybody. The arsenal literally went down to old muskets and handguns. It doesn't necessarily take a large projectile to knock an aircraft down. Remember that if a jet fighter sucks up something like an old screw or washer on the runway, that can destroy a jet engine in a matter of seconds. One small slug from a handgun could rupture fuel or hydraulic lines, and since our fuel and hydraulic lines were not well protected, a single slug could render a Thud uncontrollable and vulnerable to fire.

Since we were usually forced to visit Downtown on the same flight paths at the same times every day, it was no trick to know when to be ready, and the North planned their work schedules around our visits. An observer atop a wooden tower, armed with a bugle or a bell, was probably as effective for the villages and the workers in the rice paddies as sophisticated radar warning systems. If we went low enough, we could see them lying on their backs around the villages, firing straight up into the air.

For us the guns came in colors: white for 37 mm, blue for 57 mm, and black with orange centers for the big ones. The 37-mm guns were effective for low-level barrage type defenses and they spit puffy cotton-ball patches that gathered in dense clouds. One gun could get you, but you were more likely to have trouble when several of them, clustered along a road or around a village or a rail siding, all started to concentrate on a point just in front of your nose. They were easy to camouflage and easy to disperse along well-traveled ground routes and we could never guess where a cluster of them would appear.

The 57s were nasty. They had a high rate of fire, and they were usually dug in, though still capable of mobility. They could easily saturate our operating and bomb-release altitudes and one hit could do the job. While they would generate a blue haze at explosion, you most often saw them as red golf balls floating your way. They were tough on a flak suppression strike since the gun pits were well coordinated to insure the maximum field of fire. The gunners, often chained to the guns, hung in there until you either knocked them out for good or you beat them for the day or they beat you. At first the only thing we had to use against them were 750-pound bombs, and we fused the bombs to detonate right at ground level to produce surface blast rather than penetration damage. It required a direct hit on a gun pit to silence it, but a hit usually eliminated the pit for good.

Later we got cluster bomblet units, or CBUs, which were baseball-sized canisters filled with antipersonnel fragments.

We carried 460 of the bomblets in each of the large bomb-shaped containers hung under our aircraft on our armament racks. We aimed the containers just like bombs and released them the same way on our dive-bomb runs. As they dropped toward the gun pit concentrations, each container would open like a clamshell and drop its individual bomblets. Each individual CBU had its own propellerlike arming device that would both throw the CBUs on slightly divergent courses in the airstream and activate the fuses. When they detonated, just above ground level and in a scattered pattern, they were very effective in silencing the gunners. They often triggered secondary explosions and fires that got the guns and stored ammunition. If you only got the gunners, that was still enough to give the rest of your strike force the few seconds needed to get their bombs on the target.

The big guns went from 80 mm all the way up to 120 mm and were often radar controlled and capable of firing well above our highest approach altitudes. They spat big black puffs that looked like ragged six-foot-tall rectangular boxes hanging all around you. If they got a good bead on you the black stuff seemed to be everywhere, and if they were getting close you could hear and feel the detonations and see the orange core of explosion in the center of the black boxes. One hit or a close miss from one of those babies was enough. Their pits were sturdy but easier to see and if you were in the lead flight suppressing flak for your buddies, the satisfaction of planting six 750s or several hundred CBUs right in the middle of one of them was immense.

As time went on, the North became even more expert in coordinating their guns against our strikes and the closer we got to Downtown Hanoi the tougher they got. They would lace a defensive web for us and our challenge was to make it through the web, get the target, and beat the web back out. There is no doubt that they were well controlled. If you tried to run in too low, even the villagers would fire at you with small arms. When you pulled up a bit the cotton balls would be there. Then the 57s would cover you all the way up to roll in on the target and stick with you throughout your dive. The big guys concentrated on the peak of your arch to bombing altitude, where you had slowed a bit and were rolling for the right approach. Once you shed your bombs and pulled your guts out to avoid the ground the white puffs and the red golf balls would be back and if you climbed above them, the big guns would try you again.

Other than flak suppression bombing, which was a one-time, one-flight effort timed to clear the main strike's run, our only defense was to keep moving, or jink. Within a flight we would keep moving up and down, rolling slightly from side to side and slipping and skidding to avoid coordinated flight on a steady track—anything to compound the problem of tracking for the gunners. The intensity of jinking varied with the density of the blasts and tracers floating around you. When you knew they had you cornered you also knew that you had better do some violent maneuvering if you expected to survive. Some of the guys used to call me "superjinker." It was not too difficult for the gunners to figure out that the first guy in on the target was the leader. Since rewards for capturing a prisoner increased with the prisoner's rank, I often got as much attention as my Tail End Charlie. Many times, coming off a tough one with the 57s still chasing me, I played Thunderbird with uncoordinated rolls on the deck, inverted flight while pushing my nose up, and whatever other sloppy maneuver seemed to fit. My guys thought that was a pretty neat idea, started doing it themselves, and when they began to get the most out of what that aircraft could give them, they quite often survived seemingly impossible situations.

But jinking was only for while you were moving in or moving out. Once you rolled over the top and acquired the target it was nothing but smooth, precision tracking as you raced for a drop at about five hundred knots. That was the payoff, the reason for the trip. Sometimes that run seemed like an eternity and it was a time for the gunners to concentrate on your steady flight path. We lost lots of troops about the time they dropped their bombs, but I never saw a single one of my people flinch on the way in. Fighter pilots are a dedicated lot and those who went Downtown on a regular basis were the best.

* * *

Not everyone who had the basic credentials was up to these missions. We had a few who could fly okay, but they were just not built for the task at hand. Those of us on the first team got very emotional about those who wore pilot's wings but who crapped out when they came face to face with our true mission. I lost my cool when a Naval Academy graduate, who had switched to the air force, quit when he got shot at a few times. He told me he was afraid. Hell, anyone who wasn't afraid when he was looking down the wrong end of a gun was an idiot. The name of the game was to turn that fear into effective professional action, just like you promised when you raised your right hand. For a few days I was so engrossed in trying to punish that individual that I didn't pay the proper attention to all my charges who were laying it on the line. Fortunately for me, my wing legal officer sensed my frustration and set me straight. He painstakingly dragged me through the regulations to show me that there was no way I was going to pull that coward's wings. The regulations were specifically designed to prevent that. Furthermore, that pilot was going to be able to move on to a desk job someplace and continue to disguise himself as a military aviator and collect flight pay. To top it off, I would not be allowed to state my disgust on any official records. The rules were specific, so I abandoned my personal vendetta and got on with the things I could do something about, like leading the good troops.

More often than not, the weak sisters showed up early on, which was good. Sometimes it was a new guy who was certain to wind up as Tail End Charlie, such as the one Dave Groark ran across. When Dave went down there for his third trip, they formed a new squadron called the Thirty-fourth. It was a mixed group of pilots with varying numbers of missions, so they could build experience and have a reasonable rotation schedule that would give the squadron good balance. They took along a new lieutenant who had just reported in to Yokota. Their flight was made up of Dave, Ken Blank, Tom Curtis, Phil Hamby, and the new lieutenant. At that time people and aircraft were being juggled between Korat and Takhli, trying to keep a balance between the two outfits. Tom and Dave took their new wingman to Takhli and that's where

121

he got his first mission. He wound up flying with Cal Broadway, who had the reputation of being aggressive, and Cal took him on a supposedly easy mission to Route Pack One. Cal made several passes at a target where there was plenty of flak and the lieutenant got hit. He got part way back before he went down and the choppers got in and hoisted him out. They took him to Udorn and since he was not badly hurt, a gooney bird brought him back to Korat the next day. By that time the rest of the flight was also back at Korat, so they thought it would be fitting to greet the one-mission veteran when he returned. They painted up a sign and rounded up a welcoming party to meet him and the first thing he saw when he stepped off the gooney bird was ONLY 99 MORE TO GO.

Unfortunately, that first mission had really gotten to him. They pulled him out of the flight and put him in the command post keeping charts and records to let him cool out, but it didn't work. Ken flew with him one more time, but he was skittish, not what you need when all four pilots in a flight have to depend on each other, so they let him finish out a one-year tour without combat and sent him home. Dave and the other pilots had thought their sign and welcoming party was a good idea, and it would have been had the lieutenant's temperament been like theirs. But it didn't work that way, which was probably best for all concerned.

Sometimes those who couldn't join our Downtown Club were experienced people, and it bothered us that there was plenty of room for them to hide within the system we lived under over there. Swede Larson had a lieutenant colonel in his squadron who got there a couple of weeks ahead of Swede, was senior to him, and was slated to take over the squadron until personnel advised them that Swede was en route to join the wing. That lieutenant colonel had a very high number of Thud flying hours from his stateside experience, but he would always find some feeble excuse to abort a mission. He aborted on the ground or in the air every time they were on their way to Pack Six. If he did stay with them on an easy one when they weren't going to Pack Six, he'd roll in on a target, even in Laos, and as soon as he'd get his nose down under the horizon he'd dump his bombs off and pull up and never offer an explanation. This kept going on and got worse and worse, and of course his supposedly sick birds always checked out perfectly when he brought them back. Willy Chairsell said he was too busy to screw around with somebody like that, so he transferred him to a ground control intercept radar site and that individual left still disguised as a pilot. He wasn't sitting around the radar site more than about three or four weeks when Seventh Headquarters found out that there was a man up there at a radar site who had 105 flying experience. So they plucked him out and took him down to Saigon and they put him in charge of the section that was putting out frag orders for Pack Six. He was in Saigon, telling Swede and all the rest of us how to fly Pack Six missions.

Like most of the Thud drivers, Swede didn't have much use for those who couldn't hack Pack Six. He also didn't have much use for easy missions. When I think about those easy missions, the first thing that comes to mind is Mugia Pass. Lord, how many times have we looked at that. We used to fly over there into Laos, knowing full well before we took off that there wouldn't be any targets for us. Targets of opportunity over Mugia Pass amounted to a wasted sortie. It's hard to say how many tons we threw on that Ho Chi Minh dirt road, for all the good it did.

Those easy packs were deceptive and they got lots of good people. Going Downtown, you knew you were going to see lots of action. Going over to the easy ones, you could get complacent when you didn't see any action, and then they would gang up on you all at once. Often it was too late to avoid the consequences. My friend John O'Grady made a couple of dive-bomb runs on a spot that looked like nothing but turned out to be a well-armed battalion just waiting and hiding while on their way down south. Their supporting guns hit John and he had to eject. He got a good chute and his wingman saw him land in the trees alongside what looked like a deserted and desolate dirt road. There was no apparent enemy activity; in fact, nobody knew where the guns were that had hit him. That was the last we ever saw of John. He seemed to be okay when he hit the ground in the middle of no-place, but like many others, he never showed up on any prisoner lists. Twenty years later his family is still fighting the valiant though agonizing fight to try to account for him. The only thing we know is that he hit in a hornet's nest: We only found out that it was a hornet's nest as a result of our rescue attempt.

Part of the rescue effort over there belonged to the troops who flew prop-driven A-1 Douglas Skyraider aircraft that were so ancient that everybody automatically named them Spads after that venerable old fighter plane of World War I. They had a brute of an engine and could stay airborne for hours; thus they were ideal for covering a downed pilot while the choppers tried to get in. The majority of the Spads had the primary job of flying night air-to-ground missions around Laos, but if a rescue was in the works they had another job. They would respond to rescue calls and use the combination of the downed pilot's emergency radio beeper and steers from any other fighters in the area to spot the pilot on the ground. Once they had the general location, they would try to get a good visual sighting on the downed pilot and insure that a pickup attempt by a chopper was a reasonable thing to try.

During that process they usually had no trouble getting the enemy to fire at them and thus identify their location on the ground. The Spads then had to neutralize that fire, or at least keep it under reasonable control, while they called the choppers in to complete the pickup. They also had to cover the choppers while they hovered for the pickup and then escort them out of the area. They had a guts job all the way and plenty of Thud drivers owe their skins to them. We admired them, we trusted them, and only on the rarest of occasions did they ever falter.

That day there were quite a few of us working close to the spot where John went down and it didn't take too long to set up a rescue attempt. My wingman and I were working as low cover when the first Spad arrived on the scene, and I was able to direct the Spad almost over the spot where John's wingman had last seen him. We stayed a bit off to the side so the Spad could use the low hills for cover. The Spad driver and I decided by radio that the only way to determine if further rescue efforts were feasible or necessary was for him to take a close look at the spot where we knew John had hit the ground. We figured that if we both headed west for a few miles, he could stay on the deck with his slower aircraft and turn in toward the spot while I could light the burner momentarily and pull my element up a few thousand feet as I did a wingover to the left and lined up with the road. The burner noise and my up-and-over maneuver would get their attention; then we would roll in and charge down the road firing our cannon while the Spad came in on the deck. I would momentarily light the burner again when I got over the spot where John had touched down. After pulling up and over I would then come back down the road shooting up the south side, as the Spad passed the spot and broke north for the cover of the hills.

We went to work and as I approached firing range I could see that on either side of the road the hills sloped up sharply, making a valley. AK-47s, larger automatic weapons, and who knows what else spit from all over those slopes and we had ourselves at least a battalion of well-armed and dug-in North Vietnamese regulars. I put the target pip on a cluster of sparkling small arms fire up in front of me and pulled the trigger, only to have my cannon fire a few rounds and jam. I yelled at the inoperative cannon and I yelled at the North Vietnamese troops on the ground, but my cannon was dead and the Spad was charging in behind me still doing his job. I pulled up over John's spot as planned, reversed, and started back like a toy airplane flying into real bullets; but I pulled the trigger as hard as I could anyway and screamed, "Drop dead, you bastards."

The Spad hugged the trees to the north, while I did the same to the south, and when all the nasty tracers and noise faded the Spad driver said, "There's nobody there, no sense in losing any more birds. We better call it off. Sorry, old man, thanks for the cover."

There is no doubt that the farther north you went the rougher it got. In the earlier stages of the war, some of the pilots who were rotating in and out on temporary duty wound up with strange combinations of tours where they racked up quite a few missions against defenses that were less severe than the fierce defenses proliferating around Hanoi. That often lulled them into a false sense of personal invincibility. Dave Groark's friend Bob Jones was lucky enough to make that mistake and get away with it. Dave and Bob were sitting in the officer's club at Korat during their final deployment tour and Bob was telling Dave that he had flown seventy-eight missions, that he had never taken a hit, and that they had never laid a glove on him. Dave had about the same number but thought seriously as Bill talked and just said "Yeah," and not much else. Somehow it seemed like a good subject to say nothing about. The next day was the first time Bob went to the POL depots in Hanoi. He got shot up badly and had to limp back to the emergency recovery strip at Udorn. Dave's flight had to recover there also and when he met Bob on the ground, Bob's plane was all messed up. Dave quietly told him he should have kept his mouth shut instead of making a big deal about not taking any hits.

Having a picture taken while posing with a battle-damaged bird was another way of shooting your mouth off that I personally avoided like the plague. Some people thought it was neat to do things like sticking your head through a hole in some part of a bird you have been lucky enough to nurse back and then smiling for a photographer so you could have a horror photo to show back home. My classmate and friend from West Point, Robert Elias Spraggins, built my superstition against pictures like that back in Korea. Sprag and I were among those who had gone through flight training and won our wings while we were cadets at the Point. When we graduated, we were commissioned as second lieutenants in the army and assigned to the air corps. We flew together from graduation, through the establishment of a separate air force, until we went to Korea together. Sprag picked up a big hole in the tailpipe of his F-80 one day, and when he got it back someone had him pose for a picture next to the damage. It was an impressive picture, but when he showed it to me, I somehow felt inside that the picture seemed to be flaunting fate. On his next mission Sprag was inbound on a low-level napalm run and they blew him out of the sky. Time after time

I saw people get badly hurt or killed after smiling on a photo after being hit. Whenever I got hit I talked to the crewchief about how to fix the bird, told the photographers to take their damage pictures by themselves, and walked away, thankful and trying to figure out ways to keep that from happening again.

When one of our people got knocked down we always tried to figure out how to avoid falling into the same trap, but I never figured out how the guns along the Northeast Railroad got Art Mearns. He had been going down south since the first flights came down from Yokota and he only had a few to go for his one hundred. He had flown against every type of tough target down there and probably understood the place as well as or better than anyone around.

That morning everybody was directed against the rail line that ran along the east coast from China to Hanoi, and the weather was not good in the target area. All the flights had come up the long way: take off and fly east to the water; head north and refuel off the coast; turn in past Haiphong, then hit the deck as you make landfall. The low ridge lines between the coast and the railroad were loaded with guns and they always had a crack at you both coming and going. Art was leading Laredo flight and they were after a heavily defended railroad switching yard. He was the only one who managed to get his flight through the murk and find his target under the clouds. He pulled his flight up into the clouds and over onto the run, and they broke out of the clouds just in time to put their bombs in the middle of the yard. It was a super job, but if anyone could have pulled it off, it would have been Art.

They went balls out for the coast, still under the clouds, jinking for all they were worth with the guns on the ridge lines spitting at them from both sides. It was touch and go getting out, but they were still hacking it when Art suddenly yelled, "Laredo, take it down!"

Art was a perfectionist who was intolerant of any lack of complete attention to detail within his flight. Normally the command to take it down was associated with an approaching Sam, but Sams didn't seem to be a factor at that instant. No way to tell what Art saw, or what he was thinking, but he stuffed his nose down and wound up right in front of those guns and in an instant they had him. They shredded his belly and the aircraft burned with fuel and hydraulic fluid spewing from end to end. He managed to get to about 20,000 feet, with the coast and navy rescue in sight before she locked up, snapped to inverted, and Art punched out.

He wound up in the Hanoi Hilton, but he died there. He was a strong-willed type, and while I don't know, I'll bet he died on some sort of a rack without giving much but his name, rank, and serial number.

I hated the Northeast Railroad. For some reason there were targets and areas that I worked with enthusiasm and there were others that I just did not care for. I didn't like the long drag up the coast to get there, and I didn't like the fact that all I ever found was a railroad track, old shot-up railroad cars, and lots of flak. One afternoon Jack Hunt and I wound up way up where those tracks hit the Chinese buffer zone. We were all by ourselves with nothing in front of us but empty tracks and lots of enemy guns.

We had a double abort in our flight just as we came up on the coastline from over the water, and the other Thud flights were working farther south. Jack and I were all the gunners had to worry about. We knew we wouldn't find anything to do but cut the track, and we knew that, even with good hits from two fighters, they would have the track repaired by morning. But that was our job for the afternoon. Before we even turned parallel to the tracks we were absolutely covered with 37s and 57s. I jinked harder than I can ever remember jinking before or after, but I could not shake the ground fire. They were concentrating on me in the first aircraft and though Jack kept yelling at me, and I kept evading harder, those red golf balls just kept painting the sky right in front of my windscreen. According to Jack, "I about gave you up because it looked like lots of them were curving right up your tailpipe."

You know why that stuff was so thick? We had given them all the time they needed to bring in massive numbers of guns, and at that time we insisted on sending several flights every day, twice a day at the exact same time, to run an armed recce on that same stretch of track. Early in 1967, to complement a corresponding Sam and Mig buildup, the North got a massive increase in defense capability with the infusion of one thousand additional antiaircraft guns of all sizes. On that ten-mile stretch of the Northeast Railroad that ran between the Chinese buffer zone and the Hanoi prohibited circle, there was one gun every forty-eight feet! Imagine what kind of coverage that gave them. Jack and I were taking on that defense all by our lonesome while trying to complete a meaningless strike against empty tracks.

There was no way that we were going to find anything worth hitting and it was amazing that we hadn't already been knocked down. I picked a stretch of track and we laid twelve 750s on it and blew some track and lots of dirt into the air. We hauled ass in burner, still jinking and dodging bunches of flak. When we got back out over the water, I couldn't do much other than scream vile language into my oxygen mask and wonder.

The 37-mm guns weren't big but they were all over the areas we worked up North. They had good gunners, and they put up a dense enough cover to give you a really bad time if you got in their way. They could always give you trouble, even if you knew where they were, but you were most susceptible when they surprised you. If you went looking for targets of opportunity up North you stood a good chance of finding good shooting, but you also ran the risk of getting surprised.

After we hit our target Downtown, each flight leader in our wing was on his own and there was no reason or intent to regroup on the way out. You could take your flight straight back to the base, or you could go hunting, providing you had enough fuel left, and providing you didn't stub your toe on any of the restrictions. As long as I wasn't in a fuel panic I always took my guys hunting before I headed home. My favorite spots were along Route Six from Hoa Bin to Dien Bien Phu, and if you were eager to find something in there, you could almost always do some good work. That was partly because they didn't expect you to be off by yourself showing initiative and partly because Route Six was a prime supply route that didn't get worked over very often. It was remote enough so that it was not the type of target that would normally qualify as a strike target and was only vulnerable to armed recce by fighters who were looking hard for targets.

In Swede Larson's wing, they didn't mess with hunting tactics. You could pick up a note of envy when you listened to Swede say, "You guys at Takhli tore up the countryside up there in Pack Six after you struck your targets. That was counter to what we were allowed to do at Korat. We'd roll in on a target in burner and come out of there honking at about Mach .95 to 1.1 and jinking out, still in AB, until we got over the jungles and then we'd start climbing out. We didn't strike targets of opportunity on the way out."

There were many differences between our two F-105 wings. The pilot situation was great in our wing at Takhli. The majority of our pilots were well experienced and eager. All of our leaders flew and they led the tough ones. For us, there was no other way. Swede Larson wasn't so fortunate at Korat, and—no offense to the good guys at Korat—I've got to say that it showed around Downtown during the time I was involved over there. As Swede says, "I'd estimate that only 40 percent of the pilots we got in were fighter or fighter bomber qualified or had any previous experience to amount to anything. We had a lot of them that the personnel weenies dug out of the woodwork. I don't know what they did after you and I left there, but it must have been even worse. In our particular wing we had a wing commander who for all intents and purposes never flew. We had a wing deputy for operations who had no fighter bomber experience and who only flew as a wingman. We had an assistant DO who was a lieutenant colonel and a friend of the DO and we had to check him out with his very first ride in the Thud in the local area, if you can believe that. He also only flew wing, but he was one of the people who advised the DO and gave us squadron commanders chaff. It's pretty tough to have a first-class outfit when you've got a commander, a DO, and an assistant DO with backgrounds and flying habits like that."

While there were vast differences between the two Thud wings in leadership philosophy and how we operated in the North, we had one thing in common: visitors. If you were a politician, or a ranking civil servant or a general aspiring for more stars, Southeast Asia was the place to visit. Takhli and Korat were the only places where the offense was running at Hanoi, so to be a true expert when you got back home in a week, you had to visit the Thud drivers. Since Takhli was just north of Bangkok, we were usually the last stop on the trip. That way most of our visitors were able to finish their tour with a night on the town and a suitcase full of Thai trinkets to take home. We hated the visitor routine. Those people were a daily interference since somebody had to squire them around, and more than 99 percent of them were bored, dragged out, and ready to get back to more comfortable places. They never added anything to our effort. The public relations people from Washington loved it, and some of our eager for promotion military loved it; but for those of us involved in the shooting, the show and tell routine was an utter pain.

One visitor made a hit, a fiesty American gal of Irish descent named Maxine McCaffrey. We had no idea who she was and the fact that she was billed as an artist meant nothing to us. The first time we saw an American female in jeans and an oversize blue denim man's shirt on our airbase, with three cameras and nylon bags of film strung in reckless abandon around her neck, we had to wonder what crazy thing was going to happen next. We were soon to learn that she was one of us and that her paintings were superb. Of all the non-fighter-pilots who came our way, Maxine was one of the very few who were accepted. That was because she was really a fighter pilot minus flying lessons.

Max took pictures like a woman possessed. It seemed like her cameras were always busy and she scurried about with boundless energy and a sense of urgency second to none. She got to know us through her cameras and her penetrating desire to find out who we were and how we fought. When she went back to the States she painted us and she fought for all

131

those we left behind in the Hanoi Hilton. She was, simply, a great person who stumbled into our little world.

Her whirlwind of activity took her all over Southeast Asia, but her strongest focus was on the Thud operation. Korat was one of her first stops and she ran into a bit of flak there, but Swede Larson took care of that. On the first of April 1967, Swede got a call telling him to get up to Willy Chairsell's office right away. When he got there he found a woman in the office with Chairsell and she turned out to be Maxine McCaffrey. Willy had assigned her to another squadron, and she decided to start taking pictures that she would use to create some paintings of Karl Richter, who at that time was going for two hundred missions. But Richter got knocked down on his 198th mission while checking a new guy out in the easy packs.

So Maxine had been sitting around the other squadron with everyone ignoring her and with her project stalled out. She sat there for several days, then went to Chairsell and complained that nobody would pay any attention to her. Swede got chosen to move her to his squadron.

Swede assigned her to one of his troops and told him to make her part of the squadron. He got her a flight suit, took her to the briefings and the club, and did whatever he could to make her part of their operation. She immediately became a very integral part of the squadron and really ate it up.

The day that Swede got bagged she took a lot of pictures following him through the general briefing, the flight briefing, going to personal equipment, and then going out to his airplane. As Swede strapped in she said, "Swede, I'll meet you when you get back." So Swede said, "Okay, I'll see you in about three and a half hours." Swede was late for their appointment.

As Swede was taking the troops Downtown on his ninety-fourth mission, he had Jim Hughes leading his element. The flak was heavy as they approached town, and the first real indication of trouble came when Jim's engine died and he started down. Swede tried to cover Jim on the way down and they zapped Swede. Jim Shivley was right in the middle of it and he went down along with Swede and Jim Hughes. Things happened fast up there and we had parted company with three more of the best.

We didn't have to wait long to find out what had happened to them. The North decided to make a show of their new trio of prisoners, and even though Swede and Jim Hughes were badly injured, the North Viets dragged all three of them through the streets, accompanied by well-photographed mobs of civilians and soldiers. Swede finally collapsed on camera and all three were locked up while the pictures made many front pages throughout the world the next morning.

Most days the Bangkok newspaper printed a very short section on the war, less than half a column, containing a few bits of information that Washington decided should be available to the world. It never had much detail and usually carried some title like, IN THE WAR. It always reminded me of AT THE BIJOU, or ON THE TOWN TONIGHT. About the time that Swede went down, one of those accounts went on to say, "The Viet Tri thermal power plant was largely destroyed by an F-105 raid." Sounds mundane, but it was a mission that stood out in the mind of Hal Bingaman.

I was leading the strike force that day and Bing was flying as my element leader in the first flight. We were fragged on the Viet Tri thermal power plant and the weather looked pretty reasonable. Our wing was first in and the F-4s, which were just getting their feet wet on some of the bombing missions, were scheduled to follow us.

Bing had Max Brestel, with his super eyes, on his wing, and I had a pilot I had not flown with before on my wing. Bing, Max, and I had flown together quite a bit and always worked well together. My wingman was from Bing's flight in the 354th, and as I recall he was a nondescript who went home after accumulating eighty missions over an eight-month period. He had a few other problems while he was at Takhli so we really didn't miss him when he went home.

It would have been nice if everyone we had was a super-jock, but that was not the case. As in most outfits there were those who showed up when they were supposed to and accomplished little more. We had to use them to get the job done, so one of the tasks was to match them up with situations where they had all the help they needed to stay out of trouble and all the urging they needed to do the best job they possibly could. In this case, we had my wingman surrounded.

Viet Tri had the first large power plant ever built in North Vietnam and a fair-sized rail yard. It always seemed to be defended by an inordinate number of 100- and 85-mm gun positions. If the weather was decent you could spot it from way out because it sat right along two big bends in the Red River. It was also easy to find because the big 100- and 85-mm batteries that surrounded it always seemed anxious to shoot. There were tougher targets up there, but Viet Tri was tough enough.

Viet Tri was also the location of the "Hospital," a good-sized long gray building that ran east to west and faced the river. Most of it was about four stories high, with lots of windows, which was a good excuse for calling it a hospital. The east end went up a few stories higher and could have been an executive office section or something like that. There was a huge white circular field with a big red cross in the center painted on the south-facing wall. The thing that made this hospital different was that any time you came near it all those hospital windows spit streams of red tracers at you and more of them barked from the roof of the executive tower. Every time they shot at us from the hospital I wished I could have had Lyndon and McNamara flying my wing.

Bing still bubbles with enthusiasm when he repeats his account of that Viet Tri strike, saying, "Our flight was loaded with CBUs and our job was to hit first, hammer the guns, and let the strike flights get their bombs on the power plant. The thing that made this such a good mission was your plan for getting the job done and the way it worked to perfection. We were all fed up with doing things exactly like we had done them the day before and getting our ass shot off in the process, and we welcomed some imagination. Right from the initial briefing, our whole outfit felt like we were going to do good work on that one. You briefed that this time we were going to go after them the way we should. We were going to give those gunners an approach that wasn't in their school books and we were going to fly one where they couldn't predict what we were up to or what we were going to do. The first time they would get the clue would be when those cans of CBUs were heading their way. Even the briefing was fun.''

I could tell that Bing and all the other guys were hot to trot on this one, and that pumped me up to do the best job I possibly could as their leader. I flew down Thud Ridge just like always, and then swung just enough to the southwest to put Viet Tri off to our right front. From the ground it must have looked like we were heading for someplace south of Viet Tri. We were down low, going like hell, in a fingertip four with the element on the right side as we came up on the bends in the river. We were not quite abreast of Viet Tri when I called for the pop and we hauled 'em straight up. As we passed vertical I started rolling to my right and went over the top to inverted, heading to the southwest. As I rolled to inverted Bing kept climbing straight across my track, then crossed back over me as I went on my back. The gunners were lost already.

I kept rolling back into a giant wifferdill as Bing passed over me. Then I pulled back to the left with my nose falling through at the end of the wifferdill, and Bing turned back to the right and let his nose fall through underneath me. As we rolled out we wound up line abreast, Bing on the right and me on the left, going straight down, in the opposite direction from the way we came in. The big gun pits were lined up right underneath us and the gunners were probably looking straight up with their mouths open trying to figure it out. We each picked out a particular set of gun pits and sent eight fat cans of CBUs right down the gut into the middle of them.

If I had gone by the book I would have pulled out straight ahead after we dropped our CBUs and started jinking northward back up toward the ridge, which I'm sure any of the gunners that were still alert were expecting. But we weren't going to do that either. We all broke under the dive angle. I pulled and rolled left and Bing pulled even harder and under me, and we wound up heading back across the Red River. We were still down low, speeding along and jinking and moving as an integral and effective flight of four. I had briefed the bombing flights to split off from the standard approach well before they got to the target, and they each hit it from a completely different angle. The last flight bombed from an approach exactly opposite from the one used by the first flight.

Bing also liked the way things went as we pulled off the target. As he came back across the river, still in a pretty steep dive, he was well below me and coming up on my left side. He checked back toward six o'clock and Max Brestel was at his eight o'clock position coming up toward line abreast, just where he should have been, flying a beautiful wing. It was then that Bing saw his first and only flak of the whole day. It was moving down from about six o'clock high, big black bursts popping about every hundred yards, describing a perfect trail from where Bing had pickled his CBUs many seconds before to where he would have been if I had made a standard recovery.

Once we got back across the river, Max Brestel looked over his shoulder to the southeast and picked up a truck convoy on a hillside road. Max saw those rascals before any of us, but that was not unusual for Max. Regardless of his position in a flight, Max consistently saw things first, which had a lot to do with his Mig kills. Two pilots can check out exactly the same piece of sky and one can see things in combat that the other may never see. Max just plain had super combat eyes.

The trucks that Max called were about fifteen miles south of the Red River. I rolled us in on them and we started eating them up with our Vulcan cannons. Surprisingly, nobody shot back from the ground, so we strafed them a couple more times, got them burning, then got the hell out of there.

I like Bing's critique of that mission because it flatters my fighter pilot ego. But even more satisfying is the illustration of the effectiveness of fighter pilots using their equipment properly, without suffering restrictions imposed by nonflying commanders thousands of miles removed from the action. It is worth noting that I led that mission as I wanted to, not as I had been instructed to by some faceless administrator. I ignored all the details of altitude, airspeed, and heading that someone who knew nothing of Hanoi had prepared for me.

It made good flying sense. It did not interfere with anyone else.

It was a smooth mission and everybody did good work. The strike flights reported no flak and all bombs went right on the thermal power plant. Later on we talked with pilots from the F-4 wing that followed our wing to the target. It was their first attempt at a bombing strike up there and they were delighted to report that they didn't see a single burst of flak. That one string of black puffs that Bing had seen must have come from the last of the guns to go down under our CBUs.

All the poststrike debriefings were very positive, and the plant was destroyed as far as those of us in the fighter force who had been there were concerned. As usual, that meant nothing. Possibly the poststrike photo recce coverage didn't satisfy Seventh or PACAF or Washington, but a few days later somebody directed a special four ship strike on the Viet Tri thermal power plant. Danny Salmon, Ken Bell, and two other pilots from our wing loaded up with high-drag bombs and headed for the plant by following the Red River at very low altitude and high speed. They were briefed to come over the target right down on the rice paddies and drop the bombs directly over the target, almost like they were skip bombing. The Snake Eye bombs they were carrying had four spring-loaded plates on the rear of the bombs where the fins would normally be. When the bombs left the aircraft, the springs would extend the retarding plates, and the bombs would then fall straight down into the target.

Danny and Ken made it to the plant, but there was nothing there. The only things standing were a few of the vertical walls and everything else was a junk pile. They didn't even bother to drop their bombs there.

7 | AND THERE WERE MIGS

Washington screwed up the Mig deal, just like they screwed up everything else over there. The North didn't have much in the way of Migs and Mig facilities at the time of the Gulf of Tonkin incident; thus it would have only taken a good series of fighter strikes to have crippled their potential. We chose to allow the Soviet Union and China all the time they needed to systematically improve the Mig facilities, train the pilots, and move in newer and better Mig models. It could be argued that had we knocked out the North Vietnamese facilities, Migs would have flown at us out of China. Given the state of tension between the Soviets and the Chinese during that time, and the Chinese desire not to become "directly" involved, that might not have happened. Even if it had, the North would have found their Mig effort more fuel sensitive, more complicated, and tougher to manage than the piece of cake we presented to them by our inaction. What could have been sweeter to the enemy than to know that he could scramble his fighters at the same time every day against a strike force heading for the same area on the same course they had used the day before. The North Vietnamese didn't even have to concern themselves that their Migs couldn't carry a large amount of fuel, since it didn't take much fuel if they delayed until they saw the inbound strike leader's flight approaching the end of their runway, then rolled for takeoff, made one turn, and wound up in shooting position on the tail end flight. It also helped them to know that we were not allowed to hit their airstrip and were forbidden to shoot at them until they were airborne and ready to hit us.

The Mig operation was often quite similar to what we had encountered in Korea. In both cases many of their Mig pilots, obviously the locals, were not overly proficient pilots, but we gave them all the chance in the world to pick up experience and get better. Their instructors were obviously not locals and, just like Korea, every now and then you would see an instructor in action who really knew his stuff.

The most frustrated instructor I ever tangled with was one who had me cornered in Korea. He had four flights of four under his wing when he found me heading home from a road recce with two of us in F-80s out of what started out as a flight of four. He was good and he was looking up my tailpipe before I even saw him. You could bend that 80 into a tight turn pretty well if you knew what you were doing, so my wingman and I were able to break inside his two-ship element and make him miss on his first pass. Our evasive action wasn't the only thing that was giving him problems as his guns were obviously out of harmonization.

One of the things you have to do to get a fighter combat ready is harmonize the guns. Harmonization is a ground alignment where the armament crew jacks the aircraft up to simulate level flight, then puts the gunsight pipper on the bull's-eye of a target that is set up at the aircraft's ideal firing range. An armament man in the cockpit fires the guns, one at a time, and another man marks where the rounds hit. The gun mounts are then adjusted until all rounds fired from all of the guns cluster in a tight concentration in the bull's-eye. It can be a tedious process for the ground crew, but if they don't do it right, you will not hit what you're pointing at.

That instructor had been let down by his ground crew. He fired on that first pass, but his tracers went well past our tails in a very broad pattern with no concentration of fire. The other seven elements of two each had a crack at us, but they were obviously rookies.

We wound up dueling those sixteen Migs for about twenty-two minutes, an almost unheard-of time for a dogfight, and a real test of muscles and acrobatic coordination for my wingman and myself. I was pooped and sweating like a pig, yelling on the radio in vain for someone else to come join the encounter, when that enemy instructor sneaked in on me on his last pass. I had just gotten rid of another of his elements, and as I broke hard left I couldn't see any Migs close by. That meant trouble. I rolled to inverted and there he was, under and behind me, nose coming up on my tailpipe and closing fast.

He pulled the trigger and once again it looked like a shotgun blast of roman candle tracers spurting all over the sky with no pattern focused on me. I kept pulling and rolling left and his faster speed shot him past my right side. He looked and acted very frustrated. I got a good look right into his cockpit as he passed and he was all hunched over his gunsight, still firing at empty sky and churning the stick in hopes that he could wiggle the nose around to hit something, but it wasn't going to be me.

I kicked hard right rudder, skidded into trail, and gave him a fleeting blast of six 50 calibers right up the tailpipe. Since I was about stalled out from turning and he was going full blower, he was out of range almost immediately. I don't know if I hit him, but he did a split S and headed back to Antung with fifteen sloppy Mig drivers somewhere behind him. I bet some armament crew went on short rations when he got on the ground.

Of course, the Migs had sanctuaries in both Korea and Southeast Asia. They had imaginary lines on the map that they could move across if it proved convenient, knowing full well that we were not allowed to follow. In Korea we were forbidden to cross the Yalu River, which flowed past the Mig base at Antung. In Southeast Asia they had the thirty-mile-deep Chinese border buffer zone that started just north of Hanoi, and they also had the McNamara loop that surrounded the perimeter of Hanoi itself. Most of us loved to mix it up with the Migs, even though our leaders had made a half-assed effort out of it. But we all agreed that it would have been far better and far smarter to have wiped them and their airfields out and throttled the whole thing before it ever got into gear.

The North Vietnamese started out with nothing but Mig-15s, the same aircraft the North Koreans had used. Their main base was at Phuc Yen just to the west of Thud Ridge, and that was the base we used to fly past every day on the way in. We would watch them line up for takeoff. They had another base to the west of the ridge at Kep, and as time went on they kept opening up new Mig bases farther south. It wasn't too long before we started seeing a mixed force of Mig-15s and Mig-17s, both armed with cannon. The Mig-21s, carrying heat-seeking Atol missiles rather than guns, seemed to be slow in showing up, and even in late 1967 they had by no means replaced all of the earlier models. The 21s did provide a varied threat and far better performance, and it would have been far tougher for us if they had switched the entire fleet to the 21s.

Regardless of which model Mig we ran across, we had to fly the engagement about the same way. The Migs were all light, fast, and capable of turning inside us at altitude. The little wing on a Thud, combined with its weight, made us less than a premier turning aircraft at altitudes much above the deck, so the mid and high altitudes were usually to the Mig's advantage. But at low altitude, where it was designed to operate, the Thud was awesome. If you got into trouble with a Mig and had the freedom to disengage, all you had to do was stroke the burner and hit the deck—nothing could outdo you there.

Our mission was to put our bombs on the target, regardless of Migs or anything else. That was our prime challenge. If the Migs came out on the way to the target, we picked up another challenge: Put those bombs on the target despite the Migs. Regardless of what else happened, you won if you bombed successfully in spite of the Migs and you lost if the Migs, or anything else, forced you to get rid of the bombs anyplace other than on target. It took guts and a lot of discipline to keep thundering along with fast, maneuverable adversaries nipping at your tail. But among other things, if you didn't get the target, you could expect to have to try the same one again tomorrow. Every Thud driver over there would have loved to pickle his bombs and tanks at the first sight of Migs and have at them, but if you did, you lost the game. If you outdiced them all the way down the ridge, creamed your target, and then had at them, you won all the way.

The Migs' game plan was not as clear-cut as our game plan. Sometimes they seemed content to fly formation with us all the way down Thud Ridge until we pulled for the pop and the run, in which case they were little more than an inconvenience. Maybe somebody told them that their mere presence would panic us into dumping our load; but that was not the case in our wing, a fact that should have been easy for them to figure out.

A Mig squadron commander defending Hanoi had a lot of tactical advantages. He could put himself with his flight on five-minute alert, in takeoff position on the end of the runway at Phuc Yen, every day at one hour past sunrise and again at 2:00 in the afternoon. He could start his engines when his ground control people told him that the Thuds had turned the corner out to the west near Yen Bai, and if any of his aircraft didn't check out for takeoff he still had time to call a spare aircraft into position. He'd close his canopy and roll for takeoff to the north two minutes after control told him that the Thuds had turned south at the end of Thud Ridge. After takeoff he'd make a 90 left while climbing to 15,000 feet and start a 270 to the right as he picked up speed.

As he was turning through a heading of east, the last flight of four Thuds in the strike force would be slightly below him and heading south. He'd keep accelerating, dropping his nose a little, and continuing his turn to slide in behind the tailpipes of the last flight. Just as soon as the Thuds were in range he'd fire. After breaking the flight hard left and down to clear out of the action, he might stick around and do it again to the second wing coming in, or he might just keep turning for the traffic pattern to land.

That's all they would have had to do, and I honestly do not

understand why they didn't do it. There were enough guns and Sams around to keep us busy, and that one tactic by the Migs would have made it even tougher to maintain attack discipline, to say nothing of what the attrition factor would have done to us.

They didn't do it that way, and though they had some successes, they generally seemed ambivalent about combat. The first time any of us saw Migs up North was during a fifty-ship Thud strike south of Hanoi. The Migs made one straight-in pass at the Thuds and kept going. When the Thuds returned a day later the Migs were a bit braver and stayed around long enough to shoot down two 105s.

The Mig activity continued sporadically and it never projected the image of a fully committed, eager force. For Dave Groark and Tom Curtis, it was hard even to get close to them. When they were down there in early 1966, Mig activity was still at a low level and it was rare if someone spotted a Mig. On one trip into the Hanoi area, Doug Louck had a Mig pull up right in front of him. In retrospect he would probably say he got behind a Mig. Regardless, he was in the air-to-ground mode, which meant that his sight was depressed to provide the sight picture he needed for his bomb drop. He was not configured for Mig hunting. He frantically tried to figure out what he had to do to get a gunsight, but he couldn't get there from here. He sat behind what might well be the one and only elusive Mig he would get behind during his entire tour and shot out 1,028 rounds from his Vulcan cannon—all he got was frustration because he couldn't hit his sitting duck.

When Dave and Tom got back they gathered the squadron together and tried to figure out what was the smart way to move if you found yourself in the same situation. There were an intolerable number of switches and buttons that had to be pushed or pulled to get the system from one armament mode to the other. Unless you made the transition quickly, which was tough, you had no idea where your bullets would go when you pulled the trigger. Two days later, back in the Hanoi area, Dave was flying number four and Ken Blank was leading their flight while they were working with one of the earlier Wild Weasel strikes. Bingo, same situation except that now there were two Migs. The Migs were shooting at one of the Weasel pilots and they apparently didn't even know Dave's flight was there. Ken got down in behind the Migs and fumbled as hard and fast as he could, but couldn't get through all the required switch actions. Rather than lose the chance, he just jammed the throttle forward and pressed in until the Mig filled his windscreen, hosed off the cannon and blew the Mig out of the sky. Fred Tracey had shot one down about two months before, but it rolled into the clouds before it pranged, so Ken's was the first really visible Mig shootdown by a Thud where the Mig flamed and augered in for all to see.

Tom and Dave spent a lot of time figuring out how they could get a Mig in their sights. On one particular night they were sitting around the club at Korat discussing what they would do if they got a crack at one. Sabre Sams had recently come south and was the wing commander at the time. Sabre apparently liked to eavesdrop, because the flap started right after Tom said that everyone would know if he got a Mig because he would show them the sweetest victory roll the airpatch at Korat had ever seen. Harmless, but it sure started a childish exchange.

Sabre called Tom into his office and told him that there would be no victory rolls over his airbase. It just got worse from there. Some time later Tom was sitting at a table in the club when Colonel Monroe further aggravated the situation by going out of his way to advise him that a victory roll would not be tolerated. Mind you, there wasn't even a shot down Mig to argue about. But Tom had a couple of beers in him and he looked the colonel in the eye and told him that if he got a Mig, the colonel would see a roll and know that it was Tom Curtis. The end result was a lot of bad feelings, and Tom was grounded for a week. By the way, Tom never got his Mig.

April, May, and June of 1967 could probably be defined as the period of the most ferocious combat activity during Rolling Thunder. The weather was reasonable for a change, the aircraft cooperated, and the Thuds were Downtown constantly. As we moved closer toward Downtown Hanoi, the defenses became more intense, almost frantic. Although there were no known Chinese military units operating in Vietnam, the Chinese had sent more than fifty thousand men to maintain the railroad systems and to help develop and operate the air defense system, particularly the antiaircraft gun system ringing Hanoi. The flak was spread out all over the area and there was plenty of it. The Soviets were providing the North Vietnamese with all the Sams they could launch. By now, with the Migs, Sams, and guns well coordinated, the defense was probably as intense as the North's forces could muster, and the Migs were particularly active.

You could see steady improvement in the overall coordination of defense. The Sams were spread all over the countryside and could come after you anytime you approached a target complex. As you moved down Thud Ridge you would go through a definite Mig area where the Sams, although they might be actively operating their radar, would not be firing. Once you broke through that quadrant, the Sams would start filling the air. The ground fire was always present during this transition phase and in the area of the target itself. As soon as you came back up off the target, you would usually find the Migs shunted in against you, and you would have to fight your way back out.

The Migs found out that once we dropped our bombs, with the speed and the power we had available, we were not too attractive as targets. The unloaded Thud was more than a match for them at the lower altitudes and our buddies in the F-4C Phantoms gave them fits at higher altitudes. The Migs got a few of us, but we got a lot more of them.

The North learned and improved with every attack, and our pilots got smarter every time we went up there. We got the feeling that this could go on forever for those who managed to survive. That was not what we wanted; we wanted to win and get out of there. But our commanders in Saigon, Honolulu, and Washington wouldn't let that happen. They refused to employ flexibility and surprise and, worst of all, they refused to listen to those of us who were going Downtown. We constantly suggested better ways to get the job done and cut losses, but we were repeatedly rebuffed and often personally embarrassed by those of higher rank or greater national stature who were ignorant of what they commanded. We begged for operational flexibility but were told in effect to keep quiet. When you fight a shooting and killing war it seems like you should have somebody to hate. With leadership like we had, the easiest ones for us to hate were the arrogant bumblers who abounded on our side. If ever there was a war where brave men fought in isolation for their flag and their comrades, Southeast Asia was it.

Swede Larson spoke often of our national lack of purpose. Like all of us, Swede and his guys used to read the frag, shrug their shoulders, strap in, and fly down Thud Ridge. They would fly past the steel mill and they would fly right over the airfields. Every time Swede flew into Pack Six, with one exception, he flew the same route, mission after mission. Not only did he fly the same route, he flew over the same checkpoints at the same time every day. Hell, the gunners could set their watches by us if the weather was good enough for them to see us. Swede remembers flying the first mission where the secretary and the president allowed us to strike an airfield. That was shortly before he got shot down, so it must have been about April 1967. The frag order said that he couldn't hit anything on the end of the runway; he couldn't drop any bombs by the runway; all he could do was strafe *near* the runway. His wing was only allowed one pass and Swede doesn't know if that was in the frag or if it was a local directive. He went in with something like sixteen or twenty birds and made one pass, which he described as "ineffective, very ineffective."

Sometimes the Migs did dumb things, like forgetting where they were in their own pattern of guns and Sams. I played the game of flying down the Ridge in formation with the Migs one afternoon, and when we popped for the target all of the Migs went away, as usual, except for one Mig-21. That Mig driver must have been overeager to get me. When I came across the top I glanced around to check my wingmen, and what should I see about to roll in on the target with me but this single Mig-21. The flak started to sprinkle as I peaked, then the Mig hosed off an Atol at me. His missile popped well in front of me and way off the mark, but the Mig just hung in there to see if he got a hit or to try another shot. I continued to roll in on the target as they really put a heavy barrage all around me. That one Mig was right in the heaviest part of it. The last time I saw him out of the corner of my eye he had suddenly realized what he was getting into and made a max performance turn out of there. He started jinking for all he was worth toward the base of Thud Ridge. He looked just like an experienced Thud pilot and he didn't care for that flak one bit.

The maneuverability of the Mig-21 was a source of frustration to us. I was shooting up Route Six after completing a strike, and I swept the sky just in time to spot a 21 closing on me for an Atol pass. All four of us were carrying a bag of speed and as soon as I called him out we pulled up and into him so he couldn't get a missile off. He pulled up into a supertight wingover and came charging back in for another pass, but he apparently didn't realize that we were light, in burner, and definitely in his league at that altitude. He was trying to line up on me, but since my element had crossed under me and turned back toward him, he was looking at a perfect scissors setup and he was screwed. Whichever way he turned one of my elements was positioned to climb all over him. But with that neat little machine he was flying he didn't have to press on and expose himself to either of my elements. He just rolled to inverted and pulled through a diving turn that we had no hope of duplicating, and streaked for the Chinese buffer zone. That 21 must have been fun to fly.

One of those 21s sure hammered Spade Cooley when he was leading one of my trailing elements on a Downtown bomb run. A pair of 21s waited patiently and moved in on Spade's tail as he pulled up after hitting his target, and their leader zapped him with an Atol. One second he was starting to jink and the next second he was sitting in space. He was right over the edge of Hanoi, still strapped in his seat and holding on to the throttle. They were the only parts of his exploding Thud that departed with him. He didn't know it then, but his back was broken.

Spade undid his seat belt, pushed the seat away, pulled the ripcord and started descending by silk through all the flak that was still rising toward the rest of us. He finally decided that the throttle he had clutched in his left hand wasn't much good, so he threw it away but it just sat there and floated beside him. You can't stop for a guy in that spot without losing more birds, so we had to leave him floating toward the south side of town.

He managed to land on the only thing that looked like a hill for miles around, and found himself on a flat, dirt mesa a few hundred feet above town. Spade realized his back was broken when he agonizingly crawled for the cover of a rock pile at the end of the mesa. He activated his beeper and came up on his emergency radio, though he knew that nobody had ever been rescued from Downtown. You couldn't even expect the rescue troops to try. Two groups of local militia were starting to climb the hill to capture him and the second wing of Thuds was working over the same target Spade had just hit. The bombs and flak were only a couple of miles away from his rock pile.

Who should come rumbling into the middle of this seemingly impossible scene but four of the prop-driven A-1 Douglas Skyraiders that we called Spads. That had to be the gutsiest rescue flight ever assembled. Their flight leader acted like he was on a weekend cross-country in the States. He spotted Spade, told him to sit tight, called a chopper in, and proceeded to tear up the surrounding countryside with rockets and gunfire that drove off most of the local militia. A lumbering chopper doesn't fit into a situation like that very well, but they brought one in right through all the gunfire.

The chopper was about to hover and toss the horse-collar to Spade when a small group of enemy militia clawed their way over the crest of the hill only fifty feet from Spade. The rescue leader saw them at the same time a terrified Spade did, and he came on the radio with, "Now just sit tight. This will be a little close, but I've got them clearly in sight." A full pod of rockets flew true. The militia only a few feet from Spade disappeared, and as Spade peered up through the flying dust and dirt, there was the horse-collar. They got him out and nobody got another scratch. Spade went back to the States, recovered from his broken back, and got back into the fray.

The North kept getting more Mig-21s and more Atol missiles, and they had some good days sneaking up on us from behind. Leo Thorsness had our Wild Weasel flight out in front of the main force one black Sunday afternoon and they got to him just as I brought the rest of us onto the scene. The 21s sneaked in behind Leo's number-four man, Bob Abbott, hit him with an Atol, and Bob had to punch out. Before any of us knew Bob was hit, they fired another Atol and got Leo and his Bear, Harry Johnson, a scant few miles away from where they got Bob.

Since I had the entire strike force only a few miles behind Leo, we had the world's greatest potential rescue effort set up for those guys. I spotted Leo and Harry and circled them as they descended in their chutes. We covered them for about three hours, and we had tankers standing by to the south to recycle us when we got low on fuel. We also had good weather and open countryside with minimal flak. I was talking to Leo on his emergency radio from the time he hit the ground and got out of his chute. It was a piece of cake, but we blew it.

The rescue Spads took forever to get there, and when a flight of two of them eventually arrived it was clear that those two particular pilots didn't want to be where they were. The radio was garbaged up with Bob Abbott's stuck beeper, but that was not a valid excuse for the Spad drivers' lack of purpose. They couldn't even find Leo while he was talking to them, looking at them from the ground, steering them over the top of his head, and firing smoke flares. Our bottom cover flight was also steering them to the exact spot and even making passes right over Leo's head to show them where he was.

The choppers never showed up: First, because the Spads refused to call them in until they physically saw Leo on the ground, a task they were strangely incapable of accomplishing; second, in this case, their control group, which had to give the command to scramble the choppers, couldn't communicate with Seventh Air Force headquarters. Seventh was almost a thousand miles away, but for some unknown reason that control group said they had to have a general officer out of Seventh say it was okay for those particular choppers to go across the Vietnamese border to snatch our buddies back. It was a revolting mess of air force ineptitude at its worst. I was still talking to Leo on the radio when the enemy troops finally walked up the dirt road, under the cover of twenty armed Thuds and two stumbling Spads, and took three of our finest to Hanoi for seven years of hell. The last thing Leo said was, "Get me out of here," but I couldn't do it.

Two more Mig-21s sneaked up behind Al Lenski and Joe Abbott (no relationship to Bob Abbott) as they were headed out from the now futile rescue to recycle off a tanker. They busted Al up, but he managed to keep flying. They blew Joe's Thud completely out of the sky and he stepped out. Leo, Harry, and Bob were done in by then, so I moved our fighters farther south to cover Joe. This time we got a great rescue flight leader and his wingman on the scene very quickly. He immediately spotted Joe at the edge of a tree line. He had Joe move to an open field and spread his chute for a marker and then got him all ready to be hoisted aboard a chopper. I guess rescue control was trying to make up for the waste on Leo, Harry, and Bob as they quickly sent two choppers after Joe, but that effort blew up in our faces also. One of the choppers thought he had a rough engine, so they both chickened out and turned back from a flak-free, easy pickup. Twilight was fading fast and it was the last chance. Joe was standing there in an open field with a smoking orange flare in his hand to show them where he was and which way the wind was blowing, but the chopper pilots were gutless.

Leo, Harry, Bob, and Joe all got back when the Hanoi Hilton closed up seven years later. None of them ever needed to have gone there. We could only assume that the rescue people didn't have their first team working that Sunday afternoon.

You could tell just from his radio transmissions that our

Spad leader was as frustrated as we were when we had to leave Joe, and when you get frustrated in combat you often get into trouble. It got dark in a hurry as we turned south, then the Spad wingman split the night air with, "Mayday, Mayday, Mayday—lead's hit and he's on fire." He had wandered too close to someone on the ground and unseen small arms had scored a hit.

I immediately turned back toward our slower rescue companion, despite the fact that we were woefully short on fuel. I knew that another rescue didn't have a chance, but when the call goes out, you respond, regardless. His wingman came on the radio again, "Lead, this is four. You're on fire. Bail out, bail out, *bail out!*"

After a pause, Spad leader responded with a calm, "Negative." He knew he was on fire. He knew that if he bailed out there was no rescue possible that night. He also knew that four others had gone down that afternoon without a successful rescue in the bunch. He was not about to jump out over the black of the enemy's land and join them in death or prison as long as there were alternatives available.

He decided that he was going to try to blow that fire out. He rolled his Spad inverted and dived through the night toward the unseen jungle below, accelerating as much as his aircraft would take. That ancient aircraft shuddered and bucked as the speed increased and the altitude decreased, but the mounting force of the airstream was working. Inch by inch it forced the fuel-fed fire rearward. Then just when the ground was getting too close, the fire crept back past the trailing edge of the shattered wing and was gone.

He had to pull a bunch of gs during a dark pullout from an almost vertical dive with only the seat of his pants to guide him as a replacement for his tumbled instruments. He was a bit breathless when the radio finally spoke to tell us he had it under control. We all headed for home by different routes but it was a very dark and very quiet trip for all of us.

For a long time there was no such thing as Mig cover. We went in with our Thuds and we were responsible for taking care of ourselves. Air cover first came in the form of F-4

Phantoms. The F-4s were two-place machines, with a radar intercept officer to handle the radar and weapons systems while the pilot took care of the flying. Phantoms were far better air-to-air birds at altitude than the Thuds, but when they arrived on the scene they did not move into an exclusive anti-Mig role. They tried their hand at working Downtown, but got pretty well creamed for their trouble. The task of putting the heavy hits on Downtown remained with the Thuds. The F-4s also had other missions, such as a sizable night interdiction effort farther south, so they supported us sparingly when they first arrived. The Mig activity was moving toward its peak by the time F-4 Mig cover became a daily reality.

We gladly welcomed the help, but quite naturally we often teased each other. We told them they were prima donnas who couldn't hack it in the trenches down on the deck, and they told us that they were sophisticated air-to-air specialists and that our grubby tasks were beneath them. We worked well together and during the most active phase of the air war from January to June of 1967, we combined to account for forty-six Migs. The Thuds maintained the pace of taking the load to Hanoi and still shot down eighteen Migs. We got most of our kills with our nose-mounted 20-mm Vulcan cannon. The Phantoms got the rest of the kills while covering us from above.

Since the Thud wing at Korat liked to stagger in high and get hammered, while our wing at Takhli liked to take it to them at high speed down on the deck, the two wings presented a different Mig cover challenge to the F-4s. Swede Larson's comments verify that Korat didn't work with the F-4s the way we did. Swede said that their pilots used to complain a lot to the deputy for operations about the air support that the F-4s were supposed to be giving them. The Avis wing, which is what we called Korat because we knew that they were second best, felt the F-4s were always running off to chase Migs, and not just with an element or a flight, but with the whole gaggle chasing after them. They griped that they got left sitting there at 16,000 to 18,000 feet, hanging on a stall with a full load, wide open for other Migs to clobber them. The Migs knew this and they'd come in with a few birds and suck off the F-4s, then the rest of the Migs would scream in on the Avis troops while they were wide open. A lot of their guys would take that as an excuse to pickle off their loads and go chasing Migs.

In our wing at Takhli we didn't have those problems. By working down low at high speed we obviously didn't have to worry about being Mig bait while hanging on a stall with a load of bombs at medium altitude. Also, our discipline and dedication to our mission, and to each other, quite simply ruled out dumping our load to go chase Migs. We appreciated the F-4s watching what we were doing and taking out any Migs they could spot above and behind us while we did our job. It was a good arrangement for our wing.

When the ratio of Mig-21s to the older models got higher, the North came up with a few new wrinkles. They would send the 15s and 17s in after us first while the 21s held above and out of the fray. If we stroked off after a 15 or a 17 and got overly eager and careless, the 21s would be there on our tails with an Atol missile.

I got to personally check that tactic out on one of our better days Downtown. It was our single most active day and the total U.S. count for the day's work included seventy-two separate missions against the North, while those of us working Downtown racked up seven confirmed Mig kills along with two Migs damaged and probably destroyed.

I had the lead flight working against a railroad yard and we dropped our bombs and came racing back up to altitude, remembering the Migs we had observed minutes before as we came down Thud Ridge. The Avis wing was working over on the other side of the Ridge at the same time and the Migs were pretty well mixed up with them also. The Migs had been orbiting out to the west of us as we bombed, and as I came zooming up off the target my first view was of a head-on pass from a Mig whose pilot did not appear to be too well coordinated or satisfied with his attack. He had failed to take my speed into consideration, and by the time he actually tried to line up on me, he had already lost the battle and was all for getting out of the fray. That didn't give me an opportunity to shoot at him and the resultant head-on pass turned into nothing more than a near collision that scared me and, if he had any sense, should have scared him. We went zipping past each other canopy to canopy with a closing speed well up in the 1200 knot range.

Now my wingman, Paul Sheehy, on my west side and a little high, came into my field of view quite clearly. He really caught my attention because there was a Sam bursting directly behind his tailpipe. Fortunately, it had tried to close at a right angle to him, a difficult shot, or he never would have made it. The thing burst right on his tailpipe and covered about half of his aircraft with the ugly orange ball that was the trademark of an exploding Sam. To my great surprise, he came flying out of the explosion. His electronic jamming pod was not working. Knowing that the Sams had his range and elevation, he had no choice but to roll over, head for the weeds, and get down behind the Ridge before they tapped him. This, of course, left me without a wingman, which is not the greatest feeling in the world. My element was coming up off the target on my right side, but my left side was quite bare. Bending to the right, I noticed that I was lined up to the west of the Ridge and pointed right at Phuc Yen. In fact, I was very nicely lined up with the runway of the Migs I was fighting with. The ground gunners were lighting up the sky all around the airfield, and I was able to strafe them with my Vulcan cannon. That's not the kind of duel you engage in for any length of time and live to talk about, but it was satisfying to be able at least to give them a shot in their own backyard, even if it was off-limits.

I spotted two Mig-17s in a very sloppy echelon that put them almost one behind the other. They were under me in a lazy turn to the southwest away from Phuc Yen. I still had lots of speed and I had my cannon and a heat-seeking Sidewinder missile. As I turned onto their tails I went through a mental exercise on the Sidewinder firing sequence, since it took four time-consuming switch actions to set it up. I could have used it if I had another hand. With all the speed I had,

I closed on the two Migs like mad. They stayed in their gentle turn and didn't appear to see me. I thought, "I'll go through my switching action and set up my missile; but if I do, I'll have to wiggle around a bit and delay and they may see me in the interim and break off. If they do, I can't touch them because they'll turn so much tighter than I can. If I get the missile set up, the chances of it tracking properly are less than 100 percent. If it goes streaking across the sky, that'll alert them and they'll be off and running and I'll never get a crack at them. I might get one of them with that missile, but I'm greedy. I want them both."

So I jammed the throttle forward and got inside their turn and was closing beautifully. It was an ideal gunnery pass, just as pretty as it could be.

I started to fire as I pressed to within one thousand feet of the trailing Mig. He rolled over lazily to the right and sank like a dead fish. I figured, Okay, I got that guy; now I'll just keep pressing in and get the one up in front of him. But I had no wingman to look around and protect me. My element was now in pretty good position and John Bobel, flying number three, called me to break right immediately. It seems that a Mig-21 had entered the scene from above and was moving into position above and inside my turn and was about to have at me. I stayed until John called a second time with, "Lead, break right—get your ass out of there *now!*" I rolled down and under to the right and as I pulled through the maneuver, I threw the closing Mig-21 off and over the top of me.

While this was going on all my other flights were active, and Carl Osborne and Phil Gast each managed to get a Mig coming off the target. Paul pulled up off the deck after shaking his Sams and got himself a probable to go with my probable. Things then turned into a three-ring aerial circus as the Phantoms, who were in the area above us, wanted into the act and had come down to our altitude. They had managed to get two Migs that had been on our tails on the way into the target, and they wanted more. I spotted another Mig spinning down to earth that one of our guys had hammered. Then Bob Rilling got one with a missile and it was a beautiful hit. The entire rear end of the Mig was burning, and you could see right through the skeleton of the aircraft as it burned and went straight across the valley in a descent, never wiggling, and hitting at the base of the Ridge. I never saw any chutes from any of the Migs we hit.

The Phantom pilots got a little concerned when Bob hosed off that Sidewinder, because from some angles the Mig-21 and the Phantom look quite similar. In a fast-moving combat situation, it's sometimes difficult to tell one from the other. Once you fire that missile, it has no sense and just tries to do what it's supposed to do, look for a hot tailpipe. Once our Sidewinders started shooting through the air and Migs started falling out of the sky, one of the Phantom drivers said, "Hey, Chief, they're shooting Sidewinders. Let's get the hell out of here." They lit their burners and went back up to altitude and allowed us to finish our work.

After Bob got his Mig, he was quite low on fuel, as he had been in burner for a long time. He was also right down among them at the edge of Phuc Yen, and had maneuvered to a spot behind us where he had managed to "corner" two Migs at his six o'clock position, a move calculated to get you shot down. He called his flight and indicated that he was in big trouble. I turned the force back toward him as he pushed his bird right down on the grass and got going as fast as he could. With the speed that an F-105 has at that altitude, he was able to shake his pursuers and we again turned the force out of the area. That was quite a wild melee and I think, perhaps more than any other day, it taught those Mig drivers some respect for the combined forces that were lined up against them.

That evening I got a call from Chappie James, the deputy for operations of the F-4 wing. He had been leading our Mig cover that afternoon, and while he congratulated us on our fine work, he complained that Mig killing was supposed to be their business. I told Chappie that if he and his guys would come on down where the action was and get a little bit sweaty, they might be able to steal some of our kills from us.

All in all we did pretty well against the Migs, and it was not too often that they kept us from what we were after. But that is no register of what we could have done if we had been free to clobber their airfields, or to shoot them wherever we saw them, or chase them whenever they were running for their sanctuaries. Whatever good we did, we did in spite of our restrictions. Maybe even worse was the fact that we never met the Mig first team, yet we bragged about our record. If we ever tangle with first team in another war, I doubt that it will be as easy as our government would have you believe it was in Korea and in Southeast Asia. If we are ever dumb enough to try to go after that Mig first team with one hand tied behind us, they'll eat us up.

8 | AND THERE WERE SAMS

The SA-2 surface-to-air missile, known as the Guideline, or as just plain old Sam to us, was a two-stage rocket, thirty-five feet long, with a 349-pound high-explosive warhead. It was capable of supersonic speeds up to altitudes of 60,000 feet. It could accelerate to Mach 1.9 by the time it reached 10,000 feet and moved at speeds up to Mach 2.3 by the time it went through 20,000 feet.

But let me introduce you to Sam firsthand. It clusters in a Star of David formation scratched out on the ground, with its tracking radar van, known as a Fan Song, in the center. The radar tracks you when you're in the target area and if it can get a good lock on you, the operator pushes the fire button and Sam comes to life. If you're dumb enough to sit there straight and level, and if the radar trackers can keep you in their beam, Sam will likely get you. They can set its fuse for a specific altitude, such as the base of the clouds, or they can use a proximity fuse that will detonate when you're in range. The first-stage booster that launches the Sam creates a good-sized dust storm on the ground, so if you just happen to be looking in the right direction when it blasts off, you know that Sam is airborne and on the prowl. After the booster has done its job it drops off and falls back to earth, leaving the propulsion to Sam's internal rocket power.

If you can see Sam, you can usually escape. It has little, stubby wings and it is going like hell, so it can't turn very well. You can take it on just like another aircraft, and if you force it into a commit position and outturn it, it will stall out and auger in. If its radar guidance can't stick with you, it will just explode in the empty sky, with pieces falling back on those who fired it.

The Sam is most dangerous when you can't see it. If you're on top of an undercast you can't see the launch. If you are in the clouds, they can shoot for you there or they can prefuse for the altitude of the base of the clouds, and greet you with a bursting Sam when you dive out of the bottom of the overcast.

John Bobel and I encountered a Sam when John was flying my wing on a strike I was leading against some army barracks out in the flatlands south of Hanoi. The lake shown on the old photos the intelligence people had given us had dried up long ago and was not even there. The target was tough to spot and the clouds at eight thousand feet were too low to allow a good roll in on the target. I wound up going faster than I needed to and still looking for the target in a nose-down attitude. When I saw it, I had to pull up hard to get into some sort of bombing position, and I wound up leading my flight of four up into the clouds in an uncomfortable high-speed turn on the gauges.

We were only up there for a few seconds. While we couldn't see each other as we milled about at five hundred knots, enemy radar could see us and they knew we were headed for the flat base of those clouds. John and I came spitting out of the clouds, going straight down and fortunately pretty well lined up on the target, and we met three Sams in formation coming up. I never saw them until the first two roared between John and myself. John is as good a combat pilot as there is and was in perfect position, yet two Sams passed between our wingtips. The first sensation was the most god-awful noise I have ever heard. It ripped me way down in the bottom of my stomach someplace, like an old steam engine bursting out of a tunnel. The white hot light of two rocket engines, passing vertically only feet away, was bizarre and momentarily tumbled my emotional and physical gyros. For some reason those two were not proximity fused, but the third one was, and though I never saw it blow, its fragments knicked me, but only superficially.

We were already on the bomb run so there was nothing to do but center the pip, punch the bombs off, blow the barracks with two 2,000 pounders, and fly the bird out on the recovery. We then went to chase some Migs off the Avis wing, who once again were all screwed up in a high-altitude attempt at the same target. Between the thunderstorms and the Migs, they blew it and never got an aircraft on the target, but then I almost didn't get there either. Anyone who has been close enough to see and hear Sam's tail fire and feel the tickle of its fragments will tell you it's soul searing, or else he is a damn liar.

We could have knocked those Sam sites out as fast as they put them in, but Lyndon and Robert wouldn't have it. Billy Ellis hated it when the gears wouldn't listen to him when the war was less frantic at the start. He hated it worse when even our own lower-echelon intelligence people scoffed at our pilot reports on Sam activity. They wouldn't listen to us when we came back with specific reports of what we had seen if that information didn't match what the next higher headquarters thought they knew. In the earlier days of Sam's presence Billy came back with one of the first sightings and said, "Hey, guys, they're building Sam sites up there." He told the intelligence types just what they looked like and drew them little pictures and all that. All he got from the intelligence people was, "Naw, they're not building Sam sites up there. There's no other information to validate what you're telling us." Well, nobody would believe him, but somebody went up there and built some Sam sites and they sure gave all of us jocks a rough time when they were finished. It would have been a piece of cake to knock them out before they got operational.

The JCS were certainly aware of the Sam threat and expected to see them in action almost immediately. On

March 27, 1965, they advised Secretary McNamara that they had the capability to attack Sam storage facilities and operational sites. On the fifth of April a navy recce bird returned with photos of Sam sites under construction and there was no way that the threat could be disguised or ignored. The senior navy commander in the area went to Seventh Air Force headquarters in Saigon and he and the Seventh commander came up with a joint plan to eliminate the missile sites. Nothing happened.

New Sam sites continued to be documented and the JCS tried again on May 27, when they went back to McNamara recommending an attack on the Sam presence "as a matter of urgent military necessity." Their urgent request went unanswered until June 15, when McNamara disapproved the JCS recommendation, suggesting that the problem be reexamined "if interference is experienced with subsequent Rolling Thunder activities." General Westmoreland writes in *A Soldier Reports* that his air deputy raised the matter with Assistant Secretary of Defense for International Security Affairs John McNaughton in June, only to receive this response: "You don't think the North Vietnamese are going to use them! Putting them in there is just a ploy by the Russians to appease Hanoi." On July 21, 1965, we lost our first American aircraft to a Sam.

One of the rules we had to follow was that we could not shoot at or bomb a Sam site until it was ready and operational and demonstrated that readiness by shooting at us. The Soviets and the North Vietnamese were free to establish their operational sites and then tie them in with the Chinese, who were working the overall radar and communications networks, while we watched. Dean Pogreba thought that this was a stinking deal, and he would have been court-martialed for his affront, but he got killed before our leaders could get to him.

Pogie was a guy you couldn't overload. Since he was a major, we could and did make him everything from squadron commander to wing ops to squadron ops to flight leader to strike leader. Whenever there was a hole in the dike, we plugged Pogie in and he loved it. One afternoon on the outskirts of Hanoi he came up off the target and ran into unexpected flak from a new batch of 37- and 57-mm antiaircraft guns. He reversed, rolled in to strafe them, and saw a full crew of advisors and local workers, complete with modern earth-moving equipment, scratching out a Star of David. The 37s and 57s were deployed around the perimeter of the construction. Pogie made a couple of passes and shot the hell out of them.

When he got back to the debriefing, the intelligence troops plodded through their checklists until they came to the question, "Did you see anything unusual?" Pogie, hot and sweaty, replied, "You bet your ass I did. I caught those bastards right in the middle of a new Sam site and I blew them all over the paddies."

The report of Pogie's mission was on the air waves almost immediately. No sweat as far as Pogie was concerned; he couldn't be bothered. He had scheduled himself for the predawn mission back to the North and was airborne by 4:30 the next morning. By 10:00 A.M., a fitting hour for finishing coffee and crullers in the Philippines, we got a priority message from General Wilson: "Ground Major Pogreba and prepare court-martial action for attacking a forbidden target." The first return flights were hitting the initial approach for landing at that time, and everybody not on the mission was usually counting the aircraft as they came in and pitched out for landing. Several flights of four came in, then there was an element of two and then there was a single.

Either Pogie's aircraft took a severe hit or he had a bad electrical problem, or maybe Pogie himself got hit. When he came up off the target nobody heard from him, and his wingman saw him turn toward the north. His wingman chased him toward the Chinese border but couldn't catch up. We never knew if the Chinese Migs got him or what, but he was long gone. If there can be any satisfaction in losing Pogie, it had to be in sending General Wilson a message saying, "Sorry, General, can't comply. Pogie's missing and presumed dead."

* * *

In the early days Washington acknowledged Sam's entry into the fray with a new code word, Iron Hand, which referred to our efforts against the missile threat. Back in the States, an air force and industry-accelerated modification program turned out the first of a series of two-seater F-100s configured to seek and destroy Sam sites. They were the first editions of the Wild Weasels, and at least we got some specialized hardware into the act. The early electronic sensing gear installed in the 100s was just nibbling on the edge of missile-hunting technology, but it was a big step in the right direction.

The 100s were older and slower than the Thuds, which led to the early Weasels' macho slogan "first in and last out." It's true that from the first time the Weasels went up North, they probed in front of the strike force on the way in and they swept to clear our tails on the way out. However, in the case of the F-100s, "first in and last out" also meant that they were so much slower than we were that they had to head for the target well before we did, and once we hit the target, we flew right on by them while they had to struggle out behind us as best they could. That speed differential ceased to be a problem when the Weasels got their F-105s.

Thud pilots were used to flying their aircraft by themselves. They were proud of the fact that they were perfectly capable of steering themselves from place to place around the world, and the thought of having a bomber navigator sitting behind them was completely foreign to them. Suddenly all these two-place fighters started showing up and along with them came a bunch of radar operators with funny-looking wings. They were referred to as Trained Bears, or Gibs, and they were not immediately accepted with open arms.

Some of us who had flown with Air Defense Command had at least been exposed to the two-seat system before, but even there it was not universally accepted. Personally, I never liked to fly with anyone else, and even an instrument check flight in a two-place T-33 trainer was a pain. I hated listening to someone else breathe into my ears on the hot mike for hours, and I just didn't like someone looking over my shoulder while I was working.

It took Southeast Asia and the two-place Weasel mission, and the arrival of the F-4C, which always had two seats, to convince us that the second man had a role to play. The guys who shared combat with them in tandem seats understandably swore by them, and a single-seat strike pilot couldn't help but admire them when they contributed to taking out a Sam site that was shooting at him. But the single-seat versus two-seat debate has never really gone away.

Jerry Hoblit converted from a single-seater to a two-seater and became an outspoken supporter of the two-man concept. He got to fly two temporary tours down south when he was stationed at Yokota with the Thirty-fifth TAC Fighter Squadron. When he got back from the second deployment he was reassigned to Nellis in the States and went through the Fighter Weapons School. His plan was to get the school under his belt while Rosemary was busy having their first child, and then get back down to Southeast Asia again.

As soon as he finished school he volunteered to go back to Southeast Asia, and by coincidence they were just starting the Wild Weasel business at that time. When he called a friend in rated officer's assignments he found out that the personnel people were lining up a bunch of Weasel crews. Jerry had just figured out what that Weasel thing was all about and said, "No you don't. I don't want to do that. I want to go back and fight the war, but I don't want to commit suicide." His friend in personnel allowed that he understood and would take care of him, so Jerry went off deer hunting for a week.

When he returned to the squadron the next Monday, it was clear that his personnel friend had ignored Jerry's request to return as a strike pilot. He was greeted as one of the new Weasel pilots. It was a compliment because the Weasel assignments were quite selective and required tigers with high experience levels. Jerry had about eight years in the service with something like two thousand total flying hours, a thousand F-105 hours, and he had been an instructor pilot in the 105 both at Yokota and at Nellis. Most everyone who was selected was senior to him, and he turned out to be the youngest front-seater in the program at that time. That's when Tom

Wilson, his backseater, and Jerry teamed up and started working together with a shared ideal to become the best Weasels in the business.

Since Jerry got into the very first production increment of Weasels, he got to pick the brains of both the 100 and the 105 crews who had introduced the Weasel approach to combat. At the very start of the program the first Weasels had gone to Southeast Asia in the F-100 with the task of testing the concept and the basic equipment, particularly the backseat electronic detection gear. The next step had been an increment of F-105 Weasels, and Tom and Jerry were to be part of the third step as they progressed through the training and indoctrination for the first replacement group of F-105 Weasels.

The idea of the Weasels was that they would take care of the Sam threat and, as a corollary, they would take care of all other radar-directed threats. There had been radar-directed antiaircraft guns as far back as World War II, but the advent of Sams expanded and complicated the radar threat significantly. Weasels operated under the concept that in order for any radar site to be a threat to our aircraft, it had to transmit a signal. It could then be located, providing you had the right kind of electronic equipment. The scenario then went back to the basic military principle that once the seeker is seen he himself immediately becomes a target.

When the F-100s first took the concept over to Southeast Asia, there were not too many missile sites up and active in the North. At the start there were only from five to seven active sites, and the Weasels engaged those sites on a one-on-one basis. The Weasels would win. The sites would transmit from their fixed ground positions and see the 100s; the 100s would read the radar transmission and utilize their airborne flexibility to attack. It stopped being a simple problem as the North multiplied the number of active sites, and as the sites started cooperating with each other and with other elements of their highly efficient Chinese and Russian augmented air defense system.

The Vietnamese learned fast and became very good. They were doing so well that by the time Tom and Jerry arrived as the second 105 contingent in the theater, they were desperately needed replacements. The first 105 Weasels had arrived with five aircraft and seven crews. When Tom and Jerry got there all of the five original Weasel aircraft had been shot down and only three crews were still there. The sixth Weasel aircraft that they brought in was the only one the Weasels had to work with, and the Vietnamese Sam system had the upper hand at that time.

The Weasel aircraft had the same front-seat configuration as the other Thuds, but had a stretched fuselage with a back seat that was originally designed with training requirements in mind. The backseater had specialized signal detection capabilities that gave him a broad view of the overall electronic environment that each of the strike flights was exposed to. He could see multiple signals from all quadrants and evaluate them simultaneously. He was able to analyze the battle situation the strike force faced in greater detail and with a far higher degree of accuracy than any single-seater in the fray. The signal environment was so dense in North Vietnam that no single-seater could adequately sort it out by himself.

The man in the back seat was not a crew member in the sense that he was directing the airplane or directing the strike. What many people never understood was that he was an instant intelligence analyst. His prime job was to sort out and make sense of the dense electronic pattern and communicate the results of his analysis to his pilot. Those who could handle that back-seat task as it should be handled were few and far between. The good ones were specialists who were essential to producing optimum results. Many of the backseaters were pure technicians who never truly grasped what their mission was.

Most of the early F-100 Weasels were friends of Jerry's, and he talked with them constantly. He also knew some of the first 105 group pretty well and learned a lot from them. He did a great deal of listening and tried to correlate what he heard with his previous tours as a strike pilot at Korat and Takhli while he picked up all the Weasel combat experience he could get.

You wouldn't say that the survivors of that first 105 group

were scared, but they were obviously professionally concerned. Their attitude must have been like that of the early World War I pilots when the other guys were the first to get the machine guns that shot through the prop, which gave them a very visible advantage. Everyone knew that the Sams were in a temporary position of advantage and that the Weasels needed to figure out how to overcome that.

Tom and Jerry's first job was to learn as much as they could in a hurry from those who had been there. They were fortunate in that the crews who were left were senior majors who averaged about fifteen years of flying experience and who had learned plenty of hard lessons. They were some of the best battle tacticians who ever fought over there, and when time allowed they often spent as much as two days planning a single mission. Those guys had studied and made adjustments only to watch the Vietnamese make other adjustments in the cat and mouse game. It was a constant learning and application sequence where, at that moment, the North's learning curve was steeper than ours.

Even with the help of the backseater and his equipment it was often difficult for the front-seat pilot to visually acquire a site before that site fired a missile, as they were usually well camouflaged. When a site launched a Sam, that camouflage was compromised because the departing missile created clouds of dust and smoke. You could see where the sight was and you could go after it. Of course, you first had to deal with the missile coming at you. One of the first things pilots facing Sams had figured out was that you *could* dodge those missiles. You put your nose down and tracked the missile as it was coming after you. You waited until the last moment, always keeping it somewhere between ten and two o'clock out there in front of you. Then at the last second when it was closing on you, when you could clearly see the missile's stubby wings, properly called canards, you applied a whole lot of gs. The missile passed close to you but it would almost always fuse late and blow up someplace other than where you were. Most Thud drivers were exposed to some of that missile dodging, but the Weasels did a whole lot of it. The first time you did it, in fact every time you did it, it was thrilling to say the least. But it was something you knew that you could do if you had to. It got trickier when they learned to shoot more than one Sam at us.

Between mid-1965 and mid-1966 the North had approximately 50 Sam sites in operation. From 1966 to 1967 they quadrupled this number to 200 Sam sites, and at any one time they had between 350 and 500 individual missiles alerted and ready to fire. They operated twenty-six to twenty-eight missile battalions, each with three firing batteries. Each of the batteries filled a Sam site with four to six launchers. Strike pilot or Weasel, that was quite a bunch of Sams to face in the small area of Downtown Hanoi and the surrounding countryside.

Strike pilots had to avoid Sams that were fired at them to get their job done. The Weasels had to hunt and kill Sam sites to allow the strike pilots to get that job done, and it didn't get any easier as the defenses continued to expand and improve their coordination. The North came up with a new tactic we called Dr. Pepper, and the Weasels wound up dodging missiles coming at them from ten, two, and four o'clock at the same time. The Weasels would find a site and start their approach. Then that site would go down and another site would come up. The Weasels would have to turn to a different azimuth and start working on the second site until that one went down and yet another one came up, then went down. Suddenly all three sites would come up at once and launch simultaneously from different directions, thus Dr. Pepper—ten, two, and four. It's an understatement to say that Dr. Pepper vastly complicated the evasive maneuver.

When Jerry felt somewhat well grounded, he had a try at updating some of the Weasel tactics. The first thing he advocated was that instead of mixing in with the strike force as they had been doing, the Weasels should go out ahead of the strike force and split their four-ship flight into two semi-independent working elements during the time they were in the target area. The first time they tried it they goofed. They put themselves out about five minutes ahead of the strike force and all that did was to alert the Sam sites as to who they were. That put them in a miserable position with everyone up North looking at nobody but them. They wised up and figured out that they only wanted to be a couple of miles ahead of the main force.

The Weasels got so much help and supervision from everybody up the line that they ran into some headwind with their split-flight procedures. The four-ship flight is a conventional air force concept, and despite the face that the Weasels demonstrated the practicality of their approach in a new environment that was far from conventional, their idea was not universally well received. Never mind that a four-ship flight working in high *g* situations below and in front of the strike force most often got split up anyway.

Maintaining a position just ahead of the main force was often a tricky job. In our wing we usually had one of our flying colonels leading the strike and running the show. Despite the fact that the Weasels were just out in front, the maneuvering, timing, and weapons delivery of that force was under the strike commander's control and he did what he felt he had to do depending on the combat situation. Most of the time it worked out very well, and an efficient and aggressive strike leader plus an aggressive Weasel leader usually meant a mission accomplished.

Tom and Jerry destroyed four missile sites. That is to say, they either had film of their bombs going off on a recognizable site, or they had secondaries of bright orange smoke coming out of the site. They also threw a lot of Shrikes at radar signals, and they could well have knocked out a dozen or so Fire Can radars that directed the big guns.

They got their first site kill in March of 1967 on a mission up around Thai Nguyen, when Leo Thorsness was leading and Jerry was number three. They had briefed to split the elements about fifty miles from the target with Leo covering north of the target and Jerry covering to the south, but the weather didn't cooperate and they couldn't split as planned. They hung together as a flight of four while Leo probed for a break in the cloud cover. Suddenly they broke into the clear above some cloud-covered hills, and the first thing they saw was a Sam dead on course for Leo. Leo saw it first and rolled into a hard left turn headed for the hills with the missile zeroed in on his tailpipe. As Leo hugged the hilltops, still turning hard left, the missile swerved hard right and bashed into the hills.

Jerry broke in the direction the missile had come from just in time to see what must have been the separated missile booster splash into a small lake. He found himself looking at a side view of a camouflaged Sam site, and he was so low that he was looking under the camouflage nets stretched over the top of it. He just plugged her into burner, stayed on the deck so he wouldn't lose the site, and pressed in.

Jerry was carrying CBUs and had his site depressed for a high-angle drop. But all Thud pilots were used to making instantaneous sight corrections since we were hardly ever lucky enough to guess ahead and pick exactly what target we might get a crack at. Jerry just put the pipper on the middle of the sight and skip-bombed it when the sight picture looked good. That was a perfect example of the value of long hours on the gunnery ranges, as well as knowing your aircraft and your ordnance capabilities. As soon as Jerry felt the CBUs drop he yanked and jinked and looked back over his shoulder to see a perfect hit. The CBUs covered the entire site and two of the Sams on the launchers had already blown. His wingman put his six 750s right on top of Jerry's CBUs and that site was long gone.

Under the split-flight concept, the Weasels' optimum formation was a Y, with the strike force in the middle and one of their elements working on each side in front of that force. Prior to the actual engagement the Weasels could give each other mutual support with radio warnings, but once the real action started the radios were so overloaded that they became all but useless. If they had studied and briefed extensively beforehand it helped them to better understand the potential courses of action, but you cannot expect to have the answers stored up for all the contingencies of an environment like Downtown Hanoi.

The split-flight approach worked to perfection on one particular occasion. Tom and Jerry were leading and Charlie Hanson had the Weasel element as the strike force approached a target between Thai Nguyen and Hanoi. Charlie was going parallel to Thud Ridge and Jerry was displaced to the north of him. Jerry heard Charlie excitedly announcing that he was engaged and that Sams were about to launch at him. They hosed a missile off at Charlie and he took heavy damage in his tail section. While all this was going on, Tom and Jerry were getting lots of peculiar signals, but they weren't directed as a threat against them. All at once they figured out that they were looking at the back radar lobes of a site that was well to the west of the area where anyone expected any sites to be. That was the site that had fired on Charlie. Jerry was still up at about 12,000 feet and to the north of the site when he looked over the side and saw it as it launched at Charlie. There was nothing for Jerry to do but flip the switches to arm his bombs and roll in, since he was already in perfect attack position. He just lined up and clobbered the site. Jerry described it as "a complete no-brainer."

On the day Leo Thorsness got a Mig, he and Jerry had split their Weasel elements and were working different parts of the countryside. Jerry's element got jumped by four Migs and his wingman deserted him. That didn't surprise Jerry since he had flown with that individual before in Germany and could vouch for the poor reputation he had earned. There were a few like that around. That coward had no intention of getting into that fight and immediately decided that his afterburner wouldn't work, so he left. All fighter pilots know that if a guy craps out on you once, he'll do it again.

That left Jerry there with those four Migs all by himself. They weren't amateurs at all, and they were giving him fits. He would try to set up on one of them and *wham*, there was another one on his tail. He finally got a break when things split up for an instant, and he hit the deck and headed down the river as fast as he could go to get some space and regroup his forces, consisting of him. He had no choice but to come back into them. As he did he saw the most beautiful thing a fighter pilot can see: There was one of them looking like it was lost and confused with its wings flopping as it turned from side to side like a big aluminum butterfly. Jerry took the bait and charged his sitting duck. He told himself not to get buck fever because this one was obviously a piece of cake. He took his time, lined up, and was doing great. Just as he was gently tightening that top right finger around the red plastic trigger, *"Watch out!"* came from Tom in the back seat. Jerry turned his head and there was the Mig's leader coming in behind him.

The Mig leader on Jerry's tail must have called "Break" about that time because the pigeon out in front kicked that little Mig, and of course they had us cold on instantaneous acceleration and turning, and he was gone. Jerry was about out of fuel and ideas so he had to hit the deck again and head for a tanker. All the fuss had brought Leo onto the scene, and he surprised one of the Migs trying to surprise Jerry and bagged him.

Some of the most intense activities of the Weasels were associated with rescue missions, and Tom and Jerry got their fair share. They were still the first ones in and the last ones out, and since it was very rare that one of our wings didn't lose somebody up there, there was more than enough rescue action. On about 75 percent of their Pack Six missions the Weasels would wind up trying to locate a pilot who was down, trying to help set up the rescue, or dashing out for fuel and then trying to cover for a rescue if one got set up.

One of the rescue missions that caused a big question to hang in Jerry's mind for years came when he was flying as a strike pilot before he got into the Weasel business. He was flying number three during the attack against the Than Hoa bridge. As he rolled in, the number-two man ahead of him got hit just as the lead dropped his bombs. The number-two man started pulling away from the target, and after Jerry dropped his bombs he got the shot-up aircraft in sight and saw the pilot eject and get a good chute. Jerry kept him in sight until he touched down on a brown dirt area in the middle of the green rice paddies. Then Jerry got down as close as he could and started orbiting the area. Since he didn't pick up any ground fire he knew he could at least cover his flight mate for a while.

Jerry could see the chute lying on the ground; then abruptly the chute got pulled in and out of sight. There was no way to tell if the pilot on the ground had pulled it in or if someone else down there had. Jerry immediately wondered if he should start strafing around that little dirt spot to try and keep the ground troops away. The downed pilot never did come up on his emergency radio, so there was no way to tell what was going on down there. Jerry was in a hell of a quandary as to whether strafing would help. They never made any contact on the emergency radio and they never got a rescue set up.

Years later at the River Rat reunion, Jerry ran into that pilot after he had returned from the Hanoi Hilton and said, ''I hope you aren't going to punch me in the nose, but I was rescapping you when you got shot down and I didn't strafe and I never knew if I made a mistake.'' He replied, ''God, I was watching you and if you had strafed, they would have killed me on the spot.'' So that time Jerry had guessed right.

Most of us in the wing liked to go hunting and Jerry was no exception. By the same token, no sane strike pilot would have thought of going hunting at Yen Bai with a Vulcan cannon. But when a Weasel wound up with a chance to go hunting he sometimes found himself with an extra missile or two on board. So Jerry, with missiles plus some strong memories of earlier Yen Bai encounters, decided to go hunting at Yen Bai.

Everybody who flew up north remembers Yen Bai because of the lingering question of why they protected that empty place so well. Jerry remembers it because he seemed to have a penchant for screwing up whenever he went there. On his first Pack Six mission he was on a supervised lead mission and he didn't do all that well as he blundered into the outskirts of Yen Bai. He took the whole strike force right over the middle of town. While he was wondering where all that flak was coming from, he was losing respect from his buddies faster than those guys on the ground were firing. He thought he had killed the entire wing and even when he found out that he had not, he always wanted to hit back at some of those Fire Can radars that controlled the guns around Yen Bai.

One of the most effective Weasel maneuvers was to pick up as much speed as possible, pull the nose up real high, and hose off a Shrike missile or two in front of the strike force. The missiles usually homed on one of the many radar control sites, which were expecting the strike force rather than an inbound missile arching their way. It seemed like a good idea to Jerry to try the same tactic when he went to do a little hunting by himself.

Jerry decided he was going to demoralize Yen Bai with an Immelmann Shrike delivery. He figured he would zip in on the deck with everything to the wall, pull up into an Immelmann, and let the Shrike go as he rotated on top. The Shrike was supposed to go straight up, then come straight back down, while Jerry continued straight ahead and out of the area. He forgot that he had to cross the mountains near Yen Bai, which forced him to come in high, rather than approaching on the deck, where you would normally be if you were contemplating that type of weapons delivery. All the Fire Cans around Yen Bai came up and started looking at him, but Jerry figured no sweat because he would be going straight up and they would never catch on to him.

The idea wasn't a good one to start with, but the execution was even worse. He was heavy with fuel, having just recently come off a tanker, and since he was still about 12,000 feet above sea level when he crossed the mountains, he just didn't get enough airspeed before he got there. He started to forget those Fire Cans when the big, nasty 85s opened up. He was smooth as silk, but he came across the top with virtually no airspeed; hanging there, out of everything. Tom was watching from the rear seat with his camera poised, figuring he would get a spectacular snapshot, but zero g took over, and his camera was just floating around the rear cockpit. Just as Tom started cussing Jerry out for the idiot he was playing, a three-ring Fan Song opened up on them, but for some reason didn't hit them with a Sam. Jerry's guess was that the North Vietnamese must have figured he was too stupid to kill. Jerry also said he never heard such unkind things said between two people in the same aircraft.

Dr. Pepper was mostly a Downtown problem. But the lower route packages also had their missile defenses. Those solo Sam shooters out in the isolated areas had to rely more on their individual techniques, and they became extremely clever and difficult to battle. They were somewhat mobile and they would sneak from place to place, then launch against some unwary pilot when he wasn't expecting it. They gave out some nasty surprises.

Since the Weasels were a scarce commodity in their early days, Tom and Jerry were usually committed against Downtown Hanoi and didn't often do battle against those remote sites. But one of the best pieces of work that they did was a kill that they made near Vinh. Unfortunately, the one they got was not the infamous Vinh Fan Song, but it was right close by. The site that they got was run by one of the cleverest individual operators they had ever dueled with. They jousted for about twenty minutes, with the site's radar coming up and going down. They never did fire at Jerry, and this was the only one he ever got that didn't fire first. Despite the camouflage and natural cover, Jerry finally spotted what he knew had to be the site, went after it, and got the prettiest bright orange secondary he ever saw.

They told Jerry about the Vinh Fan Song when he was a brand-new Weasel, and he and Tom took it on one evening. After exchanging radar signals back and forth, Jerry decided to ignore it for the moment and lob a Shrike at what he thought was a Fire Can working along with the Vinh Fan Song. Jerry pulled straight up to let the Shrike go and just as he was running out of airspeed and standing on his tail, the Vinh Fan Song came up and fired a Sam at him. He felt like a real fool and figured he was done, but somehow he stumbled out of the way and the Sam missed him.

For Tom and Jerry, like all the Weasels, a site kill was a two-person kick. On one occasion Jerry went after a missile site only because Tom talked him into going after it. They were south of Thai Nguyen, and in the process of shooting a Shrike because a site had fired a Sam at them. They were at low altitude, about five hundred feet above the flat ground with nothing to hide behind, so Jerry had no choice but to wait for the Sam to get close and evade, according to script. That particular missile seemed to guide better than the others and Jerry was getting concerned. When he pulled up, the missile pulled up along with him. The Sam went off right under Jerry and was so close that the blast rolled the aircraft over on its back. It had been a single launch from an isolated site, and they had a good view of where the missile had come from. But its position was so far to the south of where the strike was headed that Jerry almost didn't go after him. From the back cockpit Tom said in a very disappointed voice, "Aren't you gonna get him?" With that Jerry guessed he had better, so he moved on toward the site, pulled up, and rolled in and bombed it. The strike film was very clear and showed that they got good secondary explosions when the bombs hit. The site was right in the middle of a village, which was of course not unusual. Putting a site in the middle of the huts and shrubs made the site hard to see and was also good for instant cries of civilian casualties when you clobbered the site.

Tom's call and Jerry's reaction illustrated the fact that the team and the personality match in the Weasel mission was something unique. As Jerry described it, "The intensity of the radio noise, the vital nature of the decisions that have to be made, right now, the requirement for accelerated brain traffic; they were often more than a guy could effectively handle. In addition to that I had to assimilate what Tom was telling me if I was to do what I went up there to do. Tom had one mission in life; he lived to be ultimately involved in the superspecialized thing that he was doing with his head locked in his electronic gear and his mind sorting out things that cascaded on him like an overpowering waterfall. He knew what he told me had to be right or else we, the other Weasels, and the strike force could go down the tube right now. He had to sort out what none of the rest of us could sort out and he had to assign the correct priorities to the realities that meant life or death over the North.

"We communicated with grunts and one-liners; there wasn't any room for more. The only way we could do it was by intensive briefing, relentless critique, and living together. I swear, he could be dead silent back there and still be communicating with me. You'll never know unless you've been there. We had matching personalities, we were both overly aggressive, both of us thought we were bulletproof and we probably had a total maturity of a nineteen-year-old between the two of us. We were both dedicated to being soldiers who knew this was our one war and we wanted to make the very best of it. As I reflect, if it had not been for the very excellent way we lived it, we both would have died trying."

9 | GRADUALISM

Most postwar analysts seem to agree that gradualism robbed air power of its effectiveness by violating the principles of concentration and surprise. If you were there, getting shot at over Hanoi, you didn't need to analyze too deeply to conclude that our misuse of airpower was more than a violation of principle, it was a disgraceful display of national mismanagement, a lack of national will, and a lack of professionalism. We were not allowed to do the job we could have done for our country, and because of that we lost the chance to alter the course and the duration of the war significantly. We took a lot of tough losses in all phases of the ground war and the air war that never should have been taken. When we were driving Thuds to Hanoi we knew our country was having big problems, but we were tied so closely to what we were doing that we had to leave the big-picture analysis for later. We were not a numerically large group, since any one wing would have been considered fat with a hundred pilots on board, even counting the noncombat pilots who had support jobs. Those of us with experience in the business had many responsibilities, not the least of which was to do the best we could to keep our people alive despite the way we were being wasted. That was a full-time job in itself.

Combat pilots are not usually big on statistics and for Thud pilots, especially during 1966 and 1967, that was understandable. Pilots who came on board at Takhli or Korat during that time knew that with the established Thud loss rate of that period, it was mathematically impossible for them to survive a one-hundred-mission tour; thus one of the phrases of the day, "There ain't no way." But those statistics were shrugged off and gave way to jokes, like the one about the Downtown Thud pilot who quit smoking because he was afraid he would get lung cancer. Sick? Maybe, but if you were fighting with one hand tied back by McNamara and Johnson, you damn well couldn't expect to get the job done and survive by doing anything other than ignoring the odds and going balls out.

Overall U.S. aircraft losses in mid-May of 1967 showed that we had lost 539 American aircraft north of the border and a total of 1,035 planes and helicopters in combat on both sides of the border, and that another 522 aircraft had gone down from noncombat causes such as mechanical failure. We lost another 150 aircraft between May and October. Statistics are not good material for combat pep talks; thus we ignored them.

We tried to pump our troops up with a medal or a decoration now and then, but even that often failed to work. All our awards had to be processed through committees of non-fighting folks at our various headquarters. They often seemed to feel that there was something wrong with giving a Hanoi jock a brightly colored tuft of cotton to pin on his chest when and if he got out of there. I thought that was what those things were designed for. It was difficult to understand the awards and decorations policy over there since it varied wildly from unit to unit and from time to time. It seemed to depend on whether or not we needed heros at the moment, and whether the work that was being done tickled the fancy of Washington or not. Some of us were lucky enough to be in the right place at the right time to be called heroes, while other deserving people lost out.

* * *

It was miraculous how some of those losses over the target turned out. Billy Ellis went in low one day. After he hit his target, he was working his way out when he saw a ball of fire from the second flight as one of their Thuds literally exploded. It turned out to be a really sharp, good-looking young lieutenant and, as usual, Billy felt lousy about it. He talked to the lieutenant's wife when he got back to the States and told her that we could always hope, but personally he would bet that her husband didn't make it. But he did make it and finally got out as a POW. So miracles do occur, but that miracle got blunted when the lieutenant and his wife couldn't get back together again and wound up divorced. Lots of sad stories came out of the war.

One of the saddest personal stories of the entire operation for me came with the abortive attempt to push those early F-111s into the act. Old Lucky Palmgren, my almost brother from the Thunderbirds, was the ops officer of that initial F-111 effort, and wound up carrying all the load of both command and ops for their detachment of six aircraft. Washington had decided that those F-111s were going to change the way the air war up North was conducted. They were supposed to move right into a low-level, nighttime, all-weather bombing role, but no matter how hard Lucky tried, the aircraft weren't ready and the black boxes didn't cooperate. The first night they launched one aircraft and lost it before it ever got across the Mekong River into enemy territory because of its own internal malfunctions. Must have been a message there. The next night, the same story, but still no acceptance of the message.

Lucky took the ride on the third night. He was supposed to fly at something like two hundred feet, using the terrain-following radar, the automatic flight control coupler, and the systems that were designed to integrate all aircraft functions into an automated low-level mission. The loss of the first two aircraft on successive night efforts, and the fact that they never even stayed airborne long enough to get to the enemy border, should have proved to someone that neither the aircraft nor the automated systems were capable of what was planned for them. But if those were the mission requirements and the flight plan, you can bet that was exactly what Lucky was doing. It always bothered me that those jungle trees used to go up to over two hundred feet, and with the equipment we had at that time, I don't ever remember getting a good clear radar paint from a tree.

Lucky at least set the course record. He got to the border near Nakhom Phenom on the Mekong River and was heading for enemy territory. The control site there told him to switch radio frequencies and check in on the new radio channel. He was cleared on his way to the first-ever F-111 combat mission. I wonder how many thousands of aircraft lost radio contact on that frequency change at that very same spot. Our ground-to-air communications were far behind the state of the art. When I told General Ryan about this problem, he personally told me I didn't know what I was talking about and that the communications were great. All flights going north and returning south had to work through that particular radio and radar matrix, which constantly malfunctioned. Regardless of what the general said, that simple channel change was unsafe and a constant frustration, but we were never able to generate any action to upgrade it through our complaints. Lucky never came up on the new channel. That was the last anyone ever heard of Lucky. Those who were left in the F-111 outfit immediately packed up and took the operation back to the States without ever having accomplished a single combat strike.

Years later, all concerned declared Lucky dead and we held a memorial for him at Luke, where he and I had flown together on the Thunderbirds eons ago. That 111 project had been some sort of a pet of General Ryan's, and he had pushed it pretty hard. Coincidentally, he was on the base at Luke the day we had the service for Lucky at the chapel across the street from the officer's club. There were a lot of old buddies and admirers at the service, but Ryan couldn't make it. Seems he had something important scheduled at the club.

There is no doubt that the losses hurt, as they do in any common endeavor, but those losses frustrated us bitterly because we always felt that we were taking them alone, with little concern on the part of not only our nation, but even our own air force. The job was made tougher because we all felt that the rules of engagement and those who enforced them were our enemies as much as or more so than those we physically fought.

It even showed up in little things. The last time I saw Swede Larson over there, he was standing on the ramp at Takhli, an F-105 combat squadron commander, trying to bum a ride back to Korat on a gooney bird so he could go fight over Hanoi in the morning. He was fuming in the hot afternoon sun. Our pilots were supposed to get a break now and then for rest and recuperation. They would want to get out of there in the worst way when they finally got off the schedule for a few days. But any of us who wanted to go someplace had to hang around someone's base operations and sit on the bottom of the totem pole to try and get a ride over to Bangkok or the Philippines or even back to our own base. Swede remembers going that route a couple of times when he had to sit in a terminal in Bangkok, or some other hot, sweaty place, trying to get a ride, last in line on priority. There was a pistol team that bumped him one time. Another time a special services entertainment group, no high-powered big-name stuff, just odds and ends, bumped Swede and a whole bunch of other fighter pilots. Our pilots used to gripe all the time about how hard it was to go anyplace and get back in those few days. The priority system was absurd as far as our pilots were concerned, and there was no excuse for it.

Things like that happened because we were split into different forces: those fighting the war in Southeast Asia and those not fighting that war. One of the forces not fighting the war was MAC, the Military Airlift Command, which expanded to monstrous proportions and finally had to rely heavily on contracts with civilian air carriers, who made tons and tons of money in Indochina off our government. You could see leased civilian superjets going where you wanted to go, devoid of anything but crews and stews. You couldn't get on one of those aircraft unless you were part of something like that pistol team, which was traveling on "funded" orders from someplace like General Wilson's headquarters. That meant that the members of the pistol team were getting paid extra money during their trip and were assured of a comfortable ride to go shoot paper targets that didn't shoot back. To make it worse, air force people scheduled the seats. A Downtown pilot, with a few days' free time, was not in the same air force as MAC and thus not welcome aboard.

Washington never did want to get around to the little things, like convincing everyone in the Department of Defense that we were all on the same team. However, they had plenty of time to get into things like minute control of targeting. If you got a go signal on a particular strike, that didn't always really mean go. If you had to abort a strike that had been approved for a specific day, you couldn't simply reschedule the strike. The entire laborious request and release process had to go all the way back up to Washington and then all the way back down the chain to the operating commanders.

But it went deeper, even to the absolutely ridiculous. When Takhli was no more than an outpost in the early days, one of our majors got a very personal phone call. He had fired up and was on the way to the end of the runway with a flight of four, armed with napalm and headed for a nondescript mission in the easy packs. The duty officer sped after him in a staff car and herded him back to the chocks, where he dutifully shut down and reported to the command center telephone. It was McNamara, none other than the SecDef himself. The major accepted his direct order to have the napalm downloaded and to change targets. Then he fired up again and dashed off to attack his secondary target, a bridge, with his cannon. I often wondered how many people above the rank of major Mr. Secretary bypassed over those ten thousand miles of phone lines.

There was no way for us to know it then, but a lot of people in Washington apparently never got over the McNamara and Johnson syndrome either. Back in 1964 I had listened to Walt Rostow speak to our National War College Class. I had an opportunity to talk with him after his presentation and I was very much impressed with his attitude. When I wound up way out on the other end of that sharp stick, I could never visualize him as buying the things we were looking at from the operator's viewpoint. Sure enough, in May 1967 Walt

Rostow echoed the view of those of us doing the job when he authored a position paper entitled "U.S. Strategy in Vietnam." He specifically gave our air effort good marks and noted that the accomplishments to date had been achieved while operating "in shackles." His comments were in vain, since at the same time McNamara's people were preparing a Draft of Presidential Memorandum that was contrary to Rostow's statements. Once again a voice within State was saying, "Go get 'em," to include closing Haiphong Harbor, but McNamara, the voice of Defense, was still saying no.

We wanted so much to be supported and to know that our national leadership was really worth fighting for that we were even somewhat heartened when we learned that frustration was showing within Congress. We were pleased that Senator Stennis and Senator Symington were the spokesmen for that frustration, since they had been around the military effort long enough to know that we were not being utilized commensurate with our potential. The interest in any news releases we could get our hands on went up when we learned that the Stennis Committee was going to look formally at the conduct of the air war.

Secretary McNamara must have felt that he needed more instant expertise before he got entangled in the Stennis hearings, because he quickly called a high-level conference in Saigon on July 5, 1967, to discuss the future of Rolling Thunder. Admiral Sharp, whose persistence in the face of constant rebuffs has to be admired, dutifully reported and tried again. He used battle damage reports of the preceding eighteen months to show that even restricted air strikes against Hanoi were crippling the North. He quoted sources from within Hanoi to illustrate the disillusionment of Soviet and east bloc officials. He again urged a campaign of concentrated air attacks to bring the effort to a successful conclusion.

Secretary McNamara returned to Washington and reported "unanimous agreement" with his views that air strikes were a waste of time. Admiral Sharp indignantly advised the JCS that the Secretary's statement was not true. It made no difference.

Swede Larson and hundreds of other fighter pilots spent

far more time in the Downtown Hanoi area than they should have. Most of them suffered for six and a half years, fighting for survival under appalling conditions. One of the things that stuck with Swede when he was sitting over there in Hanoi was that about five days before he got shot down he got called up to the DO's conference room at Korat. The wing CO, the DO, and all the other squadron commanders were there with General Ryan. No aides, just Ryan. They sat around and had kind of a BS session. Swede remembers that Ryan was elated and said, "They finally turned the targets loose for us and we have targeting now that we've been crying for. Now that we've finally got them, I feel very confident that we can end this thing in the next four to six months." Swede thought, "Boy, if anybody knows, it ought to be Ryan."

A few days later when Swede got shot down, he remembered thinking over and over, "I've got it made. Six months at the outside and I'll be out of here." As the months passed into years, he used to wonder where Ryan got his information.

Among the questions asked of Swede at the Hanoi Hilton was one put by the Polish press: "What do you think of your government's war in Vietnam?" Swede answered, "I'm not a politician, I'm a soldier. Ask that question at the state department." Another question was, "What will you do if released after the war and they let you go home?" Swede answered, "If the war goes on at its present rate, I'll be old enough to retire."

Maxine McCaffrey had planned on taking some shots of Swede when he got back from that ninety-fourth mission, but Swede was very late for the photo session. Swede says he kind of thought about her during those six years, wondering what had happened to her. He got released on March 4, 1973, and as the senior officer on the aircraft they flew out on, he had to get off first. As Swede walked down the ramp, who should be standing at the bottom waiting for him with her camera but Maxine McCaffrey. She was the first person Swede met as he got back to Clark, and she said, "I told you I'd meet you when you got back." Swede walked right past the admiral who was there to greet them, and Maxine and Swede cried all over each other.

They put all the guys returning to Clark right in the hospital, but Maxine always seemed to have high-powered passes, and she and Swede talked two or three times that first day back. When Swede got home he found that shortly after he had been shot down Maxine had painted a montage portrait with him as the central figure. It was the first picture she painted when she got back to the States and that's what really kicked Maxine off to being the most famous and respected painter of the Vietnam War. She did several paintings of the wives and kids and did everything she could to help the POW and MIA effort. In the fall of 1973, Swede got a call from Los Angeles from the people who put together the show "This Is Your Life." They asked him if he would come out to California and appear on a show they were going to do on Maxine. He went out there and Maxine's husband Dan got her to the show on some pretext. Swede stood behind a screen and said something to the effect that, "You promised you'd meet me when I got back. It took me six years, but you made your promise good." Swede treasures spending a lovely evening with Maxine and Dan. It was a really sad thing to all of us when we found out that Maxine had died.

On August 13, 1967, the *Los Angeles Herald Examiner* stated that the Stennis Senate Preparedness Committee was heating up in its far-reaching look at the government's bombing control policies, and also quoted congressional leader Gerald Ford as being in favor of lifting the tight governmental controls.

On the same day, in an attempt to take some of the heat off, President Johnson announced the release of "some additional targets" in the Hanoi area. True to bureaucratic form, it took until October 6 to get Washington's blessing for the Thuds to actually release the brakes, light the burners, and go Downtown to finally cut the center span of the mile-long Paul Doumer bridge across the Red River. The North had so much advance warning and so much time to prepare that we lost seven aircraft that day.

* * *

It seemed like Billy Ellis was destined to be a part of Southeast Asia for as long as we were there. When he went back to the States he got promoted to lieutenant colonel and went to school, and the next thing you knew it was 1968 and he was back in the flight again, this time at Korat. They were still flying the 105s but switched to F-4Es a bit later. Things were pretty much the same as they were before. They had poured lots more concrete and the living conditions were better, but by and large they were running on the same targets in the same way. It amazed Billy how little things had changed over the years. They still had problems like getting the bomb fins to match the particular bombs they happened to have available, or getting the right size and type of bombs to match the particular targets they were fragged for. But whatever they had was what they used.

The only thing that made it different from day to day was whether a "bombing pause" was in effect, how much Washington had them restricted at the moment, or whether they were going against real or junk targets. Regardless, the sorties were ground out day after day and the big difference, depending on how far up North they were allowed to go, was in the loss rate. Billy guessed that the continual action against insignificant targets was so the tonnage expenditure stayed right up there and all those people who were filling out those graphs and giving all those glowing reports could show an impressive bunch of numbers.

Having flown with both wings, Billy thought the rivalry that existed between Takhli and Korat was good. There were two basically different philosophies about how to hit a target. Takhli always wanted to go in low and fast and pop up on the target, while Korat wanted to go in high and rely on the electronic countermeasure pods to cover them. Of course, early on there weren't that many operational pods in commission, so the guys flying the high approach went through some rough rides. But Billy reflects that when there were enough pods, who knows? How do you measure effectiveness in an area like that? Who was up and shooting at you from one hour to the next and how well were they shooting? He says he could argue either side, and that you also have to consider the pilot skill level that either wing had on hand at the moment. It is also worth noting that there were some situations where our own leaders had the deck stacked against us to the point that neither tactic could be employed with any hope of success. There also were differences in how the results got reported at debriefings and how the intelligence people analyzed the strike photos. If you ever wanted to point at two areas that were subject to the whims and imagination of the moment, they would have to be reporting and intelligence. Anytime you have two teams playing the game, they'll play it differently, and that's not all bad.

The Stennis hearings boiled during August, and for Admiral Sharp there must have been a sense of both urgency and futility as he contemplated the approach of mandatory retirement at the end of the year. It certainly did not dim his enthusiasm for the cause. When the Stennis Committee report came out on August 31, 1967, it gave the administration all bad marks for its conduct of the bombing campaign. In essence the Stennis Committee deferred to the military testimony it had heard and advocated an escalating pressure.

The committee was very direct in its criticism of McNamara. During the hearings the secretary had emphasized the inability of the bombing program to accomplish much in terms of his view of the objectives. The committee commented, "That the air campaign has not achieved its objectives to a greater extent can not be attributed to inability or impotence of air power. It attests, rather, to the fragmentation of our air might by overly restrictive controls, limitations, and a doctrine of 'gradualism' placed on our aviation forces which prevented them from waging the air campaign in the manner and according to the timetable which was best calculated to achieve maximum results."

Military witnesses had told the committee that Haiphong could and should be closed, but McNamara had once again ignored that. The committee didn't buy his policy there either. "In our hearings we found a sharp difference of opinion between the civilian authority and the top level military witnesses, who appeared before the subcommittee, over how and when our air power should be employed against North Vietnam. In that difference we believe we also found the roots of the persistent deterioration of public confidence in our air power because the plain facts, as they unfolded in the testimony, demonstrated clearly that civilian authority consistently overruled the unanimous recommendations of the military commanders and the Joint Chiefs of Staff for a systematic, timely and hard-hitting integrated air campaign against the vital North Vietnam targets. Instead, for policy reasons, we have employed military aviation in a carefully controlled, restricted and graduated build-up of bombing pressure which discounted the professional judgment of our best military experts and substituted civilian judgment in the details of target selection and the timing of strikes. We shackled the true potential of air power and permitted the build-up of what have become the world's most formidable antiaircraft defenses.''

The report continues: ''It is not our intention to point a finger or second guess those who determined this policy, but the cold fact is that this policy has not done the job and it has been contrary to the best military judgment. What is needed now is a hard decision to do whatever is necessary, take the risks that have to be taken, and apply the force that is required to see the job through. As between these diametrically opposed views and in view of the unsatisfactory progress of the war, logic and prudence requires that the decision be with the unanimous weight or professional military judgment. It is high time, we believe, to allow the military voice to be heard in connection with the tactical details of military operations.''

Amazingly, none of that slowed McNamara down, and he fought against any and all proposals for escalation until the last day he was in office. Win or lose, he was determined to reject the military, whom he supposedly represented, regardless of the facts, and to use every bit of persuasion he could muster to get the president to reject any views at variance with his own.

The Pentagon Papers added a bit more perspective to the fire under McNamara's feet: "The Stennis report also raised a furor by exposing the policy rift within the Administration. In an attempt to dampen its effects, the President called an unscheduled news conference on September 1 to deny differences among his advisors and to generally overrule his Secretary of Defense on the bombing. More stinging for McNamara, however, than this oral repudiation must have been the subsequent escalatory decisions against his advice. On September 10, for instance, North Vietnam's third port at Cam Pha, a target he had specifically counseled against in his testimony, was struck for the first time. McNamara's year-end resignation seems in retrospect the only logical course for someone who found himself so far out of line with the direction of Administration policy."

On Monday, December 18, 1967, the *Los Angeles Herald Examiner* reported that U.S. fighters had struck the Mig bases at Kep and Phuc Yen and further reported, "Military spokesman said that the Phuc Yen air base had been repaired while under heavy cloud cover and was again operational prior to the raids. It had been spared from American bombs until the previous October 24 due to official fears of hitting Soviet and Chinese technicians who were helping to operate its radar systems. The system spots and tracks American war planes, enabling the Mig fighters to scramble and intercept the raiders. Officials said the radar network is the most vital air defense link in the industrial region of the Red River Valley." It was only a token attack, and even the most determined of us knew we were running at half-throttle, giving them plenty of time to fix whatever we hit, despite the efforts of the Stennis Committee and other strong voices who had tried and not made the grade. Even though McNamara was on his way out, he was leaving a shambles behind him and Lyndon Johnson was still the commander-in-chief.

By the time 1967 drew to a close, the Thuds and their fellow fighter pilots had put on a heroic and dedicated show against the North. The statistics were impressive, especially considering that we had generated them the hard way, but our leadership and their restrictions had ensured that the full job would not be done. As the normal cry for a Christmas truce was dusted off again, nobody who knew anything about the situation thought that the North would do anything different than what it had done during past respites, like restock, repair, improve, and get ready to go again. Sure enough, when the white flag of indecision was hoisted again, the trails and waterways from China and Hanoi to the south were clogged with men and machinery hustling to position themselves to wipe out more of our ground troops. The North Vietnamese had absolutely no idea of approaching a conference table, and they must have realized that not only did they have the Americans buffaloed, but they had a great chance of pulling off an ultimate victory in the South. This was essentially the windup of any effective action under the banner of Rolling Thunder. The fighter pilots had given it their best shot but their bosses wouldn't let them win.

John Colvin, observing as consul general at the British mission in Hanoi, verified our fighter strike effectiveness: "The strength of the American bombing campaign of summer 1967 had rested not only on its weight but on its consistency, hour after hour, day after day. The strategy, as well as damaging or destroying—in ports, on railway lines, and on storage areas—the capacity of the DRV [Democratic Republic of Vietnam] to feed itself and to maintain invasion, had also, for the first time, allowed the North Vietnamese no time to repair war-making facilities. No sooner were they repaired than they were struck again; Tonkinese ingenuity had been defeated and, by the remorseless persistence of the campaign, their will eroded to near extinction.

"But although some spasmodic bombing in the northeast quadrant took place after September, it was on a greatly reduced scale and frequently interrupted by long periods of inactivity during 'peace initiatives,' all illusory if not contrived. . . . Above all, that factor—the persistence of the campaign, which had sapped North Vietnamese endurance—was discarded. And at the end of March 1968, all bombing of North Vietnam north of the 10th parallel was discontinued. Victory—by September 1967 in American hands—was not so

much thrown away as shunned with prim, averted eyes. . . .
Nor could a war be won by men familiar with computers and
academic theory but not with the battlefield or the ageless
facts of Southeast Asia.''

It is obvious that President Johnson was confused and behind the power curve throughout his tour as commander-in-
chief. It is equally obvious that Secretary McNamara and
those whom he gathered about him were dangerously coun-
terproductive to the national resolve. Had the president employed the forces immediately available to him with firmness
and determination on any one of several occasions, it is highly
probable that the entire course of Southeast Asian involvement would have been altered significantly. A fighter pilot
gets behind the power curve when he allows his aircraft to
assume an attitude or position that he cannot match with adequate engine power. In a fighter you can stay behind the
power curve for only a very short time before you lose control
and the aircraft augers in. The tragic crash of U.S. efforts in
the final surrender of Saigon many years later was the same
situation.

As skilled fighter pilots we knew that the national resolve
was inadequate, and that there was a weakness within our
civilian and military channels of leadership. As a group we
longed for a charismatic air professional at the top of our
ranks who shared our desire to fight to win, but we didn't
find him. As an individual I was disappointed with the general officers who commanded, and my expectations were not
unreasonably high in light of either our national history or
our air force tradition. We served our country with pride and
we hoped against hope that we could somehow use our bodies
and our machines to make our country victorious. The fighter
pilot ranks are still full of people like that. Cultivate them
well, America; you just might need them.

10 | TURKESTAN

As for me, I fought that war as hard as I knew how, and I found that the harder I fought the war, the harder I fought the system. I never was a system man, and in retrospect, if I had been, I would have snuggled down in Washington after National War College and gone star hunting in the General Officer's Group or in Legislative Liaison. I wore my wings to fly, fight, and lead my troops. Anything less was for someone else. My discontent had been simmering for a while, and I finally took three days off over Christmas in 1966 and checked in with my wife AJ and the four kids in the neat little place I had rented for them so they could live in Hawaii while I was down south. I bummed a ride back to Hawaii in the rear of one of our tankers that was heading back to the States, so I didn't have to mess with the military airlift people. We refueled one of our Thud strikes on the way out and I got to play the boomer game from the other end. Then I slept like a baby on a canvas bench while we droned across the Pacific.

I had the family in a small but gorgeous place on the windward side of Oahu that overlooked the lagoon and the Rabbit Islands. The house had a deck that stuck out facing the islands, surrounded by sweet-smelling flowers and bushes. It was different from what I was used to. You can't turn Hanoi and Washington off in a day, but I damn sure wanted to try. I was sitting on the deck, in my shorts and sport shirt, mixing martinis, when a big, bright, silver moon rose out of the far side of the ocean. It climbed splendidly over those two little islands and paused to shine right onto my deck. It cooled me instantly; I just drank it all in and said, "What the hell am I doing in this mess?"

I decided that I was fed up with stupid men trying to direct people and control fighting that they didn't understand. I told AJ then and there that I was going back to Southeast Asia to fight even harder for my country and my fighter pilots. I would continue to contribute my full energy to the air force as long as I could do some good for the operational people and as long as there was some sense of accomplishment, but I would stay no longer. I knew at the same time that I was aching for a fight.

I went back to Takhli the day after Christmas and flew and fought to the maximum for the next six months. Then I got the fight I was looking for. Two of my guys were under attack by the guns surrounding a Russian ship that was unloading in the port of Cam Pha, inside McNamara's sanctuary. My pilots shot back to save their hides and they got out of there alive. The Russians complained loudly that their ship had been hit, and Washington transferred the complaints and pressure to General Ryan. General Ryan hastened to respond, and since he found nothing to substantiate the claim, Washington was ready to forget it; in fact they had forgotten it. In his book *Confirm or Deny,* Phil Goulding, from the viewpoint of the office of assistant secretary of defense for public affairs, wrote, "But we did put it out of our minds, and the press, swept up in other news events and particularly the Middle East war, did not pursue it." That is exactly how I had hoped it would go, but that was just the start of what came to be known as "the *Turkestan* incident."

June 2, 1967, was simply another day in the war in Southeast Asia. I would have to go to a calender to tell you what day of the week it was, because days of the week made no difference over there, except that *Stars and Stripes* printed its headlines in red on Sunday. The roar of the afterburners on the first predawn takeoff jarred me awake at 4:00 A.M., but I was not flying the early mission that day. My feet hit the floor, and as I switched the light on I noted that the date window in my watch said the second and the thought flashed through my mind that it was exactly twenty-two years ago that I got my wings. At that instant my title was vice-wing commander and I was second in command to the senior flying colonel on the base, Bob Scott, the wing commander. Scott was in Okinawa for several days, this time not on one of his public relations boondoggles, but taking care of his divorce. The huge load of administrative baloney, really too much for one person, forced me to spend the morning playing paper shuffler, but I managed to get airborne on the second set of missions for the day. We had several different targets, with most of the flights working north and east of Haiphong and Cam Pha, while I drew an ammo storage area about twenty miles south of them.

The guns around the port of Cam Pha always shot at us, both inbound to our targets and outbound, but most of those guns, and the harbor and the ships they protected, were in forbidden territory. Some of the guns were just barely outside the restricted lines and were thus open to attack, though it was tough to know exactly where those imaginary lines were on the ground. Major Ted Tolman was leading a flight of two that had shrunk from four because of aircraft problems en route, and the gunners fired at Ted and his wingman, Major Lonnie Ferguson, on the way in. Ted was able to pinpoint their location exactly, and he decided that if things went okay he would hit them a lick on the way back out from the target.

They hit their target, regained some altitude, and then Ted spotted the gun pits that had bothered them on the way in. He swung his nose up and over the top and into a steep, high-speed strafing run with Lonnie following him. As Ted approached firing range and prepared to pull the trigger, he found himself in the midst of heavy and accurate fire from the ground. It is impossible to appreciate the intensity of this drama unless you realize that the entire *Turkestan* incident transpired within five seconds! The closer he got, the more apparent it became that there was a surface vessel in the center of the gun activity. By then every gun in the ring surrounding the vessel was barking at once, and Ted disappeared in a black cloud of fragmenting projectiles. From his perch above and behind, Lonnie realized they were in bad shape, punched his radio mike button, and yelled, ''Let's get the hell out of here.'' Lonnie was just along for the ride for the rest of the *Turkestan* incident.

As you can know only after experiencing it yourself and watching others fall from the sky, Ted knew that one or both of them was very close to going down. He could have hung in there for another second and become one of those little mundane statistics on page four of the local paper: ''The U.S. command reported the loss of an F-105 today. The pilot is listed as missing.'' He chose not to become a statistic and did the only thing he could do to live. He lit his afterburner for extra power, pulled and rolled his aircraft as hard as he could to change position rapidly, and fired his cannon to unleash a stream of lead at the gun complex that was trying to kill him. I suspect that the Soviet ship *Turkestan* was in the center of his gunsight. Somehow Ted and Lonnie both made it back to the coast, climbed for altitude, and headed south toward the billowing thunderstorms in front of them.

I was also on my way back from my target, heading into those thunderstorms that hid our base from us. I cursed our inadequate ground radar control system. It was undermanned and the equipment was not state of the art. We sent pilots to talk to them and they sent controllers to talk to us, but the system was horrible. We were unable to get any improvement, or even interest in the problem, by our repeated complaints. If the guys flying the missions and the guys trying to exercise radar control of the launches, refuelings, and recoveries agree that the system stinks, there must be some truth to the complaints. When the nonflying experts, thousands of miles away, shrug off the complaints of the operators, you have a sick system.

That system was at its stone age worst the afternoon of June 2, and the controllers could not find my flight on their scopes. I dodged storms and did identifying turns until I was critical on fuel, and they finally said that they had us identified. They gave me a heading to fly toward the recovery pattern at the base and instructed me to start letting down through the thunder bumps. The blip they were looking at on their scopes was not me and thus they gave me an improper course to fly, but I had no way of knowing that they had made an incorrect identification. In a case like that you turn your fate over to ground controllers you don't even know, your flight does what they tell you to do and goes where they tell you to go. I took their heading and we proceeded to ricochet through one of the biggest, blackest thunder monsters I have ever been forced to enter. As I was following false instructions, that monstrous combination of rain, lightning, and wind spit me out of its southern side into a clear area about three miles wide. I almost died right there. As I made the transition from black to visible gray, at about 350 miles per hour, heading south with my nose down, a twin-engined B-66 reconnaissance aircraft, departing from Takhli, the same airstrip I was trying to find, under the direction of the same control agency, was heading north with his nose up. We missed colliding by a few feet.

I finally got my flight out underneath the main storm with minimal assistance from the ground controllers. By then they had me properly identified, but they wanted to set me up on an approach for landing that would take me right into the middle of a second huge storm in the area. They had jazzed me around so long and taken me so far south with their bad steer, not to mention the near midair collision, that fuel was becoming a real problem and I couldn't accept their long, stormy approach route even if I had wanted to. I outsmarted them. I figured I was pretty close to the base and switched to the Takhli control tower frequency. I told them I needed a direct steer to the base, and then held down my mike button so they could pick me up on their direction-finding set. A huge storm system was moving along a course that took it right over the center of our airstrip at Takhli. The airmen in our control tower started giving me steers, but after a couple of minutes they said that the wind was switching directions and they had to alter my course to bring me in from the opposite direction. The storm center was passing overhead, but since I was wrapped inside its low-hanging clouds I could not know that. I took the new steer, sweating my fuel situation like crazy now, only to have them come back with a third steer as the stiff winds at the storm's center again favored the original landing direction. The eye of the storm had passed. We only had a few minutes of fuel left and I don't think we could have kept the mills turning through another altered approach. Suddenly a small segment of cloud underneath me turned thin, and there was the southern third of the runway in view below me. There was an absolute wall of water about halfway across the runway with a black, billowing storm cloud on top of it, but the near end of the strip was open. I wheeled the flight to the left, dumped the nose, held down the mike button and in rapid sequence said, "Speed boards, ready, now—gear down, ready, now—okay, back off and get some spacing, end of the runway dead ahead."

The tower, which was still behind that wall of water, panicked with, "Lead, it's zero-zero down here with severe rain and wind—we don't have you in sight."

"I don't have you in sight either, tower," I responded, "but I've got the end of the runway—so turn the runway lights on full bright." We touched down in sequence on the end of the runway and a couple of seconds into landing roll-out I penetrated that black wall of water, zero-zero all right, at a hundred-plus knots with only the runway lights whizzing by to help steer me to the opposite end. Another day, another dollar, in good old Southeast Asia.

I promptly drove to the radar controller's shack across the runway and played full colonel with gusto for thirty minutes. When I left, it was with a feeling that things would be no better the next day.

As Ted led Lonnie through the same storms, his actions were by rote and his mind was whirling. If he had violated somebody's rules, so be it—he and Lonnie were alive and they were bringing their aircraft back. But he was already aware that someone would complain about that ship. He might have been able to claim inadvertent strafing, but he knew that such a claim would be doubtful, since gun camera film would show that ship in the center of a gunsight. Ted was confused and panicky. The weather was bad all over Thailand, and gigantic thunderstorms bouncing between Takhli and Uben caused delays in recovering all our fighters. The weather forced our traffic controllers to divert some of our flights, including Ted and Lonnie, to land at Ubon for fuel. That's where Ted, as it turned out, screwed the works up for sure.

Ted and Lonnie had threaded their way through awesome weather to land at a strange base, after a strange mission that had almost cost them their lives, in this strangest of all wars. They were sweat soaked, tired, a little confused, and a little lonely. It may seem strange, but in a venture where you bet your life each day, you lean heavily on the few constants you can find. You identify with your base, your squadron and its pilots, and your commander. None of those anchors were there when they climbed out of their aircraft at Ubon.

Ted was the boss of this duo, and he would speak for them at the mandatory intelligence debriefing they faced while their aircraft were refueled for the trip back to their home base. Ted had been responsible for their efforts in the air and his was the voice that would now relate those experiences to a nonflying debriefing officer. The debriefers were simply administrative collectors of information who would turn the pilot's accounts into black and white history. Ted's encounter with that strange ship was about to become official written history and once it did, there would be no changing it—ever. The big man in Honolulu could read about it within the hour.

But Ted was not particularly well equipped to make the decisions that now faced him. Ted was a fighter. He was fearless in aerial combat, and his score against the enemy's Mig interceptors and his constant bombing accuracy attested to the fact that he was trying very hard to win the war he was fighting. He had spent most of his career with operating fighter units and that was what he knew best. He did not understand the intense oversupervision of the war, and he did not understand why his part of the war was constantly being interfered with. He did understand that several of his comrades had been severely disciplined for honest errors made under the worst of conditions. He did know that four of his fellow pilots had been disciplined when they dropped their bombs in the jungle across an imaginary line while they were fighting for survival in a fierce thunderstorm and while the ground controllers who were supposed to advise and assist them would not talk to them on the radio. Those four had received, as part of their punishment, what to Ted would have been the worst sting of all. They had been restricted from leading flights and had been relegated to following. Ted knew that certain kinds of ships were taboo, and he knew that he had fired his cannon at an unknown ship. He had made a quick decision and he was afraid of the consequences.

At the intelligence debriefing the exact details of when, where, and how were chewed over in great detail. One of the mandatory questions was, "What armament did you expend and where?" The next question was, "Did you fire your cannon?" That was Ted's moment of truth. Ted answered no. In answer to the next question he denied seeing anything unusual during the mission.

It would be fair to describe Ted as different, or as a loner, but those terms are too much of a generalization. The only thing that Ted lived for, in fact, was obsessed with, was to fly and lead fighters in combat for his country. At that moment, this life goal was in jeopardy. If Ted went down the tubes, Lonnie was probably going along, if only by a combination of association and acquiescence to the false statement.

Forty-five minutes later they were rolling down the runway for the short flight back to Takhli. By the time they had lifted off the ground and retracted their wheels into the bellies of their Thuds, the intelligence report was formalized and on its way to the world. A false official statement was on the wires and as they probed the black moonless Thai night, they brought that statement and the ship incident to lay at my feet.

When I got back from my talk with the controllers I headed for my office to work over the bale of paper that I knew would have arrived during the afternoon. By about half past eight I found the combination of drivel, cigarettes, and coffee to be depressing. I quit for the night, admonished my helpers to get the hell out of the office, and headed for my trailer. I considered cleaning up and changing clothes, but measured the thought against the hour and gave it up as a bad idea. I stomped across the small courtyard to the officer's club, where we all had to eat, three times a day, every day, intent on forcing myself to eat a good meal. As I walked in the door I received a phone call.

The call was from Ted, who had just landed. He said that he had a problem that he needed to talk to me about at once, so I told him to come ahead and that I would wait for him. As I hung up the phone I thought the request rather strange, especially with the sense of urgency I read in Ted's voice. I had done a lot of fighting up in Pack Six with Ted and Lonnie, and on one occasion Ted had saved me from being killed or captured. On one really rough mission he hung it way out for me as he came across the hottest set of big ground guns northeast of Hanoi—where Art Mearns got knocked down—and wiped out a large gun emplacement that was in the process of shooting me out of the sky. Still, it was unusual for a flight leader in one of the squadrons to come directly to the wing commander with a problem. His normal contact would have been with his squadron commander, since the two of them had been through the mill up North together. But Ted's old squadron commander had finished up his tour and taken off for the States that very morning. Ted did not know if his new squadron commander could or would understand his desperation. His next step might have been our deputy for operations, who was sort of a super-squadron-commander, but here again there had been a change and the new man had not been up North yet. It would have been tough for Ted to hang everything on someone who had not been there. There was only one person with any degree of local authority with whom Ted and Lonnie had faced the enemy. Who better to approach than one who flew the rough ones with them and understood their war up North? Ted knew his own neck was on the line.

Didn't he have a right to seek help from a boss whose neck he had saved?

They were still in their flying suits, just like me, and we went outside the club where Ted indicated that he thought that perhaps he had been involved in an incident with a ship. The rules of engagement covered a multitude of restrictions, including ships, and were difficult and complex. They were confusing even when you were sitting on the ground reading them. All pilots had to review them once a month and certify that they understood them, and I guess we all understood them as far as reading a piece of paper was concerned, but the cumbersome directives did not transpose well to a fast-moving combat situation. Ted went through a detailed description of the mission to the point of his attack on the flak site when he figured he was about to be knocked down. He said that he then reacted with his basic sense of survival and pulled the trigger, fired a good-sized burst in an attempt to get the gunners' heads down, and lit his afterburner and moved out of there as fast as he could. As he moved out he saw the wake of his bullets in the water and did not deny the possibility that he might have struck the ship. He thought that either the ship was firing at them or it was in the middle of the guns that were firing at them.

When he told me that, I questioned him in more detail. I said, "What kind of a ship was it?"

Ted said, "Well, I don't really know. We were going so fast—but it was a relatively large ship." That conceivably could make it a North Vietnamese ship, but they had so few ships fitting that description that it was far more likely to have been a commercial ship of another nation.

"Was it marked?" I asked him.

"No," he said. "It was unmarked. It had no flags or standards or anything that I could see." He could give me absolutely no information as to what kind of a ship it was other than to say that it was sort of a dirty color. All he knew was that he had been covered with gunfire and had fired a burst and gotten out of there as fast as he could.

Then I asked him what he had said at the intelligence debriefing at Ubon. He said he had not reported the strafing and while I already knew the answer I asked why not. He said, ''Hey, boss, you know they'd throw the book at me and even at Lonnie for just being there. Somebody up the line would call for an investigation and we'd wind up grounded and probably court-martialed.'' This had happened to others in the past and he had a valid fear. We all feared our own system and those who controlled us.

The picture was quite clear. Ted and Lonnie had been caught in an untenable situation. They had responded force-fully in combat. They were petrified that they would be cas-tigated for breaking a rule in order to save their lives. They knew that if they had reported the incident the very least they could have expected was a formal investigation by one or all of the headquarters, with resultant disciplinary action. They could hardly expect to fare better than their comrades who had been personally and professionally embarrassed and restricted for bombing the wrong portion of the jungle in a thunderstorm. But their situation was now even worse. The intelligence debriefing message was a fact of life docu-menting a false official statement. Regardless of what else transpired, Ted's statement made him liable to trial by court-martial and subject to dishonorable discharge. In the environ-ment of the day, one strip of gun camera film could make that a real and frightening possibility.

Their problem was now my problem. Basically I had to acknowledge an unauthorized action coupled with a damag-ing false official statement. Then I either had to expose this combination of facts or somehow try to make them go away. I made a decision and I stuck to it, but it was not an easy decision nor was it made lightly. Over the years I have had hundreds of suggestions as to how I could have reacted dif-ferently, but none of the advice givers was there.

How did loyalty apply that night? From the beginning I always thought that loyalty was a two-way street, and I used to think that all of the air force felt that way. I know for a fact that parts of the air force used to think that way. I had visualized it as one big effort, run by smart people who cared about individuals and who only wanted to utilize the talent at their disposal to better serve our nation. I jumped in with both feet from the time I was a brand-new lieutenant, and I never worried about stubbing my toe, because the good guys for whom I was giving my all knew that loyalty had to go both ways and would give their all for me.

I had learned many of my loyalty lessons early in my flying career from Colonel and later General C. T. Edwinson, the greatest leader of them all and my first group commander during my P-47 days. He was "Curly" to those of his rank, but "Big Ed" to those of us who flew for him. While we idolized him there were plenty of others who hated his guts.

He was fiercely dedicated to his flying and to those who flew with him. That was it—absolutely everything else was secondary. He expected that same dedication from all those he commanded, and he either got it or the individual not demonstrating that dedication was gone. Talk about an all-volunteer force; we were it in spades. We were the elite of the flying business. We loved it, and loyalty both ways was an integral, unquestioned part of the wild life we lived.

The first time I was ever involved with him, he was flying with our squadron as he led the group. As a new second lieutenant I only knew him as a legend, and I was awestruck when the schedule showed me flying on his left wing with the call sign of Rupert Red Two. I was petrified as we taxied out and I glanced across his wing at the profile of his hawk-like features, but I lucked out and flew a good wing for him—he was so smooth it was easy. After we landed he told me that he was pleased with my performance and that if I liked, I could have that spot and do some of his light work for him. For the next two glorious years I reveled in being Rupert Red Two, and I fully subscribed to his edict that if he augered in and bored a hole in the ground, there had better be three other holes in perfect formation. In return, I knew that he would never let me down.

A couple of thoughts about Big Ed went through my mind that night. One was of his World War II story about how he was on a road recce in Italy in his P-38, late in the war, when he saw a big, black sedan coming down the road. He said that he pulled the trigger and just before that sedan blew up he noticed a big red star on the side. Russian military personnel had apparently been invited to tour the battlefield. Whenever he told the story he was usually cackling with glee. He said he felt so badly that he thought he had better find another target and do something good. About then a second sedan, bigger and blacker than the first, came into view and he figured surely it must be full of bad guys. Just before it blew he noticed that it also had a red star on the side. His boss sent him back to the States for a month's vacation to allow him to escape the heat the Russians created.

The other thought was of my standing beside the ripped-up left wing of my P-47, about a year and a half after I started flying for Big Ed, as a stuffy major, who later became a stuffy general, laid a blistering chewing on me. I had been flying right on the deck with John Karr on my wing as we sneaked up on the city of Augsburg in a mock attack. The German countryside was laced with large high-tension electrical lines that drooped toward the ground as they stretched between their supporting towers. I had been careless and had not seen a particularly low-slung section of line until I was too close to get either over or under it. John saw them snap apart after they sawed my left wing almost in two and he pulled up just before they swung back together with a blinding flash that shut down all the lights and electric streetcars in Augsburg for that evening's rush hour.

The major was just going through the part about how the European commander, who happened to be Curtis LeMay, had issued an edict that accidents were career terminating, when Big Ed cruised up on his motorcycle. He fixed me with those one-of-a-kind steely eyes he had, and almost chuckling because he already knew the answer, said, "Well, Moto, how'd you manage to screw that up?"

There was no sense in giving Big Ed dumb excuses; besides he knew I was dying a thousand deaths to have to admit that I had goofed on something connected with my flying. All I could say was, "I was practicing low level—trying to get right over the center of Augsburg before anybody knew I was there—and . . ."

He cut me off, almost gently with, "Yeah, yeah, yeah—I

keep telling you those damn high lines can slice you to ribbons.'' Then he turned to the major and asked him if he had a spare wing available. That was not what the major had in mind, but he managed a red-faced affirmative on the spare wing. Big Ed told him, "Get it on there tonight. I want that Jug flying in the morning." Then as he kicked the starter on his motorcycle he added, "And, Major, get that clapped-out old wing out of here and put it someplace where nobody will ever see it again."

That's how I was brought up in the air force in general and the fighter business in particular. We had lived in a system that demanded your all, but protected its own. Had Big Ed been running the show in Southeast Asia, I have no doubt how the events of that day would have ended. But by the time we were in Southeast Asia, all that Big Ed represented did not seem to mean as much as acting for personal gain. My codes were different from many I worked for. Did my feelings about two-way loyalty make me a dinosaur within the present American military? I hoped not, at least not within the fighter fraternity I grew up in. But I had to remember that I was not operating within the fighter fraternity I grew up in.

Those early dreams had faded grudgingly with the years. When I was a junior officer a colonel told me that I would never know what relative rank meant until I became a colonel. I didn't believe him then. I thought that surely when you got to be a big deal, hotdog colonel you didn't worry about rank. You just went around doing all sorts of good things and all the generals were your buddies. Not so. For some the quest for stars becomes an all-consuming obsession, and two-way loyalty often becomes an early casualty. By the time Ted, Lonnie, and I stood together that evening I had strong indications that there was no two-way loyalty above wing level in the air force of that day, especially in Southeast Asia, but I just did not want to accept or believe it.

What could I see for myself as I reviewed my career that night? Things looked pretty rosy, I thought. I was disillusioned with our leadership and the way the war was being run, but I was due to leave in a few weeks and I had made it through the roughest missions of any air war. I was the hottest fighter bomber leader in the business, and I had the medals to prove it. I had been to all the right places and I knew all the right people. All I had to do was keep my nose nice and clean. Looking the other way, however, I saw two sweaty, frightened fighter pilots, men with whom I had fought the war up North. What did I owe them?

What of my country? I had raised my right hand on the plains of West Point when I was a boy of seventeen, and there in the steam of Takhli, Thailand, twenty-five years later, I still had my hand raised. Two things I had learned at the Point clashed head-on: Don't ever get tangled up in the details of the regulations, and always take care of your people.

I had proven my love of country in battle and by the dedication of my physical being to the effort I was now so deeply involved in. I felt the presence of my country's flag very strongly that black night. I had seen respect for it shrink throughout the world as one nation after the other thumbed their noses at us whether we aided them or not. I had seen the ships of nations we succored, our "friends," lolling at anchor beside those of the Soviets in the sanctuary of the North's harbors. I hated the fact that my pilots and I felt like the sole standard-bearers heading North and knowing that our nation, and even our own air service, cared little. I bitterly resented my flag's defamation, and that very night, if I was a good little boy and played by the absurd rules, I could give somebody, very possibly the Soviets, another tidbit to cackle about. Somebody in Washington could deeply regret that the Lend-Lease ship we gave them got shot up while delivering munitions to the guns shooting at us. Or I could insure forever that the gun camera film provided no evidence. My commanders could truthfully tell their commanders that they could find no indication of a ship being attacked.

I never even considered that damn ship. I didn't even know for sure to whom it belonged, but we had been sent to war and that ship had been sent to war. Our job was to attack Hanoi and its job was to supply Hanoi. There was no doubt in the minds of the gunners surrounding that ship that the situation was real war. Those gunners were at war, the ship was at war, and—phony rules be damned—the 105s were at war. There was only one physical piece of evidence that could hang Ted, and that was the gun camera film from his aircraft. Because the gun camera has a very narrow field of vision, it only looks along the line of the gun and would not show all the metal being hurled skyward at Ted and Lonnie. The evidence on that film, if in fact the film had run properly and Ted had hit the ship, could only be one-sided.

When you returned from a mission, a group of airmen from the photo lab were among those who met your aircraft. Their job was to remove the film magazines from the various cameras mounted on the aircraft and return the magazines to the photo lab. The photo lab at Takhli did not have the capability to develop our particular type of gun camera film, and the normal procedure was to load it onto a courier aircraft to be flown to a nearby base to be developed, and then immediately sent to Seventh headquarters. We had no control over that film; in fact, we did not even get to look at it. The primary purpose of gun camera film is to provide pilots with a means of assessing their techniques and effectiveness, and to make changes in the way they shoot at their targets, should the film show that to be necessary. In Southeast Asia this sound principle was discarded. Gun camera film was for the various headquarters to monitor what fighter pilots fired at, to be sure that there were no violations of the off-limits rules. To hell with the pilots and assessment of their techniques; who cares about that? Once that film was placed on board that courier aircraft, it would be forever lost to us. At that instant Ted's film was sitting on the floor of our photo lab awaiting pickup.

This was the time of decision. I could have let that film go through its normal channels and thrown Ted and Lonnie to the wolves. I would have been clean, but I would have surrendered any possibility of further action on my part. I would have been passing the buck up the line, and with evidence in hand those up the line would have been forced to act, and to punish. The false official statement would also have immediately surfaced and that would have been it for Ted and Lonnie.

I could have pleaded their case up through the maze of

supervision. "Perhaps we struck a ship—it was all a mistake." I knew that would not work. I had been through several investigations where our people had been dealt with severely for minor infractions of Washington's restrictions. Even then we had pilots in the wing under such punishment, and across the way two F-4C Phantom crews were fighting for their military careers for a similar combat mistake. Pleading was a waste of time. We just did not care that much about our own.

But I cared. I thought: I could stop that film and forever rule out any positive evidence that any of our people had done anything to an unknown vessel. If it turns out to have been a North Vietnamese vessel, chances are that there will be no noise and the false official statement will disappear along with the rest of this mess. If it turns out to be the vessel of another power, there will surely be noise but there will be no evidence. If my leaders choose to fight the war along with us, they will ignore the complaints of those supplying the enemy. I had to remember, if I followed that course, that I was in as deep as or deeper than those I commanded. It was the only course that was remotely acceptable to me.

I directed the sergeant running the film crew to bring the film to me and I took care of it. I had the sergeant open the containers and pull the film out. Then I directed him to expose it in the headlights of his truck. I helped him a little bit and Ted helped him a little bit. Lonnie was completely in the background, along for the ride as he had been all day. I told the sergeant to take the exposed film and burn it, as he would any other exposed film. Then he was to get on his way and forget the entire thing. As far as I was concerned, nobody could ever establish firmly that we had done any damage to a ship that was delivering weapons to be used against us.

General Ryan called me from PACAF in Hawaii at 2:00 A.M. with nothing more than a curt demand to "check and see if there is any possibility that Kingfish Four could have bombed a ship in the Haiphong area this afternoon and call me back immediately." Obviously he had received an inquiry and was doing the detective work, on the wrong track, all by himself, which typified our command structure. Kingfish Four had experienced a hung load of bombs that wouldn't come off on his dive-bomb run that afternoon, and that had almost caused him to auger into the target as he fought to pull out of his dive. I woke everybody up and verified that the other three members of his flight had watched him manually dump those bombs on a dirt road after they got out of the target area. Then I called Ryan back and said, "There is no possibility that Kingfish Four could have bombed a ship. You have nothing to be concerned about as regards the question you asked me." Ryan wanted to know where Kingfish Four's film was. I told him that he was not carrying film, since the maintenance crews had not had time to load it in the quick turn-around to get that particular aircraft on its second mission of the day.

Had Ryan asked me if there was any possibility that *any* of our aircraft had attacked any shipping targets, I would have been forced to answer differently. That would have shut down Ted, Lonnie, and myself. I was not about to volunteer something I felt could harm my people. I had an idea that General Ryan might still be personally concerned, and I knew that he could well make his concerns my concerns in the near future. I had not constructed an elaborate plot nor had I attempted to hide my tracks. As Phil Goulding said from his viewpoint with the assistant secretary of defense for public affairs, "It all went away, for a while."

11 | FLAK FROM WITHIN

From June 2, 1967, until June 17, I was very busy trying to win my segment of the war. We saw a few squibs in the Bangkok newspaper to the effect that the Russians had claimed that a ship called the *Turkestan* had been attacked in Haiphong Harbor, and that our people in Washington had said to forget it. That sounded good. I wrongly assumed that the *Turkestan* incident was something way in the past, and since there were so many important things that needed doing, I dismissed it from my mind. I was suffering from a bit of naiveté as I went my merry way, leading my people in combat and running my personal mission total for that war up to 102 missions. I became a bit distracted on the eleventh and twelfth of June when my luck ran out.

We came up off Phu Tho the afternoon of the eleventh after a good strike and since everyone in the flight had bags of fuel, we went hunting. I had a good solid flight with Ted Tolman leading my element, and it wasn't more than five minutes before we picked up some poorly camouflaged trucks and large supply containers along the edge of a dirt highway. We started shooting them up with our Vulcan cannon, with no flak in sight. Something must have been screwed up within that convoy, since they usually covered up better than that.

Everything we shot at blew up big, like it was fuel and ammo, and I called another one of our flights in the area to come in and join the shoot-up. We had uncovered a significant amount of explosive supplies and when a few wooden shacks down the road a mile or so blew with only a few cannon rounds, we knew we had found a very worthwhile target area.

As I pulled off a strafing pass I spotted an uncommon sight. A couple of miles to the north six overloaded army trucks were parked in a straight line right in the middle of a valley floor. The convoy was apparently split up and part of it was completely in the open. The trucks had tarps lashed over them and were so full they looked like six fat toads squatting in line.

I pulled hard to turn and line up on them and dropped the target pip on the line of trucks. As I squeezed the trigger the last two trucks in the line burst into flames, the third crumpled, and all hell broke loose. I found myself surrounded by 37-mm gunfire. I was in a sea of white puffs, right at their optimum firing range, and they hit me hard. They ripped through my vertical fin and tore out a huge chunk that left the fin hanging on by a single one-inch leading-edge strip. They also got all the electrical flight control components, and I was off on a wild ride that damn near caused me to buy a chunk of North Vietnamese hillside at the end of that valley.

Once again, I couldn't shake the groundfire and it just kept coming. I didn't have to worry about jinking since my beat-up Thud was tossing me around harder than a sane person would or could jink. There were lots of 37s and they were still all over me. Nobody had to say a word on the radio. We all knew the drill by heart and we knew that I was in trouble. I needed help that very second or I was done, and that help, once again, could only come from Ted. Ted instantaneously forgot about the trucks, clamped down on the trigger, and kicked his rudder pedals from side to side as he hosed down the base of those white puffs with hot Vulcan cannon rounds. Ted made them duck their heads and get off the guns for a few seconds, saving me for the second time. I had my hands full with a bucking, swaying Thud that was too close to the ground and whose flight controls were far too unstable. Had I been able to examine my subconscious at that moment, I suspect I would have been patting myself on the back for not having turned Ted in to Ryan nine days earlier.

As soon as I got on the ground at Takhli, I got on the phone to General Momyer and his staff and did something unique in the annals of Southeast Asia. I talked them into letting us design and execute our own strike against what we had found along Route Six. I took the whole wing up there at the crack of dawn and found just what we had hoped for. They hadn't moved out and there were more targets to be bombed and shot up than I had imagined.

I took my flight in first and the same 37s that had hammered me the afternoon before lit up just like I wanted them to. We saturated them with our flight's load of cluster bomblets and they went out like a light. Then I moved to the side and directed the other flights in. Everybody scored big and the flak in the area decreased with every explosion. I did notice persistent activity from one 57-mm site, but it was over in a corner and we were pretty busy. I had one flight hit him a quick lick from their cannons, but they were about out of ammo and that 57 kept pecking away.

When the last flight was out of ammunition, that section of North Vietnam was a smoldering mess, and lots of ammunition and fuel headed south never got there. I was elated. I still had some 20-mm ammo left for my cannon and nobody had silenced that 57, so that seemed like the thing for me to do before I left.

I lit the burner and rolled over the top at about 12,000 and pointed her straight down with the pip on the spot where those red golf balls were starting to rise. I tracked for a second or two as I screamed straight down, and they just shot my ass off. All the fire warning lights came on and everything in the cockpit went ape. I thought, "What the hell, those bastards may have me, but I'm going to get them before I go."

I was able to hold the pip on target and the red balls were still floating up as I pulled the trigger and fought my sick aircraft. I kept pushing forward on the stick to hold my target pip in the middle of their fire, and I spit the better part of two thousand rounds of 20-mm ammo down their throat in a couple of seconds. The last thing I noticed before I babied the stick back, draining the last of my main system's hydraulic pressure, was that their firing had stopped.

I was in tough shape with a sorely wounded bird trailing black smoke as I laboriously cleared the ground and tried to see what kind of problems I had on my hands. For one thing I was obviously on fire. As my wingman pulled into a wide wing position—not too close—he told me that my right rear end was perforated, with one hole large enough for him to look inside my engine at the fire. Both my main hydraulic systems were gone, and the little standby system gauge was bouncing on and off zero. Zero on that emergency system meant good-bye flight controls and good-bye Thud. Every slight control pressure I had to apply drove it back to zero.

From the wing came, "Better bail out, chief. I think she's about to blow."

For some reason I looked at my watch and it was a quarter to twelve. I looked at the valley below where I had been shooting them up for two days and said to myself, "No way. If I bail out here those bastards will eat me for lunch."

Ken Bell had my element and he took command. He sent our two wingmen on ahead to see if they could find a tanker and refuel, so they would be available for a possible rescap. My rear end continued to burn and the last thing my wingman said as he left was that I looked like a pot-bellied stove. Once again, Ken and I were in the barrel together.

Since I was on fire, no tanker would have me even if I could hold still long enough to let the boomer stick me. But it turned out that the tankers were spread too thin and there were none available anyway. Every time I had to move the flight controls, the emergency hydraulic pressure went to zero and my hands dropped to the ejection handles. I took my feet off the rudder pedals and put one finger on top of the stick so I wouldn't overcontrol. The nearest emergency strip at

Udorn was about three hundred miles to the south. They had a low ceiling in rain, and there was a wall of thunderstorms between them and us. I was not flushed with overconfidence.

I didn't dare light the burner and pour raw fuel on the fire, so I had to limp to altitude, risking the hydraulic system by ever so gently slipping from side to side in the hope of blowing the fire out. At about 22,000 feet, the thin air and the side slipping worked as the fire lights flickered for a few minutes and went out.

The two wingmen that Ken had sent ahead had scrambled a rescue Spad for me. Once we contacted him he helped me steer around the worst of the storms, and I threaded my way between layers of cloud and through valleys of rain. The meandering around meant an extra hundred miles, but no way could I have hacked a head-on thunderstorm penetration with those flight controls. Ken and I had our usual fight with the ground controllers, but they finally set me up on a good instrument letdown. I locked onto the instrument landing system and fell through the bottom of the clouds with a few hundred feet to spare and nothing between me and the end of the runway but a rainstorm.

With Ken hanging in there as mother hen I blew the gear down with the emergency bottles and lined up with the runway. After all that, I scared Ken silly. My radio was garbled and he thought I said my gear was not down. Since I didn't know if the emergency brakes would work when I pulled the "one time only" handle that activated them, I was dragging in low and flat, heading for the very end of the runway. He thought I was going to undershoot.

A few hundred feet out from the end of the runway I got a blast of heavy crosswind that tried to roll my right wing up and push me off the runway heading. I had to roll aileron into it and had to hit the rudder pedals. Out of the corner of my eye I watched the emergency hydraulic needle drop to zero and stay there as the controls stiffened. "Not here, baby—hang in there."

I touched down right on the end of the runway and held my nose off as long as I could. When the nose gear fell through, it held up, and a pull on the emergency brake handle worked. As I turned off at the end of the runway I punched the mike button and said, "Thanks a lot, Christ. I'll take it from here." Ken whistled over the top of me in burner and headed for Takhli.

I had plenty of fire trucks and emergency recovery people for company as I taxied in. They parked me way down on the end of the hardstand. Since I had so much fuel running out of the 57-mm holes they were not sure that I wasn't still about to blow up. The colonel in charge of that outfit figured it was the worst one they ever caught coming back, and they towed her straight to the boneyard as I was catching a ride back to Takhli in a T-39 courier aircraft that was passing through. She was one hell of a super Thud to have gone through what she did and to have gotten me back. Like I said, those 57s were nasty.

While I was going about my business of shooting and getting shot at by the North Vietnamese, the gears at PACAF headquarters, and General Ryan in particular, were busy figuring out how they could keep the *Turkestan* pot boiling. There were a few seemingly routine queries as to munitions expended on the second of June, and we provided the required answers, but gave little thought to the prospect that the secret service of the Pacific was in action. It was in action because General Ryan wouldn't let the *Turkestan* go away. He was sure that there must be someone to punish. He spent the next two weeks crisscrossing the Pacific with a C-135 full of PACAF detectives, personally searching for an answer. That film was never developed and nobody ever saw one frame of it. That was not enough for General Ryan; he wanted someone to hang.

We were expecting Ryan to stop by for a routine visit about the twenty-sixth of June, but on the seventeenth we got a call that he had moved his schedule up and would be there that afternoon. He would have Generals Vogt and Chandler from his staff in Hawaii with him and Mike Ingelido would be there representing Thirteenth in the Philippines. There would be nobody from Seventh, our operational headquarters in Saigon, in the crowd. Bob Scott and I needed to prepare a briefing within a couple of hours. Scott was calling the shots and knew we could expect little more than another unpleasant encounter with Ryan.

On his one previous visit since taking command of the Pacific air arm, Ryan was given a briefing on the specific tactics we used to accomplish our mission. At that time he had a golden opportunity to become everybody's big man of the air war, since people throughout the theater were anxious to get him involved in what we were doing. Instead, it seemed to me that he exuded a senior bomber general's inbred animosity toward fighter pilots. He did not appear receptive to our briefing on his first visit and showed little appreciation for what we were doing. We did not know why, but we knew we did not have an appreciative CINCPACAF, and nothing we said or did seemed to change that situation. Since Ryan had been such a pill on his first visit, nobody was eager to go through another session with him. Scott gave the briefing chore to me.

It would not have been much effort to give him a briefing on the mission we were flying that afternoon, but I did not want to do that. I told Scott I would give it a little thought, then check with him at lunch to be sure that I was going to approach Ryan the way Scott wanted me to. I had hopes that the briefing would provide the basis for an exchange of ideas and a discussion of concepts, tactics, and equipment, with an end goal of better prosecution of the war. I had never worked with Ryan as an individual, nor was I familiar with the details of the SAC mentality of the times. I assumed that Ryan and those who were not fighting the air war, and who did not understand the details of the operation, would want to learn more about that air war and hear our ideas on how to improve the way we were fighting it.

I wanted to come up with an approach that would excite Ryan, especially since the first meeting with him had been so disappointing. During that first briefing he had gotten off on a tangent, telling us all about our gross bombing errors, which was not true. Our attempts to tell him that perhaps he had given his intelligence people and photo interpreters an impossible task were to no avail. We tried to tell him that when we were directed to use instantaneously fused bombs, those bombs detonated **at** or slightly above the ground. They did not leave a hole in the ground, nor did they show up as a hole on anyone's pictures. Thus they complicated photo interpretation, but did not indicate gross error. He was used to looking at pictures of the thousands of holes the B-52s left scattered across the soft jungle floors down south. I'll admit they really tore up some desolate sections of southern jungle. We called them monkey killers and toothpick makers. But that was a completely different league; we worked a league where there were targets to hit.

We had wisely abandoned that early attempt to talk to Ryan about the different types of bomb fuses we used. We backed off because he obviously did not understand us. He did not want to listen to us and became very visibly disturbed. By the end of that first briefing we knew it had been sour on both sides, and we immediately sensed that Ryan did not care for us personally, or for our concepts of the war—but we did not know why.

I knew that Ryan as an individual was my prime audience and I knew that he would be a tough audience, but I felt confident. I was the one leading my troops Downtown and I was the one who knew what the air war in the North was all about. My audience had never been up North; he had never been to war in a fighter, and in fact he had not seen a shot fired in anger since the straight and level bombing raids of World War II. The responsibilities assigned to him were vast multiples of my own, thus I could not imagine that he would not be interested in what I had to say.

I wanted to talk about things that could be done better throughout the entire system to give us more positive results against the enemy. I wanted to lead him through a searching look at the mechanics of how we struck the enemy, including the capabilities and shortcomings of our present weapons versus available weapons, and I wanted to discuss the tactical capabilities of our aircraft, as opposed to how we were actually using them. I very much wanted to inject some of our ideas and thoughts, from our vantage point over Hanoi, into his headquarters in the hope that his far-removed, noncombatant staff would more closely align itself with our real-life goals. I accepted the fact that if I went with that approach I would have to be critical of some of the things that were being done at that time. I thought I owed it to my country to speak forcefully; I knew I owed it to those who flew with me.

As I finished my briefing Bob Scott gave me a big thumbs-up and a happy smile. I asked General Ryan if he had any questions and got a curt, "Not now." But he wanted Scott, plus our new DO and me, to remain behind as the others were dismissed. I received all sorts of positive comments from my troops as they filed out after the briefing. My three squadron commanders came up to me and told me that it was the best briefing they had ever heard and that the suggestions for improvement were great.

As soon as the others had left, Ryan began to tear into me on a personal level. He hammered me for making the points I had made, and it was immediately obvious that he would not even consider them. He said I was talking like an idiot in bringing up those points and that I did not have all the facts. He said that I was wrong to talk about those things in front of my people, as that could create doubt in their minds that things were other than absolutely correct. He quickly skimmed through each of my points saying that they were incorrect.

General Vogt and General Chandler sat there in the front row as Ryan lashed out. At each of Ryan's attacks they would say, "Yes, that's right," and throw a barb or two of their own, nodding in agreement with Ryan's every word. Ryan had obviously closed the door on any constructive thought.

Ryan, unfortunately, personified a type of general officer who had risen rapidly in rank with the wave that carried those on duty at the start of World War II to the top, or close to it. He had spent little time at the intermediate levels, and he had little feeling for anything but his own level. He had adopted LeMay's devotion to SAC, as well as LeMay's gruff mannerisms, and had added a bit of his own screaming and abuse. It had worked well for him. He was tyrannical, successful, and completely unfamiliar with being opposed. But here he was not in a familiar SAC situation. He was in a down-and-dirty combat situation that he did not understand, and that was bothersome and potentially embarassing to him. He was uncomfortable with the situation and with the people who symbolized that situation, and the only things he could attack were the people.

I, of course, was the Thud spokesman, the closest target Ryan could find. I was not reluctant to accept the leadership mantle; in fact, that seemed to be the reason I was there. I felt that, in spite of rank, Ryan should defer in some degree to me and those I spoke for since we knew the air war first-hand and he did not understand it at all. He had been absent from combat for over twenty years while advancing his personal position, and his credentials for running this air war stunk. My people and I faced death daily while he treated us as no more than stepping-stones to the chief's chair. Since he refused to share our knowledge of this war and the suggestions we proffered, I felt that it was my duty to antagonize him and show him up as not knowledgeable of what he commanded. We all knew we were expected to genuflect at his manufactured excellence, but those three generals didn't know what they were talking about. We did, but they would not listen to a word we said.

Ryan knew that I was a lowly colonel who was six years behind him at the Point, and that he had been dropping bombs over Europe while I was still getting my wings. He considered me to be the leader of the local resistance but that did not concern him since he was one tough four star who had never been denied for long. Having to listen to a briefing by Jack Broughton was a demeaning experience, and I'm sure it aggravated him that my people showed such open dedication to me.

The more I talked, the more antagonized he became. He could see my people were supporting me with enthusiasm; they were all pumped up. Obviously they thought just like I did. He thought that I couldn't be right about the things I was talking about. His staff would have told him if I was right.

The more I talked, the more Ryan showed difficulty in refuting my statements, because he had no knowledge of the specifics I addressed. His lack of knowledge was embarrassing to him, and his only retort was to scream that I did not have all the facts.

After Ryan had made the point that he did not like the briefing, he directed that Scott and I go into Scott's office. There he pulled up a chair, crossed his legs, leaned over, and started shaking his three fingers at me again. He spoke about the telephone call I had returned to him on the night of the *Turkestan* incident, saying, "I'm still pissed off at you about that phone call." Then he switched abruptly and launched directly into another tirade about the presentation I had just given. He summed up his feelings by saying, "Broughton, you have diarrhea of the mouth and constipation of the brain."

Without another word, he strode to the front door. We all raced out the door, jumped into our automobiles, and whizzed off for a tour of the base.

General Ryan rode with Scott and I had Vogt and Chandler in my car. I had no desire to contain my feelings in front of that pair of two stars, and as I slammed the car into gear, I said, "Boy, now isn't that something. Twenty-five years of dedicated service to your country, 216 fighter combat missions with 102 of them over here, looking at the very things we were talking about, and I get treated like a complete idiot and hollered at for trying to make constructive comments."

"Don't feel badly," General Chandler said. "Join the club. We all get the same treatment." They added that Robin Olds, the wing commander at Ubon, and even three-star General Momyer in Saigon, had received the same treatment the day before.

We spent a couple of uncomfortable hours roaming around the base and Ryan did not like anybody or anything. Sometimes Chandler and Vogt would get out at a stop and talk to people, while other times they sat in my air-conditioned car, too lazy to make the effort. At the tail end of the afternoon we went back to the operations building at about the time the afternoon mission was landing. We figured this would probably be another difficult stop as the general had summarily announced that everyone was mishandling their bomb assessment film. We were all making gross bombing errors according to his photo interpreters, and the pilots were doing this because they were not paying any attention to their film.

Nothing could have been further from the truth. We waved the red flag, saying that instantaneously fused bombs don't leave deep craters, as we had told him on his last visit, but we retreated at his first sign of apoplexy. The bomb film was a different kind of film than the gun camera film and could be developed locally within a few minutes. Looking at that film was the payoff for everyone on the mission, and you had to fight your way in to get a look at what was on the viewing machines. Those of us looking at that film were far more interested in the technical detail, and far more capable of assimilating what we were looking at, than Ryan and his photo people. Ryan wanted to find something to complain about, but as usual, the film drill went perfectly and the hits were terrific. Ryan looked but never said a word. If he didn't raise hell you assumed he was out of ammunition; nobody even expected him to say anything positive.

The next stop was right around the corner in the flight-planning room. One of our squadron commanders was there planning how he would lead the early morning strike, fighter-pilot style. He was introduced to Ryan and enthusiastically described how he would work the next morning. Ryan thought all targets should be hit from a high altitude, with straight and level mass formations, like the B-17s did it in Europe. Our tactics bore no resemblance to that, and Ryan challenged everything our squadron commander told him. Our squadron commander was still pumped up from my earlier briefing. He knew nothing of the ensuing nastiness, and was a positive type. He said, "Oh, no, General, you'll get killed if you try and do it like you're talking about—and besides, you won't get the target." Ryan spun on his heel and stomped out to Scott's car.

We delivered all our visitors to the various spots where we had them set up for the night. As soon as we had everyone positioned I swung by Scott's trailer both to see that everything was in order for the quick cocktail and hors d'oeuvres session that came next, and to attempt to get in a quick private word with him. I asked him if my pitch of the afternoon had been correct. I wanted to know if I had said the right things. Scott replied, "Hell, yes, it was great."

Then General Ingelido stuck his head out of the room in Scott's trailer where he was staying and said, "You get the egg off your chin yet?" It was a friendly inquiry from a man I had known for about twenty years. I didn't know it then, but that was our last truly open and friendly exchange.

I had been through enough conversations with Ryan for the day to suit me, but shortly after he appeared for cocktails it was me, not Scott, who got dragged into rebutting a ridiculous accusation by Ryan that our pilots were jinking on their dive-bombing attacks. From the time we arched to inverted over the defenses of Hanoi until we plunged our right thumbs onto the red bomb release button on the stick, we didn't wiggle or alter our dive-bomb run regardless of what was whistling around us. We had long since raised our right hands and sacrificed those seconds of our lives to the mission, regardless of the risk. Once the bombs left, we pulled and jinked and skidded and slipped as hard as we knew how to, trying to insure that we and our Thuds would be able to return in one piece.

We had a camera pod faired into the bottom of our aircraft with the lens angled downward and backward, toward the tail. That camera started taking pictures only after we punched the bombs off, and it would thus look back at our target and trace the flight of our bombs, allowing us to review impacts and damage to the target. Just like everything else on the aircraft, the camera went through a wild ride on the egress from the bomb run, but its wide field of view provided very good target coverage.

Someone had shown Ryan some egress camera footage. He assaulted me with, "The reason you people aren't destroying more targets is that you're doing all that damn jinking around instead of aiming your bombs at the target." I was flabbergasted, insulted, and hurt for my troops. I tried to explain that the camera was looking backward. I tried to explain how an attack and escape were flown. I tried to explain that the ground images on the film got smaller as we pulled away, not larger as they would if we were taking pictures as we approached the target. Ryan wouldn't even listen. He cut me off with, "Don't give me that crap. I've dropped bombs before and I know."

We had two tables of visitors for dinner and I hosted the second table with General Chandler, whom I had met before. He was apparently quite interested in what we were doing. I suppose because I felt wounded from the afternoon, I was quite eager to talk with him and get some feeling of decent rapport.

During the conversation I talked about the kinds of missions we were running and the kinds of opposition we ran into up there; how we were getting shot at from all over the place and how it was often quite difficult to keep track of the details when guns were fired at you from all around. Feeling that I was talking with a friend who was interested in the problems we faced, I really poured it on. I alluded to the fact that it seemed like even the ships were shooting at us.

Later I learned that other members of their group were well advanced in their detective work, gathering all sorts of mundane facts, like how many cannon rounds were fired on June 2. It could not have been too challenging a task, as nothing was hidden. Theoretically we had all been working for the same side on June 2, so why hide anything from each other? But there was that naiveté of mine again.

My mention of ships was what Chandler was after. This was his portion of the assignment; he was the good cop, the one to work from the inside. He had the lead he was after and did not let go of me until four the next morning. He was looking for information and he thought, correctly, that the way to get it from me was to involve me in a conversation about my troops and the good work we were doing up North. He accomplished his assignment of suckering me in. I sometimes wonder if he was proud of his work that day.

When the dinner broke up, General Chandler invited himself over to my trailer, and the rest of the generals disappeared to let him work. He told me that he wanted to talk about some intimations I had made in our earlier conversations. He sat in the little kitchen area of my trailer and harangued me about my obligations to my country and my duty to tell everything I knew, to expose anybody who might be exposable. I realized that they had pretty well completed the task of pasting together the events of the *Turkestan* incident. The realization that I was the criminal the system was after was heavy.

I kept looking at Chandler and thinking, "Judas, you are here to screw me."

He kept repeating, "We just want to get this thing straightened out. Don't worry, everything will be okay. We'll take care of all the details and nobody will be hurt." The phone in my trailer rang and we were summoned to Scott's office to talk to Ryan.

Ryan sat at Scott's desk and had a map of North Vietnam stretched out in front of him. Generals Vogt, Chandler, and Ingelido, and Bob Scott sat around Ryan as he called people in from various sections of the wing and questioned them. When my turn came I offered nothing and was not eager to talk. This routine dragged on and on throughout the night.

During the next to the last session Chandler sat against the wall as Ryan was grilling me and blurted out, "It's your duty to your nation and your air force to tell everything you know, everything you intimated to me. And besides that, if you don't, we're going to get you up on the stand one way or the other, swear you, and make you answer any questions we ask."

Ryan turned to Chandler and said, "Oh, shut up."

Since Scott had been in Okinawa on the second, he was beyond Ryan's suspicion. Both he and Ingelido looked quite contented sitting on Ryan's side of the room. Suddenly it came through to me loud and clear. There was a big line drawn across that room. I was on one side of that line, and Mike Ingelido and Bob Scott were on the other side. I asked to be excused for a few words with Scott and we walked out into the hall. I asked him how he wanted me to play it and he told me to go tell Ryan everything. That figured; Scott was protected, and thus a good guy in Ryan's eyes, or so he thought. I returned to the office and told Ryan that the two-ship element he was interested in was Weep Three and Four.

His immediate response was, "Where's their gun camera film?"

I snapped right back with, "I destroyed it."

Ted was in Tainan picking up a battle-damaged bird that had been repaired, so Ryan alerted the entire Pacific to locate him and return him to Takhli at once. They dragged Lonnie in at this point. He had not strafed anybody and I felt great waves of emotion as Ryan called Lonnie a liar, which he was not.

Lonnie kept saying, "General, I did not strafe any ship. The only time I fired my guns was to suppress flak on my bomb run. I did not strafe any ship." General Ryan really beat him up verbally. It was bad. While I can't remember any direct reference to race, I could feel it there.

About six in the morning, as the early mission was taking off for the North, I was released to return to my trailer. All was unhappiness, disillusionment, and disappointment. I hoped the guys going North for the morning did good work.

I didn't know it until much later, but all that grilling was a waste of time. H.K. White, a Wild Weasel from Korat, had routinely reported dropping CBUs on some guns at the east end of the harbor at Cam Pha while the *Turkestan* was in the area. H.K.'s film showed his CBUs well clear of the *Turkestan* and he had no gun camera film showing any involvement with the ship. But he had been close, and to Ryan that meant that he was the best one available for hanging at the moment. H.K. was grounded and the machinery to press charges against him was set in motion. Even if Ryan had never come to Takhli, had those charges against H.K. been formalized I would have spoken out. Probably with Lonnie's concurrence and probably without Ted's concurrence; but regardless, I would have immediately involved them and myself the moment Ryan moved against any of us. H.K. told me later that he was resigned to a hopeless, one-way ride before the events of the seventeenth. He knew he was innocent, but he also knew that it made no difference.

I made a pot of coffee and sat around my little kitchen wondering what my next move would be. It was bound to be a tough, uphill battle, since Ryan had taken such fanatical, personal charge of the whole thing. As I sat there, to my surprise, General Chandler came into my trailer and wanted a cup of coffee. I had little choice but to give him one. He persisted in patting me on the back and said, "Everything is going to be okay, no sweat, you did right. You did a beautiful job. You came through for your country when we needed you. As soon as we get this squared away everything will be okay. Don't worry about a thing, we'll take care of you." He didn't stay very long and I was glad to see him gulp his coffee and leave.

I got on the phone to our base legal officer, a fine young captain named Joseph A. Carretto, whom we called "Judge," and solicited his help in my defense. While I waited for Carretto to arrive, a very impressive young captain hurried up to the door of the trailer. He was General Ingelido's aide, and while we did not know each other well, we had associated professionally throughout our mutual tours in the Pacific. He knew full well that my trailer was not the best spot for the general's aide to be at that moment, but that was of no concern to him.

I offered him a cup of coffee but he declined saying, "Sir, I've got to leave quickly to file our flight plan back to Clark, but I just wanted you to know that, as far as I'm concerned, you did the only thing that a man with any guts could do. I'm behind you one hundred percent and I know that all the people who are allowed to think are behind you one hundred percent."

When the Judge arrived I gave him a quick thumbnail sketch of the entire episode and told him I wanted him on my side. He accepted. Then Scott walked in with General Ingelido along to observe and to be sure that Scott did what he had been told to do. Scott said, "Jack, I hate to do this to you, but by order of General Ryan I have to relieve you from your position as vice-commander of the wing. Further, by order of General Ryan, I'm appointing you special assistant to the combat support group commander."

Well, that was about as low as a snake's belly. Any time you're special assistant to anybody in the military, it just means that the people in charge don't know what to do with you and hope they can shuffle you off into a corner until you go away. Scott said that he had told General Ryan that he would prefer to have me as his special assistant, but Ryan had said no, absolutely not. There were a couple of reasons for that decision. First, Ryan wanted to embarrass me to the maximum. The combat support group commander, who was several years junior to me as a colonel, was the guy in charge of housekeeping, and he already had a lieutenant colonel as an assistant. He knew nothing about fighters. He was a tanker driver out of SAC. So I was given the title of assistant to the assistant of a guy who used to work for me. But Scott was trying to protect me and keep me in his immediate area because I had run that wing for the past year. All the administration, the nasty little details, all the writing, all the editing, all the action on the incoming and outgoing messages—all of those things I had done. Scott needed all the help he could get from me and did not want to lose it, but Ryan had ignored Scott's request.

When Scott told me, I just stood there for a few seconds, then looked at Scott and said, "For Christ's sake, Colonel, what am I, a goddamned criminal? You know perfectly well that if you had been there instead of me you would have done the same damn thing and it would be your ass they were firing now instead of mine!" Ingelido left, silently.

Then came the only real display of emotion I had seen from Bob Scott in the tough year we had spent together, and in the many years we had known each other before that. Tears welled in his eyes and his face flushed and he had to turn away. He walked away from me around the front of the trailer. He couldn't stand the truth. That cleared the room, and the Judge and I sat down to come up with a defense.

General Ryan had decided that he wanted the three of us charged with conspiracy against the United States Government. That was it; all else was simply administrative detail to accomplish the general's wishes. Absolutely nothing else mattered. His decision was common knowledge from day one, and his subordinates stumbled about to make their findings match Ryan's conclusions.

The interim before the trial was nasty. General Ryan and his associates did their utmost to humiliate us. Even though Ryan ran the court-martial very personally, it was technically an administrative matter, so we were under the jurisdiction of General Wilson in the Philippines, which had to be bad news. Most of Wilson's staff really enjoyed it, since it was as close as they ever got to combat. They secretly read our mail and listened to our phone calls, they constantly searched our belongings looking for the destroyed gun camera film, which they were convinced I was hiding, and they locked us up in the psycho ward on the far side of the airbase at Clark in the Philippines. It was very easy to sort out your friends during that period. It was amazing how many of those who used to pat you on the back were no longer around.

There was no doubt as to the outcome of the legal proceedings; they would lead to a general court-martial. The course ahead first involved an operational investigation. That was supposed to establish what had happened and form the basis for someone charging someone else with an offense. After charges were preferred, there would be another investigation under Article 32 of the Uniform Code of Military Justice, which was supposed to satisfy General Wilson that he had a case and that he should convene a court. Then there would be a trial. Theoretically each step depended upon the outcome of the previous step, but in this case that was hogwash.

Command influence had a lot to do with the way people acted. Once Ryan established himself as the prime prosecutor the ducks lined up quickly. Those wishing to make personal points out of the case found it expedient to credit all their actions as something "General Ryan wants." Many of those caught in the middle just wanted the case to go away without hurting them personally. General Ingelido had been my P-47 squadron commander in Germany; we had many personal associations over the years and our wives had known each other for twenty years. A week before the *Turkestan* incident he had inspected Takhli and told me what a superior job I was doing. When the *Turkestan* news broke he kept me somewhat informed on command developments. By trial time he was to tell my military lawyer that he had no use for me. His wife ignored my wave and hello as we passed in the Clark officer's club.

As far as Bob Scott was concerned, I believe that his behavior stemmed in great part from a fear that some of the *Turkestan* flak would hit him and thereby lessen his chances to become a general. Scott was a master of ambivalence. But in reality, the way the steamroller was moving, with Ryan at the controls, there was little if anything that anyone could do to produce effective resistance. That was unthinkable. I knew that Ingelido and Scott had no heart for my fight.

Ryan put General Lindley in charge of running all the people they sent into Takhli for their operational investigation. I had only seen Lindley once before, and that was when he came to Takhli for a show-and-tell visit. He didn't even fly in; he rode in sitting in the back of an old gooney bird. I put him in my staff car and drove him around to show him what we had scratched out of the jungle and how we operated; and got chewed out for my trouble. I had been chewed out for many things, but that was the first time I got chewed out for something being too good.

Lindley had said, "Hell, these buildings are too good. Your operations center is first class, better than in the States. And those sleeping quarters you have the pilots in, and even the sergeants—they're just too good. Someone is going to look at them and you'll be in trouble."

He refused to accept my explanation that we had plenty of cheap teakwood and cement block, and that it cost less to build with that and with Thai labor than it did to mess around with the termite-prone pine we could get from the States. His counter was, "Things here are supposed to look like Thai hootches—you know, like shacks."

Lindley hustled into Takhli as fast as he could get there and took over Ryan's investigation. A very tired, frumpy old lieutenant colonel named Posey, a legal officer from Saigon, showed up to assist him, and a young woman court recorder was dispatched from the Philippines to document the proceedings. The first thing Lindley did was to order our first sergeant to get all my things out of my office. He had decided that he was taking it over. One of the sergeants who worked for me in my little command section, John Tomkowski, was a very sharp artist, and he had done a fine job on a steely-eyed water-color portrait of me in my flying suit with a Thud in the back-ground. I treasured it and had it hanging behind my desk. My guys went through the motions of throwing me out, but they were visibly bitter about the entire affair. Lindley settled in, and the next time I got into my office I almost cracked up suppress-ing a laugh. My sergeants had rehung John's watercolor. Every-one facing Lindley did so looking at a mean pose of me staring down at the back of Lindley's neck.

The investigation got under way. I was the first man up. I knocked on my door and was advised to enter my office. I had covered one entire wall of the office with the most de-tailed map available of Pack Six. You could walk from wall to wall and mentally plan and fly a mission in front of it. General Lindley, sitting at my desk, was directly opposite my map, but he didn't have the slightest idea of what he was looking at. Posey was perched at the end of my desk, ninety degrees to Lindley, and he was terribly busy with rumpled papers while the court recorder sat slightly off to the side. She was a trim, well-dressed young woman whose husband had been an air force pilot who had been killed in a flying accident—which may have accounted for the fact that hers were the only civil eyes that greeted me. I saluted and re-ported to the general, who promptly told me that I was being investigated for possible court-martial for conspiracy against the United States. He directed me to face Posey, who was having a tough time physically as he struggled to his feet while fumbling with his law bible. Posey mumbled that I should raise my right hand and be sworn. Lindley proceeded to repeat the Ryan line and I could see that he had studied his instructions well.

As soon as I was given a chance to speak, I recited the full chronology. My open dialogue left no room for probing, and Lindley acted deflated.

"Well, ah, is there anything else you would like to say?" Lindley asked.

As a matter of fact there was. I concisely stated my views on how and why people fight for their country and why loyalty to your people, strong leadership, and guts were important. I said that the actions I had taken were from a position of direct command over fighting men, and that I believed them to be sincere and dedicated combat pilots. It was not the kind of statement that invited further questions and I was excused. I would have liked to quote from my statement exactly, but Posey and Lindley made that impossible by classifying it as top secret, which was ridiculous.

Ted was up next, and the details he recited added little that was not already documented. But his reactions seemed strange. It seemed as if Ted did not understand what was happening to him, and that he was not making an effort to understand. He was under the illusion that he would get a fair trial, and that the fact that he was a dedicated American officer would in itself acquit him. He never realized that he was battling a system that was geared to gobble him up. When he reached the point in his story where I entered the picture, he wanted to stop talking. General Lindley said, "And what did Colonel Broughton do?"

Ted said, "You'd better question Colonel Broughton about that. I don't consider it proper that I discuss his actions under the implications of this investigation."

Lindley fired back, "Major, I asked you a question, answer it."

Ted said, "General, I think I'd like to have legal counsel." That was his right. I had not felt the need of legal counsel when I confronted Lindley, since the Judge and I had already worked out our approach. Ted could have had, and on that request should have had, legal counsel. Military law is very clear on the point, but that was only one of a multitude of abuses of the Universal Code of Military Justice that the *Turkestan* travesty was to expose. Ted had a perfect right to remain silent, but he was denied that right. Lindley growled, "Major, I advise you to get with it and answer the question." Ted was overwhelmed and proceeded as directed.

Lonnie was next and his approach was different from Ted's.

It did not take him long to analyze what was happening to him. He knew that he had been in the background of these events, and he knew, after his pasting from General Ryan, if he had not known it before, that Ryan wanted his scalp. He knew that I was to be the standard bearer in this thing and that from my command position I intended to accept the responsibility for all actions and decisions. Anything he said could do us no good and could be twisted by the considerable forces aligned against us so that it could do us harm.

Lonnie had said to me earlier, "Colonel, you're the one who stands to get hurt the worst out of this. You call the shots and I'll respond all the way." I never worried about Lonnie after that, but I did learn to respect his understanding and his reaction to pressure more and more as the weeks wore on. He didn't take any of Lindley's crap. Lonnie demanded legal counsel and he got it. He clammed up and played it cool all the way, just the way the Judge and I wanted him to.

It had been an awfully long and heartbreaking day. But Bob Scott, who enjoyed the protocol, had a few visitors on base and insisted that I help him host his dog and pony show for cocktails and dinner. It was all I could do to sit through the dinner routine and I left at the first excuse. The young woman who had been recording for the court was one of Scott's guests for the evening, and the fact that a young, attractive American woman was on board was one reason that the dinner dragged on and was still in progress as I left. I had a few words with her as I departed, and I guess I must have looked as beat as I felt. She gave me a few moments to get to my trailer, found a phone, and called me. She said that as little as she knew about what was transpiring she was tremendously impressed with the sincerity we had shown in the statements that we had made. She thought our dedication to our mission, especially in the face of the odds, was great. She expressed sincere hope that things would work out for us. I was most pleased and thanked her for her consideration in calling. I went to bed feeling a bit better in that someone had said something nice to me.

* * *

The three of us were in limbo. General Ryan had grounded Ted and Lonnie, and this was a severe blow. A combat pilot can ill afford to lose the sharp edge of proficiency. Ted was our wing weapons officer, charged with the responsibility of investigating and planning techniques for weapons delivery on our targets, so he managed to find enough homework around his office to keep him busy. Lonnie was working in the operations and scheduling section of his squadron, and while he filled his days, much of it was busy work sitting and waiting.

General Ryan had forgotten to ground me. I guess he thought I'd be so busy dodging his legal bullets that I wouldn't have time to think about flying combat. I had 102 missions and I wanted to make it 105 in the F-105—just because it seemed like a good number. I asked Scott if I could go get three quick missions before the legal rains came, but he said he couldn't make a decision like that since there was so much general officer pressure in evidence. So when he passed the ball to Ingelido in the Philippines, I knew I was in trouble on that request.

I called Ingelido several times, to no avail. Finally he talked to me and said that since his next higher headquarters was run by General Ryan he was afraid to let me fly. He said that if I went up and got killed he would never know if I had done it on purpose or not. How idiotic. He was obviously incapable of analyzing what I was made of. He was really afraid that if he cleared me to fly and I did get killed, Ryan would have lost his number-one candidate for hanging. It really gave me a warm feeling to know how much they cared for my personal welfare. One of his statements was that three more combat missions were the least of my worries at that stage of the game. It was a losing battle. Those who didn't fly for real seldom understood why some of us really wanted to fly.

It was pathetic in some ways. One colonel from Ryan's staff at PACAF, who was in the aircraft requirements and planning business, a position where he should have known a lot more about airplanes than he did, could hardly wait for the chance

to tell me that we were in big trouble because a Soviet dip-
lomat had produced 20-mm shell casings that had fallen from
a strafing F-105 onto the deck of the *Turkestan*. The 105 does
not eject fired shell casings. It spits everything that passes
through the firing cycle into a big can in the nose of the
aircraft and stores the brass there until the can is unloaded
on the ground. I don't doubt that they had 20-mm shell casings, but they must have come from one of the 105s they had
shot down around the Cam Pha or Hanoi complex. There
were lots of them up there. I started to explain that to the
colonel, but he didn't much want to listen, and I really didn't
care if he listened or not.

The architect of the prosecution was Judge Advocate General Colonel Morrie Benson, who technically worked for Wilson in the Philippines but who worked for and reported
directly to Ryan in Hawaii throughout the *Turkestan* proceedings. Morrie Benson and Ryan insisted on classifying the trial
top secret, which was ridiculous since there was nothing even
remotely classified involved. But it insured that few people,
especially the press, could look into what they were doing.

Despite the lid that Ryan had clamped on the affair, the
word had traveled far and fast. I had three separate offers of
top civilian legal help, and I had two offers of political help
from close to the highest national level. One of the most
impressive offers came from a group of senior officers just
under the level that was prosecuting us. They knew that if
their support was ever recognized by their superiors, they
would be in the same career boat that I was in. Regardless,
they offered to pool every cent they could get their hands on
and retain top civilian counsel for me. I was most humble in
the face of these offers and I spent many hours mulling over
the possibilities. Although I knew that it was not to be, I
subconsciously wanted to believe that because of my record
of the past twenty-five years and because of my actions in the
face of the enemy, someone up the line would take care of
me and put an end to this farce. From a practical point of
view, I felt that if and when this did come to trial, my best
chance would be the straightforward, combat commander ap-

proach. I was suspicious that the introduction of high-level legal and political help at this stage of the game would create more problems and more antagonism.

We had been checking every news release we could get our hands on, and as the air force finished its operational investigation, our navy buddies got into the same act by unintentionally bombing a Soviet freighter in Haiphong Harbor. We heard through the fighter-pilot grapevine that the navy had told the Washington gang to kiss off; their pilots were busy fighting the war. That's what our air force would have done if there had been one brass ball among all of our leaders. The news releases said that the Soviets were demanding payment for the *Turkestan* and that the flyers be punished. The U.S. supposedly rejected this demand. One state department spokesman, Robert McCloskey, said that the issue was closed. Not so. With twenty-five years in uniform I was as callused to official misrepresentations as anyone, but this one got to me personally; it was a direct lie.

As all the investigators put the finishing touches on their report, Benson relayed the information to Scott that Ted, Lonnie, and I were to be put in the custody of a flight surgeon and transferred to the psychiatric ward at Clark in the Philippines. The personnel people cut a set of orders putting the three of us in the custody of our local flight surgeon and friend, Lieutenant Colonel Gould. He was to insure our safe retention pending transportation to Clark, where we were to be locked up in the isolation ward of the psychiatric facility for examination and evaluation. The three of us walked in the front door of our dispensary at Takhli and asked the startled airman at the desk for our Seeing Eye nurse. The Doc promptly threw us out the back door and told us to meet him at the aircraft the next day. He threatened to bring handcuffs and straitjackets if we didn't stop calling him our Seeing Eye nurse. The whole thing was so absurd that you had to laugh to avoid numbing bitterness.

A plush little T-39 headquarters jet arrived to pick us up at about three the next afternoon. I don't know what they had told the pilot to expect, but he was amazed when he found that his cargo was three lean, healthy fighter pilots and the Doc, who just happened to be an old friend of his. One of Benson's legal messengers had hand-carried the pretrial report to Seventh for General Momyer's signature, so our first stop was to be Saigon where our pilot was to sign for and assume custody of that paperwork and hand-carry it to the Philippines.

We landed in Saigon at dusk, in a thunderstorm, and our pilot departed for General Momyer's office to pick up his top secret package. We hung around the dumpy terminal and watched the rain. I got on the phone and contacted General Ed McGoff, a fighter pilot I admired who was working there, and advised him of the current developments. Eddie had commanded the 355th, our wing at Takhli, when they got their first F-105s while they were at McConnel Air Force Base in Kansas. He was aghast when I told him we were en route to the nut house.

"Jack," Ed said, "every pilot who is fighting this war over here, anybody who knows anything about it, knows that you have balls of steel and we're for you one hundred percent. But don't forget that we're all pawns in this great big game, and they're liable to handle you pretty roughly as a pawn." He was right. I knew I had lots of support. I also knew what was happening. I felt very much like a pawn.

I had known from the start that things were going to get nasty. Early on I was made aware that we were subject to constant search and censorship. After I relayed that fact to my wife AJ, she started out her next letter with, "To whoever is reading my letter to my husband—go to hell."

We waited for our pilot for a long time before he returned with his package. It had been wrapped, sealed, and stamped TOP SECRET—RESTRICTED ACCESS. That meant that it was so top secret that only Benson or Ingelido was supposed to see it. Our pilot knew that Ingelido would not be available that evening. So having signed for and accepted that package, our pilot was responsible for hugging that report all the way into Benson's arms in the Philippines.

When we arrived in the Philippines our pilot set out to find Benson, while our flight surgeon herded us to the remote area on the other side of the base where the psychiatric isolation ward was hidden. Our pilot found Morrie wrapped around the poker table in the middle of a big game. Morrie didn't want to be bothered accepting the top secret package, but the pilot had his orders and he insisted that Benson sign the receipt and take the package. Benson grudgingly exchanged a signed receipt for the package and our pilot left.

Early the next morning our pilot was called by the command section of Thirteenth Air Force with a frenzied query as to where the TOP SECRET—RESTRICTED ACCESS package was. He announced that he had personally delivered it to Morrie Benson, as instructed, and had a signed receipt to that effect. Benson had no idea where the package was. They retraced Benson's steps of the previous night, and when they got to the poker area in the club they came upon the Philippino janitor. While sweeping under the poker table he had found the TOP SECRET—RESTRICTED ACCESS package and Benson's copy of the receipt lying among the butts, spilled drinks, and garbage of the night before.

12 | OUT OF BURNER

Our flight surgeon had to get us signed for just like our pilot had to get a receipt for his classified package. After a long, dark ride in a station wagon, we wound up on the far side of the base at a foreboding facility known as Ward Nine. It was drizzling lightly as we looked up a narrow gravel walkway to the entrance of a white stucco-faced structure that looked like the wicked witch should live inside. All the surroundings were very black, and the jungle vegetation hung along the edges of the building. The area was heavily fenced and all windows were shuttered closed and covered with bars. The only light came from one very bright spotlight focused on a heavy green wooden door. That door looked like an afterthought carved in the face of the white stucco, sealed in place with a large iron bar and guarded by an armed air policeman. We were not among friends.

My religious beliefs and habits have always been strong and have helped me through some rough spots. I learned way back in pilot training that there's time for everything, and when it's time for flying, there's no time for anything else. High-performance machinery is not tolerant of minds and bodies bent on anything other than dedication to the machine and the task at hand. Ever since the early prop days, regardless of the anticipated difficulty of the mission, I made my peace as I rolled onto the takeoff end of the runway and trusted that it would last the mission. Of necessity and purpose it was short: "Oh, God, please help me concentrate on my flying. Help me to really put out and do a good job for the air force." That seemed to do the job for me. I said that almost every day for about twenty-five years, and I meant it; but suddenly, looking at the scene in front of me, I knew I would never say it again.

That green door creaked open, we entered, then it creaked closed. That big iron bar clanged down and the locks snapped shut. The guns carried by the guards were loaded, and while it was obvious that they did not understand who we were, it was equally obvious that they had been trained and instructed not to like us. It was mutual.

The first things to go were our clothes and most of our personal belongings. They issued us little two-piece pajamas that didn't fit, shrunken white cotton sandals, and one government towel, well laundered. While we stripped under the watchful eyes of the attendants and guards and struggled into our blue suits and white booties, one of the attendants pawed through our wallets and other belongings. Lonnie smoked a pipe and he carried one of those little shovel things that pipe smokers use to clean their pipe bowls. They confiscated the pipe shoveler because patients were not allowed to have sharp objects. I thought Lonnie would die on the spot. Ward Nine had two private rooms and one large open bay. Since there wasn't anyone within the iron bars above the rank of corporal, I got one of the rooms and the two majors got to match for the other one. Ted lost and wound up out in the open bay with all the sick people, kooks, and nuts who were awaiting treatment, confinement, or discharge from the service. They were a spooky bunch. The little attendant ordered us to wait until eight in the morning when the psychiatrist would make his rounds and give us further instructions. All three of us were beat and terribly disgusted, so we crawled up on our cots and allowed ourselves to be locked in for the night.

At 5:00 A.M. we went through the normal hospital wake-up act, had a nauseating breakfast, and waited. At eight our head-shrinker came around. He was a captain and a very nice young fellow who looked all of eighteen. He was openly amazed at what he had inherited and had no idea of what was going on. He took one look and surmised that he had something unusual on his hands, and that we were not psychiatric patients. He beat a hasty retreat for instructions and said he would be in touch.

We waited for a few more hours, then were told to walk the half mile to the main building and pee in a bottle, get an X-ray, and have some blood let. We begged the corporal on duty for our uniforms, but he refused and we were forced to march along the street in our blue pajamas and white booties. When we got back and we waited for a few more hours and then were informed that our shrink was ready to see Lonnie. While Lonnie pranced back up the street in his pajamas, Ted and I drank more coffee and waited.

At this time two Filippinos representing themselves as interns approached me. The air force had a program where they dragged in medical students from local areas and let them stick things into the military patients for practice. Those two were a wild-looking pair. One of them was round and dirty-looking and the other was frail and as weird as a nine peso note. The weird one announced that he wanted to give me an examination. He also wanted a bunch of information. I told him in no uncertain terms to get lost.

It seemed that he could not understand my refusal and he just kept pressing. He asked a bunch of stupid questions like, "Do you have a hernia?"

"No, I don't have a hernia."

"Are you sure you don't have a hernia?"

"Yes, I'm sure I don't have a hernia."

"How about if I give you just a partial examination?"

"No," I said. "You're not giving me anything. My flight surgeon can direct me to take another physical if he wants to, but you're giving me nothing."

With a pleading, plaintive voice he cocked his dirty little head delicately to the side and said, "Well how about if I just give you a rectal examination?" I told him to get the hell out of there before I knocked him through the big glass medicine cabinet behind him.

Lonnie came back from his interview. I asked him how it worked out and he said, "Well, the doc told me that I don't have a complex—I really am inferior." That perked us up, and Ted's interview turned out about the same. I decided that, since it was now my turn to go see the shrink, I would keep it light. To the dismay of the guard who opened and then locked the green door behind me, I cinched my PJs and white booties as tight as they would cinch and jogged off down the road to my appointment, genitals flapping.

The young doctor knew absolutely nothing about what was going on in Vietnam and Thailand. I explained our story to him and emphasized that we were in fine shape and eager to get back to duty. At the conclusion of my ten minutes with the doc, he said, "Obviously there's nothing wrong with any of you guys and I don't know what in the world you're doing here. As far as I'm concerned you can go anyplace you want, but to make it look good I have to talk to you one more time. To cover me, how about just sleeping in the ward at night so it looks like we're playing the game, and I'll see you one more time tomorrow and put whatever you want on the report, and you can take it back to Takhli." I figured that was about as good treatment as we had been offered in the recent past and accepted his deal. I went back to the ward, and since the three of us were now free and no longer under lock-up restraint, we showered, reclaimed some of our civilian clothes, and I gave the guard a full colonel direct order to open the green door. I scrounged us a ride to the other side of the base and we all went to the officer's club. We had drinks and dinner but found it impossible to relax, so we went back to Ward Nine to go to bed.

When we got back we found that they had admitted a blithering idiot, who was strapped down with broad nylon belts in Lonnie's sack. Lonnie moved into the big room full of kooks, and I stayed awake all night listening to that poor demented soul as he moaned and thrashed endlessly. That was a terribly long night, but I kept thinking how short those hours were compared to the endless years my friends were spending in the Hanoi Hilton. I did not need to be in Ward Nine, humiliated and disgraced by gutless, make-believe military and political leaders. Like it or not, I understood now that there was no such thing as two-way loyalty in the military. Our national leadership was morally bankrupt and cared naught for those of us who believed we were fighting for our flag.

We had our second round of appointments with the head-shrinker that afternoon, and I was sitting around Ward Nine in the morning trying to figure out something constructive to do when I got a phone call. Scott had arrived at Clark to go through the formalities of a noncombat aircraft accident report that had to be made to the commander of Thirteenth. Ingelido was to receive Scott's briefing. The call was from Scott and the message was that he and Ingelido wanted to see me. I said great and allowed that I was on my way to Ingelido's office. That brought forth a reply of, "Oh, no, we'll meet you on the balcony on the back side of the officer's club that overlooks the swimming pool."

Okay, so they were ashamed and afraid to be seen with me. We met, had coffee, and talked for about an hour on how we might resolve the case. Ingelido volunteered that Ryan was personally running the show and that everyone else was absolutely powerless. He said that Ryan's interest was so intense that he demanded a minimum of one personal telephone report each day from Benson. The message they were passing to me was clear. I had been a swell kid and a peachy dancer who had done about all I could to make them look good. They had no desire to buck Ryan; and it would, in truth, have been a waste of their time. So they were telling me to buzz off. We were ex-friends for the duration, but if I somehow made it through the threshing machine, then we could be buddies again.

Since my mail was being censored and my regular phones were tapped, it was difficult to communicate with anybody representing the outside world. While Scott was at Clark he was staying in the VIP guest suites and he had a private phone in his room. He left me the room key when he finished his briefing for Ingelido and went back to Takhli, and I used that phone to call AJ in Hawaii and give her the straight story. This thing was a bad deal for AJ and the kids. They had been sweating it out while I was in combat over Hanoi; now all they knew was that my homecoming plans were destroyed and our own air force system had me locked in its grip.

Had it not been for my great personal friend Charles Blair, my communications with my family would have been nil. Charlie was right up on top of Pan American's list of captains, and at that time he was flying Pan Am Two, a globe-circling flight that came through Bangkok. When he landed in Bangkok we would send an aircraft down there and pick him up and bring him up to Takhli for a few hours. He held a reserve brigadier general spot, but mainly he was just interested in what we were doing. He was one of the nicest people I have ever known, and was no stranger to adventure, having among other things proved the validity of good navigational gear by flying a single-seat P-51 Mustang across the North Pole. Charlie visited us shortly after the *Turkestan* affair broke and he was shocked at the handling of the case. He offered all sorts of help, which I readily accepted. Among other things he acted as my newsbearer to AJ.

When Charlie got back to New York he would have a break between flights. He would go to Washington and assume his role as a reserve general officer, while trying to get all the latest information he could from the military. Then he would meet with our mutual friend Senator Barry Goldwater, who had been in my corner from the start, and who was thoroughly disgusted with the way both the war and now the *Turkestan* fiasco were being handled. From there Charlie would go to the Virgin Islands, where he owned an amphibious airline called Antilles Airboats, and wait for my prearranged phone call to bring me up to date. I always hoped that one of those phone calls would tell me that the nightmare was over, that my country did admire me. It never happened.

Every time we thought we had reached the peak of foolishness, something more foolish would surface. When there was no possible justification for continuing to hold us in Ward Nine, Ingelido and Lindley panicked. They called Bob Scott and told him that any time the three of us were at Takhli together, we represented a potential for riot and insurrection among our pilots and crewchiefs! They were afraid of us! They wanted me to go to Udorn as a special assistant to Lindley and sit there doing nothing during what had become an interminable wait, and they did not want more than one of the majors on the base at Takhli at any one time. That was so silly that we openly defied them with no difficulty. Any time the subject was raised I simply said we had business to discuss with our legal people and they were afraid to force us to leave.

We did have one three-day break in the monotony. One of our pilots had an engine seizure over friendly territory in northern Thailand and had to bail out over deep jungle. The choppers got him out but that was only part of the problem. We needed to find out what had caused that engine to seize. Also, the six bombs he was carrying north had time delay fuses on them. That meant that if those fuses had activated on impact with the ground, the bombs could go off at any time. The situation in the jungle looked like both a break in the routine and a challenge, so Scott put me on orders as accident investigator and gave me Ted and Lonnie as assistants. We gathered up some helpers, broke out our jungle gear, and headed for the bush. It was a hot, demanding three days, and we saw some strange jungle sights and some unbelievable jungle people, but we found the wreckage and dug the engine out of the ground in two large pieces and got it lifted out with a chopper. We finally located all the bombs by probing around in the mud and peering under bushes. After making sure that all the jungle people were well clear, we detonated the bombs and got out of there. Trudging out of the bush after a smooth operation, we had a good laugh wondering what General Ryan would have done had one of those delay fuses gone off and killed a bunch of natives with his three favorite people running the show.

* * *

When we got back from the jungle we found more evidence of General Ryan's determination to enforce his will on the tactical approach to bombing the North. He caused an operational analysis team to be formed from a group of nonpilot statisticians from his headquarters, and ordered them to statistically evaluate three past strikes and determine the best tactics for the F-105 wings to use. Here again we could see Ryan's craving for the SAC bible that no longer seemed to work. He wanted something that standardized combat, a ridiculous thought. Even his own statisticians recognized that every combat strike is different. When they came to Takhli to brief us on the study, they told Scott and me that they had made that specific point to Ryan, but he ignored their comment. On a specific strike against Thai Nguyen, we had been the first wing on target, running in low and fast and popping up to clobber the target. In the process we had soaked up all the enemy missiles and intensive gunfire, and we lost three aircraft while getting the job done. The Avis wing followed us to the target using Ryan's straight and level bomb run and did not see a single missile. They encountered only light ground fire, and did not lose any aircraft. Had the positions of the wings been reversed, obviously the results would have been dramatically different. Had the massive number of Sams that were fired at us been fired at the Avis wing, they would have been virtually wiped out. But Ryan had the statistic he wanted. The word went out that our tactics had been proven unsound, and that all wings would now fly the general's World War II bomber formation.

During their briefings at the forward bases, the statisticians openly apologized for decisions based on inadequate information from an inadequate sampling. We were shocked to find that they had made a gross error in their arithmetic and had credited the bulk of our target hits to the Avis wing. They agreed on the spot that their analysis was worthless, and together we hastened to advise General Momyer at Seventh in Saigon of that fact. General Momyer immediately dispatched one of his colonels to Hawaii to present a revised briefing to Ryan. Ryan did not accept the colonel's briefing. Three-star General Momyer had lost. Tactics were dictated down to the most minute detail of formation, altitude, heading, and airspeed. All flexibility was lost. The loss rates soared again.

General Ryan sidestepped the military justice system, but there was nobody to stop him. General Ingelido had personally admitted to Colonel Scott and me during our poolside visit at Clark that Ryan was controlling all the details of the case. However, when my military lawyer questioned General Ingelido later on the same subject, he denied any improper command influence. The procedures at Takhli were a perfect example of command influence. Bob Scott was still my immediate commander, and according to the Uniform Code of Military Justice he was supposed to investigate, prepare charges, and all that. In actuality Scott was not even remotely involved; Ryan, Ingelido, and Benson did it all. Benson had one of his legal lieutenant colonels appointed as Scott's legal advisor. The advisor prepared whatever Benson told him to prepare, then took it to Scott and told him to sign where appropriate. Scott never questioned the procedure.

The first time Scott saw any paper on the case was well after the operational investigation, when some of Benson's gang showed up with the formal charges. The advisor directed Scott to call me in, read me the charges that Scott had supposedly prepared, and then sign them as my accuser. Scott stumbled through them, since he had never laid eyes on them, and signed where Benson's people had placed the red X marks. As I listened to Scott meander through four paragraphs of military legal jargon, replete with phrases like "conspiracy against the United States Government," I can recall the bitter thought that this formally ends any obligation I might have felt toward the system.

Once he had completed the same task for Ted and Lonnie, Scott's obligation would normally have been to deliver the charges to the officer exercising court-martial authority over the three of us.

Scott was the senior officer on the base, and was supposed to be running everything at Takhli. However, Thirteenth Air Force in the Philippines had somehow set up the organization in the wings under their administrative control, so that court-martial authority was vested in the combat support group commander at each base, the housekeeper. He worked for Scott and until recently he had worked for me. But the combat support group commander really had no court-martial authority over us by virtue of yet another Thirteenth directive. The second directive stated that court-martial authority for all officers under Thirteenth was specifically delegated to the commanding general in the Philippines.

Benson had designed his case so that the charges would go through the combat support group commander and, legal or not, that was the route they were going. When Scott had finished signing, he punched the squawk box to his combat support group commander and said, "Ollie, come up here and pick up these court-martial papers I've just signed as the accuser and endorse them as to whether you agree with me or not." Ollie could have thrown the Pacific into an uproar if he had refused to agree. Legally he could have simply endorsed the papers, saying there did not appear to be any grounds for further legal action and the thing would have been dead. But Ryan would just have restructured and started over.

Benson and company had left nothing to chance, and Scott's assigned legal advisor accompanied Ollie and the papers from the scene. The endorsement was all prepared for Ollie, and he dutifully signed it, stating that he recommended that the guilty bastards be brought before an Article 32 Investigation Board to evaluate further court-martial action. By the strangest of coincidences, that entire panel had already been flown in from all over the Pacific and they were assembled, briefed, and ready to have at us the next morning.

It seemed to me that the whole world was out of focus. Our war in the North was being forcefully misdirected. Old friends were turning against us, and common sense was not to be found. All the nonflying and nonfighting people I had been in contention with since I arrived were now united against me, and they were firmly in command. Having been a combat fighter pilot and having repeatedly put my life on the line over Hanoi for my country meant nothing, even in my own air force. In fact, it was a handicap, because it identified me as not in the camp of those who were running the show. It took little perception to see what the course was to be, and I agonized that I could neither change it nor move it at better than a snail's pace.

The Article 32 investigation was in fact a dry run of the trial, complete with prosecution, defense, and all the trimmings, except for the court members who would sit in judgment at the actual trial. Each of the three of us had a defense counsel that Benson was obligated to provide from the sizable legal staff assigned throughout the Pacific. My guy was Major Jerome S. Cohn. Jerry was a very competent gent who tried very hard and who worked well with the judge and myself. Major Charles Stewart was assigned to Lonnie, and again it was a good match. Major William Jicha, who was assigned to Ted, was different, just like Ted was different. That developed into an increasingly difficult situation as we got deeper into the ordeal at hand. There were numerous individuals involved on the prosecution side, but Major Alfred Harston did most of their talking. I had met Harston in Japan a couple of years before and I do not ever remember seeing that man when he was not talking too much and too loudly.

They held the Article 32 proceedings in the first-class conference room that my first sergeant and I had put together, so once again I was on trial in my own facility. They had me sitting opposite the main door, so every time they called one of my troops as a witness, the first thing he saw was me. All of them looked like they were about to go into shock, but I always gave them a thumbs-up or a wink to relieve their pain. It was an extremely humiliating experience for them and for me.

They called in Lieutenant Colonel Jim Markey and showed him a piece of paper. He allowed that it meant that Ted and Lonnie had indeed flown two specific F-105s on that day. Same routine with Lieutenant Colonel Ed Miller, who added that those two aircraft had fewer cannon rounds on board when they came back than they had when they left. A wiseacre airman no class testified that Ted told him to hold onto his film rather than send it for processing. Next came a captain who was the photo officer at Takhli. He was also shown a piece of paper, and judged that the numbers on the paper meant that there was less unexposed film after the mission than there had been before the mission. He hastened to add that nobody could tell what, if anything, had been on that film. The captain was in a delicate spot, as he had signed the routine film accounting sheet the day after the *Turkestan* affair, knowing that in the interim I had destroyed the film. In return for his testimony, nobody bothered him about his involvement. That was great, since he had only been trying to help us. The sergeant from the photo lab who had helped me strip the film just repeated what we had told them about exposing the film in the headlights. Next a seemingly confused captain from Udorn said that he had debriefed Ted and Lonnie at Udorn, and they had not said anything about strafing.

Then came Paul Sheehy, the one bright spot during two days of sheer crap. He was a first lieutenant in the 354th squadron, and one of the greatest wingmen we had. He flew beautifully, had a great pair of eyes, and was violently aggressive. I used Paul as my wingman whenever I could. He was the sole surviving lieutenant pilot in the wing, since all of the other lieutenants who had come in with him had been shot down. When the last one before Paul went down, we decided that the air was unhealthy for lieutenants and made him an imaginary captain for the rest of his tour. Paul needed only one more mission to complete his one hundred, and we had been pushing him so he could get home and move his wife to their new assignment before their first child arrived. It was bound to be close, but he wanted to try. He had grown a huge lieutenant's mustache and his eyes glinted with distaste for the ground-pounding administrators who were raking his commander and two of his majors over the coals.

The only reason that he was even there was that he had walked past as we were stripping the film. Major Harston tried to make something out of Paul's testimony, but Paul would not give him the right time of day. He sat there and twirled his mustache as the major paced and probed.

Harston wanted to know if Paul had seen us. Yes, he had.

Where? He told him. What were they doing? He answered that we were looking at gun camera film.

Harston rose to the bait and asked if Paul meant we were looking at it or exposing it. When Paul reiterated that we were looking at it, Harston wanted to know how he knew we were looking at it.

Paul faced his adversary squarely and said, "Well, Major, they were holding it in one hand—like this—and pulling it through the reel—like this—and looking at it toward the light—the way you always look at camera film."

The major's pasty complexion was rising to the healthiest color I had yet seen it. "Didn't you think it unusual for them to be looking at—er, ah—I mean—oh, whatever it was that they were doing in front of a truck near the officer's club, at night?"

"No, sir," Paul replied. "If my commander wants to look at combat film in front of a truck, near the club, at night, that's okay with me."

With a sigh the major continued, "And what did you do then, Lieutenant?"

"I nodded and said good evening, sir."

Harston made one more try with, "What did they say, Lieutenant?"

Paul hit him with my reply, which had been, "Get lost, Lieutenant."

Harston wanted to know what Paul did then, and Paul said, "I nodded again, kept walking, and said good evening, sir." Harston quit, but he and Benson got to Paul a few days later.

The hearing wound down at the end of the second day. Paul flew his hundredth mission the day after he testified, and we all toasted him in the traditional manner that evening, congratulated him on a truly fine tour, and wished him well on getting home to his wife and almost baby. I saw him about noon the next day as he was getting ready to leave for Bangkok to catch a commercial jetliner home. He had shaved his moustache and looked absolutely sparkly.

Scott was off on another protocol trip that afternoon and since I had been deposed, that left the new DO, or number-three guy, in charge. It was one of those awkward situations we ran into quite often during that period. Many people were extremely uncomfortable or under strain when talking to me, Ted, or Lonnie. Some were obviously concerned that they might become contaminated, while others were so frustrated they found it difficult to express their support properly. Lonnie and I learned to live with it early in the game, but Ted never did.

Later that afternoon I was sitting in the DO's office yakking about the war when he got a panic call from Benson's office in the Philippines. Someone had brought it to their attention that Paul was about to go home. God knows Paul's testimony was the epitome of nothing, and could have no possible bearing on the outcome of the case. Nevertheless, the DO received instructions over the phone to hold Paul—not to let him go home. The DO told them Paul had already departed, but Paul had told me his flight might be delayed a few hours getting out of Bangkok due to mechanical problems. Sure enough it was delayed, and it had a scheduled stop in the Philippines. That's where Major Harston and Colonel Morrie Benson, and all they represented, got to First Lieutenant Paul Sheehy and all he represented. They took some air policemen, with their little guns and all that, boarded a commercial airliner, and pulled Paul off. They put an administrative hold on him for possible future testimony. In this case administrative hold was the same as administrative arrest, and Paul sat there for a month, confined for nothing.

Sometimes Bob Scott really got to me. He was good at arranging all sorts of fancy trips and social functions for himself, and was looking forward to a deal he had arranged to go down to Australia for a visit. As the *Turkestan* pretrial proceedings dragged on endlessly, he became concerned that the trial itself might interfere with his vacation. I repeatedly assured him that we would not call him as a witness and that his presence would not be required.

The day before I had to leave for the Philippines for the trail, Scott was in Bangkok where the chief of staff of the Thai air force was giving him a set of Thai wings, for some reason. Al McDonald, a friend of mine from Japan, was passing through Takhli in his T-39 executive jet and decided to spend the night there. I put him up in the spare sack in my trailer and he offered me a ride to Clark the next day. Mac and I were having a few drinks that evening, trying to set the world straight, when Scott returned from Bangkok and found out that Mac and his aircraft were on board and headed for Clark in the morning. Scott needed to get to Clark as well, so he could catch his ride to Australia, and he talked his way into the last open seat on Mac's aircraft. Another officer was going along on the Australian trip, and he and Scott had both been scheduled to ride the all-day C-47 courier to the Philippines. There was some slight pressure for me to give up my seat on Mac's aircraft in favor of the fellow vacationer, but neither Mac nor I would allow that to happen.

It was a long haul back to Japan, and Mac had been very explicit that he wanted to have wheels in the well at seven in the morning. Mac and I got up early, ate breakfast, grabbed our gear, and went down to the aircraft and waited and waited for Scott to show. He finally arrived, very late, which sure disturbed Mac. Once on board, Scott and I sat on the soft seats in the back, facing each other. As we lifted off the runway, he said, "How about this: eight days in Australia for me and a court-martial for you." That was tough to stomach.

The next morning I went to Jerry Cohn's office at Clark and we checked out several last-minute details. We were about as ready as we were going to get. The rest of our tribe was en route from Takhli on a gooney bird, and they were not expected until evening. Since it was midmorning with nothing to be done on the case for the day, I figured I could have some fun. I collect musical instruments, and I had made friends with Pexie Toledo, the conga player in the band at the Clark club. He had agreed to meet me in Manila on his day off and take me to where I could buy a set of congas and a new set of bongos. Colonel Chuck Yeager and I had shared many mutual friends and experiences over the years, and Chuck commanded the 405th Fighter Wing, which was located at Clark. He had been put on orders as one of the members of our court-martial board. I called Chuck at his office to see about a ride down to Manila and back. Since they had an old gooney bird that was used to bore holes in the sky and to get the headquarters staff officers their flying pay, the ride was no problem. Chuck arranged for them to pick me up at one o'clock, drop me off in Manila, drone around for four hours, then pick me up for the return trip.

Chuck had just received word that a general who was an old mutual friend of ours was due to land at Clark shortly for a refueling stop, and wanted to see me before the trial if possible. Chuck invited me to have lunch with him at his house and made arrangements for a car to bring the general to his house when he landed. Chuck picked me up and we drove to his house for a couple of drinks and a delicious lunch in elegant tropical surroundings. The general arrived, and since he had to fly on as soon as he was refueled, and since I had a one o'clock takeoff, we quickly renewed our friendship and he gave me a great pep talk. He explained the intensity of feeling and support for me that the case had aroused in Washington and in the Pentagon, and the widespread but helpless resentment of the Ryan steamroller. I was left with no doubt that while I was understandably on my own and due for a rough ride, I was carrying a large load of the true tradition of the fighter fraternity of old. I was the standard-bearer again.

We split, and while not one word was ever said about it, Chuck and I knew that in spite of our friendship, we were off-limits to each other until the trial was over. He had a job to do and I had a job to do and we would both do it like fighter pilots—professionally.

Pexie and I got together in Manila as planned, and spent a wild afternoon hauling drums through the packed, bustling streets. I got to meet his family, and after briefly enjoying their hospitality we managed to coax his ancient car to life and get back to the airport. It was good to shake loose for a few minutes, but I couldn't get very far away from the issue at hand.

Jerry Cohn lived in a house only a few doors from the quarters we were staying in, and after dinner I gave him a call. Ted and Lonnie had arrived from Thailand, and Lonnie, Major Stewart, Jerry, and the Judge were having a discussion. Ted and Major Jicha were not there. Jerry said that they had a problem they needed to discuss with me, and I hurried over. I was informed that Ted, under advice from his counsel, was considering going for severance and asking for a separate trial. Ted was long gone someplace, among the missing, as was Jicha, so we couldn't talk to them at that time.

All our planning had been based upon the assumption that we were to face a common trial. To sum up our approach, I was to take the lead and assert that I was the commander and that I accepted full responsibility for the actions of my people. I destroyed the film because I thought that to be the best course of action for all concerned. This approach was calculated to get Ted and Lonnie off the hook completely and, I hoped, to get me some sort of favorable consideration. Strategy was not to be taken lightly, as Ted and Jicha seemed to be doing. Each of the four charges against us could translate into dishonorable discharge, plus loss of all pay and allowances, and in my case loss of retirement pay and benefits—not to mention confinement at hard labor for many long years. We were not playing a kid's game.

One danger to the defense in a common trial is that the participants will start eating each other up under pressure and thus fall victim to the prosecution. I had no fears along that line at the start, but I had become increasingly concerned over Ted's apparent confusion and lack of ability to keep up with the action. I was also very concerned over what I perceived to be the strange, withdrawn attitude of his appointed counsel and Ted's susceptibility to poor advice. This announcement confirmed those fears. They had every right to ask for a separate trial. All they had to do was state their desire and base their contention on their belief that they could not get a fair trail in a group, and it would have been granted.

Such a move would have negated our entire effort. If Ted had wanted to stand alone, I could have arranged that for him on the black, thundery night of June 2. I could have stayed clear of the whole bloody thing and wiggled Lonnie out as well. I could have turned Ted and his film over to Ryan along with the false official statement in his intelligence report. I had become deeply involved by taking the burden on my shoulders, and I had been willing to take the chances that went with that choice. Now I shuddered and wondered if everyone had gone insane. If Ted went for severance he was done. And if he was done, this entire horrible nightmare was a waste. I knew the prosecution, and I understood the validity of the circumstantial evidence they had produced. Without me as a shield, Ted was a lead-pipe cinch to get a guilty verdict. With my protection and with the prosecution unable to use anything effectively against the others, I knew I could get them both off.

At this late stage of the game, severance would not have made much difference for Lonnie and me as far as trial results were concerned. I figured all Lonnie had to do was keep quiet, which he intended to do, and he would come out okay. My fate would be the same whether I was shielding one or two of my people.

Nobody could understand Ted. He had nothing to gain and everything to lose by severance. His counsel was inexperienced, a fact that we had only suspected until then, and Ted seemed to be coming unglued. I had accepted Ted as a personal responsibility many weeks ago, and I couldn't change now if I had wanted to. I announced that I would meet with him the next day and straighten him out, one way or the other.

I was upset that Ted and Jicha were acting so dumb. I was frightened at the prospect that the whole thing could become a debacle, with Ted losing and me in turn losing twenty-five years of a distinguished career for nothing. I was mad at Ted for having gotten me into this mess, and I was furious because he was turning into a wimp. I was mad at the air force for not being the gung ho fighter force I wanted it to be. I was mad at my nation for running a screwed-up war. I had a restless night.

The next morning after breakfast I had Lonnie get Ted up to meet me and review the situation. I was alarmed when I met him. He looked like hell. He was pale, shaky, looked like he had dropped a fast ten pounds from his already scrawny frame, and his eyes were sunken and dark rimmed. He was so nervous he could hardly stand still and he was not thinking clearly. In my admittedly nonmedical opinion, I had on my hands a major who was frighteningly close to a nervous breakdown. I had twenty-four hours left before we went to the docket, so I decided to work on him calmly at first and see if I could get him back on course. I was amazed as Ted told me of the advice he had received from his counsel. Obviously Jicha was as confused as Ted, and was advising him as he would advise an airman basic being tried for failure to report for guard duty. For example, the uniforms we would be wearing for the trial consisted of short-sleeved shirts and slacks. Jicha had advised Ted to wear all his formal dress ribbons and medals on his short-sleeved shirt to impress the court. He was talking about the long, dangling ribbons with the metal pendants on the end. In the first place, that makes an obscene-looking costume, and second, this court knew exactly who we were and what we had done and did not need a medal display. He had also advised Ted to go it alone, to stand as a combat hero by himself. Jicha was obviously out of it and I wished we were rid of him. I lectured Ted in great detail on the realities of the case, but I could see that he was incapable of assimilating what I was saying. After a lengthy talk I told him to go walk around the block for a while and I would meet him along with the others in an hour. I was sincerely concerned about his emotional health.

When all of us got back together, Ted was still floundering. To make it worse, he had Jicha with him, and Jicha was pouting because I did not appreciate his legal expertise. After a very few minutes I could see that I had to play colonel. I let them have it with both barrels as to why we were there and what was involved personally and professionally. I guess I must have been relatively impressive because nobody else had anything to say after I demanded a decision from Ted by early afternoon. Jicha suggested that Ted go lie in the sun and think, since that was what Jicha did when he was confused. He said that some unsympathetic people criticized him for spending so much time at the swimming pool, which he considered unjust, since he was really working. I doubted that. We split up to meet again after lunch.

As I wandered through the club dining room looking for a table I spotted our brevet captain, Paul Sheehy, still under administrative hold, and I joined him and a classmate of his who was flying F-4s up North. For the first two weeks that Paul had been there he had tramped to the legal office twice a day to try to get released and go home before his baby arrived, but to no avail. His wife's doctor had sent a message to the effect that she was not doing too well and was under great emotional strain because of Paul's absence. The doctor recommended that Paul be sent home immediately. Morrie Benson decided that Paul's wife was in no danger and denied the doctor's request. Even if Paul's testimony had been worth something, restraining him was unnecessary. They could have taken sworn testimony from him and used that, but Benson and Harston had decided that they would hold that smart young combat pilot and show him who was running the war—and they did. Paul had given up and taken up tennis to maintain his sanity.

As we ate and talked, a strange-looking man dressed as an air force lieutenant came up and asked if he might join us in the fourth chair at the table. His actions were most unusual, and he immediately got into the conversation with stupid questions about our aircraft and our operations out of Thailand. When he misidentified a couple of aircraft types and made a few wild statements about combat operations, we shut up like three clams. Paul and I compared notes later and our thoughts were the same. The first thing that crossed my mind was that he was a plant, who for some insane reason had been sent to check on what secrets Paul and I were exchanging before the trial. Perhaps we were getting spooky, but I remembered the advice from way up the line to watch my step. That clown was so clumsy and was groping so ineptly for information that the job had to be credited to the office of special investigation. Just to make it more like a B movie, as this officer left Harston walked up, as if he had been watching the scene, and told Paul he would like to see him in his office right away. Paul said that he couldn't make it until after his tennis game.

After lunch the counsel all met at Jerry's house and tried to talk some sense into Jicha. They apparently had little initial success. While this was going on, Ted just stayed in the club dining room and stared into his coffee. Finally he called Jicha and told him he wanted to go along with the original plans and the common trial. We were all relieved. Even though Lonnie and I would have come out the same, or perhaps better, if Ted had tried to go it alone, it would have made a mockery of the entire effort and surely would have resulted in Ted's being hammered.

That evening, when I was satisfied that all the last-minute details were lined up as neatly as possible, I headed for the club and dinner. My conga buddy Pexie had the bill for my congas and bongos, and I went to the club cashier's window to convert the necessary dollars into pesos to pay him. As I was standing in line I got a big clap on the shoulder and heard a hearty, "Hi, buddy."

I swung around, instinctively sticking my hand out. Who should it be but General Lindley. He was there to be the star witness for the prosecution at my trial the next day. And who was his companion as they set out for a night on the town? General Pitts, who was scheduled to be the president of the court-martial board. That was bad news seeing those two so buddy-buddy. Lindley jollied it up for a few minutes and asked me if I had met General Pitts. As we shook hands General Pitts said he didn't think we had met, but I reminded him that we had met when I was supposed to go to work for him in legislative liaison in Washington. After a few minutes they caught a cab and left, and I went on changing my money and muttering to myself about this crazy, mixed-up mess. Walking away from the cashier's cage I laughed heartily at myself as I thought that maybe if I had stayed in Washington and gone to work for legislative liaison I could be a general, court-martialing some stupid bastard who thought it was important for flyers to fight for their country. I paid Pexie and went to bed.

The morning of the trial rolled around and our counsel picked us up for a grim breakfast at the club. Ted, however, looked much calmer and better organized.

The court-martial was held in the lounge area of the bachelor officer's quarters. It was a massive five-story building, and what they called the lounge was really an auditorium with a roof two stories high. Our entire show fit nicely into one tenth of the huge room. The entrance was through large double doors at the rear of the room where two short sets of steps led down to the sunken main-floor level. As we walked down the long center aisle I noticed that the rows of seats on either side could have accommodated several hundred people, but they would not be filled that day. There was no coverage of the trial by the news media. Probably very few people outside those involved knew the exact time and place of the trial. While some documents had been declassified, Benson insisted that others retain their top secret designation, though there was nothing that resembled classified information. That meant that portions of the trial would have to be closed sessions, and it meant that air policemen had to guard the doors of the auditorium. I guess Benson liked the fact that the top secret classification made it seem spookier and maintained some aura of intrigue, though there was none.

The side walls of the rectangular auditorium were lined with narrow windows that stretched the two stories to the roof and made the place quite bright. At the far end of the aisle was the massive concrete wall that formed the end of the building. It was bare except for a lonely round electric clock. Directly under the clock was a long, narrow wooden table with chairs behind it that would seat the court with their backs to the wall. To the right and front of the court there was a place for the court recorder, a small table for the law member, who was another military lawyer charged with advising on legal details, and back toward the center aisle there were chairs and a table for the prosecution. To the left of the court was another long table and chairs for us, the defendants and our counsel.

There were a few spectators on hand, notable among them Morrie Benson and friends. He had brought his wife and another woman, both dressed in their Red Cross uniforms, to watch the fighter pilots get stabbed. Ted and I walked up to the coffee urn and drew ourselves a cup as Benson and the two women approached the urn. Ted sparked to his caustic best, stirred his coffee slowly, fixed Mrs. Benson with a piercing stare, and asked, "What did you do—come down to watch the circus?"

As the members of the court milled around the long table that would split them from us, I knew that in addition to General Pitts there were two other very problematical personalities on the board. One was Colonel Bill Harris, a headquarters administrator who traveled in very close trail behind Ingelido and Wilson, and who had no understanding or feeling for our war. I had been involved in routine dealings with Harris in the past, but he had almost died of embarrassment when I said hello to him in public when we had been at Clark during the Ward Nine fiasco. The other was Colonel John Shumate, who was head of the air police for Thirteenth, and I don't think he knew which end of a fighter the gun was in. I imagined he was still mad at me because I had run his people off months ago when they came to Takhli and wanted me to shut down a JCS Hanoi strike so he could hold an air police drill. The rest of the board was as good a shuffle as we were likely to get.

Court members can be removed in three ways. They can challenge themselves if they feel they can't do a fair job, either side can challenge them for cause, or each defendant can exercise one peremptory challenge, without explanation. Colonel Robin Olds, whom I first met when we were cadets at West Point and who had the F-4 wing at Ubon, was on our board. We had counted on Robin as a sympathetic person but he shook us up by challenging himself off the board. He said he knew all about Ryan's methods and the improper command influence in the case. So what? So did everybody else in the Pacific. But Robin didn't choose to remain involved. Too bad; his help would have been appreciated.

Getting the court seated had been a bit of a problem at the start of the proceedings. The rules are that the ranking man, who is known as the president of the court, sits in the middle of a long table. The remaining members are lined up by seniority and are seated on alternate sides of the president. Thus you have number two on one side, number three on the other side, and so on. After some shuffling of chairs Pitts thought everybody was in order and they all sat down. The first thing that was brought to the court's attention was the fact that Benson had not lined the court up properly when they had cut the orders, and some of the colonels farther down the list were actually senior to some at the top of the list. That resulted in a discussion of who got promoted to colonel when, and a new game of musical chairs. General Pitts was not pleased. Then when Robin Olds decided he couldn't hack it, they had to play musical chairs again.

After Robin walked out, General Pitts was left sitting in the middle of the long table looking very efficient and apparently happy that he had cleared the procedural hurdles. The defense was then asked if there were any challenges for cause, and we said no. Just as Pitts again smiled broadly, Major Cohn popped to his feet and said, "However, Colonel Broughton challenges General Pitts peremptorily."

General Pitts looked surprised, even shocked, and started to struggle to his feet, trying to figure out what to do and where to go. As Pitts rose, my lawyer sat and Major Stewart bounced up and said, "Major Ferguson challenges Colonel Harris peremptorily."

Before they could recover their cool, Major Jicha did one thing right when he said, "Major Tolman challenges Colonel Shumate peremptorily."

When the challenged court members found their way out, there was a gaping hole in the middle of the court. Another round of musical chairs followed, and we wound up with Chuck Yeager sitting in the center as president, surrounded by Walt Brown, who commanded the 432nd TAC Recce wing flying RF-4s out of Udorn; Jules Junker, who ran the combat support group on Taiwan; Hugh Boyd, a headquarters aircraft maintenance type from Clark; and Heinie Aderholt, commander of the 56th Air Commando wing, the Spad guys who hurled themselves at the ground in Laos, at night. I knew them all fairly well, but make no mistake, for the next two days those colonels and this colonel were on opposite sides of a formidable and frightening line.

The prosecution led off and it was dull. The entire thing was nothing more than a rerun of the pretrial investigation. Jim Markey looked at the same piece of paper again and said that it meant Ted and Lonnie had been on the flying schedule that day. Then Ed Miller came on again, but this time he livened things up a bit. There is a rule in the court-martial book that says a form or a record can't be introduced into a court case if it is not a standard form that is required by some official regulation. Ed was an old guardhouse lawyer, and he knew that the piece of paper they were going to hand him was not a standard form. He had known it back at Takhli when Harston had handed it to him during the pretrial investigation. He had not made a move then because he knew the prosecution could manage to get the same information, which did nothing more than indicate the aircraft had less ammunition after the mission than they had before the mission, transferred to some sort of standard form that would be acceptable to the court.

When Ed took the stand, they handed him the sheet of paper and asked him if he recognized it. Ed just sat there for at least a minute with his head down, looking at the paper in front of him. Then he slyly cocked his head, taking in Harston and the court in the same glance, and said, "Oh, yes, I recognize this paper. It's the special piece of paper that I prepared for General Ryan for his personal investigation."

Harston screamed. "Objection, objection," and the law member advised Ed against making improper responses. Improper, hell. It was just the truth, and once said it could not be changed. When Harston ground to a halt we simply challenged the admissibility of the paper as a nonstandard form and the court agreed and refused to accept it. What was on the paper didn't mean beans, but Ed had done a nice job of compressing the whole stupid mess into one clear little picture. As he stepped down and left the room he and I exchanged a quick wink and thumbs-up signals.

The dull morning ground to a halt for a lunch break, and we went to the club's open-air snack bar. That was a mistake.

I was soaked in frustration at the slowness and the smallness of the prosecution's effort, and my frustration doubled as I tried to eat a less than good sandwich on a hot, sticky patio under constant attack by droves of big black flies.

When we returned after the lunch break, Paul Sheehy was finally called after a month of waiting. He said just what he had said before—nothing. We had a short break after he appeared, and I collared Benson in the hall and asked him if he had made any arrangements to get Paul a flight back to the States. He had not, but Paul was able to catch a ride out of there that night on his own.

Though General Lindley was supposed to be the star witness for the prosecution, his testimony went over very poorly. They brought out the statement I had made to him at the operational investigation, and he identified it. Then they introduced only parts of the statements that Ted and Lonnie had made during the operational investigation. Both our counsel and the court members, Chuck Yeager in particular, ate Lindley up on the fact that he was introducing only edited versions of what Ted and Lonnie had said. Lindley, overimpressed with himself, did not take kindly to being questioned about this. He made the mistake of playing Ryan's big man with the court, and they, with Chuck doing their talking, cut his buttons off and left him standing naked.

It was about three in the afternoon when the prosecution rested. The court took a ten-minute break, and I thought we would then get rolling and finish up the trial that afternoon. Not so. The law member had not done his homework on a few legal points that he was required to discuss with all of us, so the court recessed until the next morning.

We huddled at Jerry's house and reconfirmed our plan. The prosecution had produced nothing that would indicate a requirement for testimony on our part. When the court reopened, Jerry would simply make a short statement, Major Stewart would say nothing for Lonnie, and Jicha would keep quiet regarding Ted. But Ted and Jicha were not there. Still, if I could keep Jicha from giving Ted any more bad advice for another day, it would be over.

Since our assigned counsel were basically a part of Benson's tribe, we usually had pretty good info on what Morrie was up to. We were a bit disturbed that he was still stumbling around, poking his nose into everything. Their office had told our counsel that Morrie had sent a long, personal message to Ryan right after we recessed for the day, covering the day's actions in great detail. Benson had also told his helpers that he would need a complete written rundown of the case by the following Tuesday, since he had an appointment to brief Ryan on the outcome personally.

When we arrived in court the next morning I was most disturbed. Jicha had Ted all shaken up again and was doing his utmost to louse up the works. We gathered in the hallway outside the courtroom, and Jicha said he wanted to put Ted on the stand. That would have been the most stupid move possible. By taking the stand he would open himself to questioning, and Ted could deny nothing. He could well become more deeply involved, and stood a good chance of alienating the court by getting up and telling them what a combat hero he was. Ted had only been able to keep his cool for one day. He seemed to be confused again, and he made little sense even talking to us, to say nothing of what he might do on the stand. I just plain shouted Jicha down.

Then Jicha wanted me to take the stand. I said, "Are you nuts? What the hell do I want to take the stand for? They already have my statement from Lindley's investigation, and if they hang me with anything, it will be that statement. I explained my position at the start of this thing and that position stands. I'm taking care of Ted, so just shut up and let me carry the load."

Reopening the court was laborious, but Jerry finally got to stand up and speak for us. He made a concise statement to the effect that as their commander I took full responsibility for the action of my men in combat. He added that the prosecution had failed to prove that the film in question had not been previously damaged, had failed to prove that there was anything on the film to hide, and had failed to prove that Lonnie had even been there. He argued that their entire case was characterized by a general lack of substantive evidence. Stewart waived argument on Lonnie's behalf.

Jicha had one more chance, and he did his best to screw it up. He tried to make a closing argument for Ted, which was both unnecessary and undesirable. He demonstrated again that neither he nor Ted truly understood what they were involved in as he started through a tedious repetition of facts. Harston did his one good turn for us at that point and challenged the argument as not an argument but a mere recital of facts. Mercifully, the objection was sustained and that destroyed Jicha. He just slumped down and faded, and I breathed a sigh of relief that he was out of the picture.

The prosecution presented a closing argument that lost Harston some more points. Without any combat or flying experience himself, he referred to "stupid actions by fighter pilots," and I would have punched him in the nose if he had said it to me on the street. I glanced quickly at the court officers, three of whom were fighter pilots, and noted the same reaction in their eyes. Harston tried to gloss it over but failed miserably and sat down. That was it. It was over and we went out into the hall to sweat it out.

We waited for the rest of the day before we got the final word. We had to wait in the hallway outside the auditorium in an area that served as an entrance and a lobby for the people who lived there. There was an elevator against one wall, and a few chairs and benches scattered around the room. I found it impossible to sit and spent most of my time pacing the room and the adjacent hallways. We would gather in little groups and talk about most anything for a few minutes, then disband to pace some more. The people who lived there moved in and out, some in uniform and some in casual clothes. They opened the court for a few minutes to ask the law member a question, then closed up again. Then they opened so they could close for lunch, and we paced some more. The more I watched the flow of people up and down that elevator, the more I realized how little those people knew or cared about the war over Hanoi, or us, or the court-martial.

Finally they opened for business. As I walked toward the benches, that lonely little clock sitting on that huge blank wall said two minutes until two. Ted and Lonnie were found not guilty on all the charges against them. They were excused from the court; they could go where they wished. The *Turkestan* incident was over for them and they could never be tried again, and it would never appear on their records. I had protected my comrades.

They found me not guilty of the first two charges, but guilty of the last two. However, all references to "intent to deceive" had been removed from the last charge. In plain words, they found me guilty of destroying $42.50 worth of government property in that I had stripped and exposed the film and not processed it in a standard manner. Hell, I had admitted that to Ryan many long weeks ago.

Everybody on my side of the long court table left except Jerry, the Judge, and me. I was now in the position where I could legally call for a delay, and call people in from wherever I chose to testify as to what a good sport I was. I could also submit written documents stating the same thing. When I had submitted what I wished, the court would close and come up with a sentence. Calling people in from all over the world was obviously not the answer, primarily because those on the other side of the table already knew who I was. I had three good letters from three stalwarts that I submitted. Actually I had been called and told that several more had arrived at Takhli five days ago. They had been dispatched by courier, care of Morrie Benson, so that I could use them as required. I never got those letters from Morrie.

The court accepted my letters and closed to determine my sentence. As I turned and started down that long center aisle again, I popped my chest up as high as I could and strode along like I really meant it, with my heels cracking off that terrazzo floor as hard as I could make them crack. The air policemen who had been guarding the inside of that big double door had been slouching around for two days. I must have impressed them as I came pounding down the aisle, because they popped to rigid attention as I approached and passed them. It was the only time in two days that I saw them look alive.

The entire tribe was waiting, and Ted and Lonnie were congratulated on their verdict and I was consoled on mine. I wasted no effort accepting sympathy. I went out of my way throughout the rest of the afternoon to goad both Ted and Jicha about how fortunate they were that I had carried them through the whole thing on my coattails, and how stupid they would have been to go their own way. I doubt that I made any impression on either one of them. Ted never understood what was going on. He never understood the charges. He never understood the factors boiling under the surface.

After another terrible wait, the court called and I tromped down that aisle again. I walked to the center of the court table and saluted Chuck as he said, "Colonel Jacksel M. Broughton," and I mentally said, "That's me," as I looked up to see the round clock telling me it was twelve minutes after four. I felt a strange affinity toward that little clock, as if the two of us were the only real things in the room. The rest of what was going on didn't mean all that much.

Chuck was talking to me. "It is my duty to inform you that you will be fined one hundred dollars a month for six months and admonished."

I saluted again and returned to our little table as Chuck was going through the routine about "there being no further business, this court is dismissed." The court filed out and Jerry, the Judge, and I picked up our papers and left.

Everyone was waiting outside the big doors and I gave them the word on the outcome. Lonnie immediately came up with a handshake and a thanks for carrying the load and wanted to split the fine with me. I declined with appreciation. I never even got a thank you from Ted. But then, I don't remember if I ever thanked him on either of the two occasions when he saved my life way up there in Pack Six.

13 | MOVING ON

Once the trial was over I wanted to contact Ingelido and see what our status was. I wanted to get Ted and Lonnie back into the flying business, and I wanted to fly three more missions myself, just to make it 105 in the F-105. My desire was strictly a personal one, but Ted and Lonnie were in a different boat. If they did not get back up there in the air where they belonged, the personnel weenies would expect them to be put in some ground job and to sit there doing nothing for a year. Ingelido was off station until the next afternoon, so it was more waiting.

I told Ted and Lonnie to stand fast and keep in touch. Then I called AJ in Hawaii and gave her the word on the trial. I still couldn't tell her when I would be there, but it would be soon. She advised me that Charlie Blair was in Honolulu and had called three times that day to see if she had heard anything. Charlie, in his reserve general role, had made an appointment with General Ryan and was going to both probe and express his views. I told her to call Charlie and give him the outcome; tell him thanks, express my gratitude for his help, but not to bother to embarrass himself with a visit to

Ryan. The trial and the outcome were history. The course for appeal lay in Washington, and I would give it a try.

I needed to get over to Jerry Cohn's house, where he was waiting to prepare our brief. This was simply a short statement that we were required to file the next day if we did not agree with the trial results. Naturally we would file it; but since it went to Benson for review, naturally he would disapprove it. It was all such a farce, but filing the brief was a required step in the game of appealing the verdict.

As Jerry and I roughed out what we wanted to say and he agreed to have it ready for my signature in the morning, Chuck Yeager came by looking for me. Since the trial was in the past, Chuck and I could now talk to each other and be seen together in public again. I often thought back to that scene by the club cashier's cage with Lindley, the chief prosecution witness, and Pitts, the supposedly unbiased head judge, off on the town the night before the trial. Obviously they had a different interpretation of the code of military justice than Chuck and I did.

Chuck was on his way out to a place called Tony's Island for a few hours, and he thought that I might want to get away for some fresh air. It sounded great to me, and we jumped in his car and blasted off, leaving the mess behind. Tony had a great house that was located in the middle of a lake. When you threaded your way through the jungle and arrived on the shoreline opposite his house, he sent a boat after you if he wanted to have you on board. We propped our feet up on his porch and sipped a cool drink as we watched him fly his radio-controlled model seaplane around the house and shoot landings and takeoffs on the lake. Tony kept telling me that Chuck came lower than the model airplane when he buzzed the house as he returned from each of his flights out of Clark. It was the break I needed. Before long one of Tony's neat-looking girlfriends arrived in the boat, and Chuck and I headed back for shore. We drove back to Chuck's house and had a really good dinner, the first time food had appealed to me since Chuck had fed me lunch earlier in the week. We were both pooped, as the trial had not been easy for either of us.

The next day I went to Jerry Cohn's office and signed the legal brief. We both knew it was a waste of time. I found out that Scott was due back from Australia that afternoon, with Ingelido due to return about thirty minutes later, so I figured I would meet them both and get all the details thrashed out at once. I also hoped to get some feedback on Ryan's reactions to the trial. I knew he was looking for dishonorable discharges with big fines and sentences for the three of us. Two not-guilty verdicts along with my minor sentence were bound to drive his blood pressure upward. He certainly knew that I could hack the six hundred dollar fine, and the admonishment was simply an opportunity for Benson to tack a few nasty sentences onto the tail end of the court-martial order.

Scott and I met Ingelido when he arrived, and so did Morrie Benson. Morrie had to brief his boss on all the good things he had done. We got Ryan's reaction. He was furious and he wanted me out of his ocean as rapidly as possible. The answer was clear: I could not fly three more missions, and I was to pack my bags and leave the banana and coconut air force behind with the utmost dispatch. There was no sense asking further questions, and I accepted the edict. Scott then asked permission to get Ted and Lonnie going on their missions again, and he almost didn't get it. There on the flight line at Clark, for a few minutes it looked like those two dedicated fighter pilots were doomed to a worthless year as nonflyers. Scott talked pilot shortage and the lack of qualified flight leaders, and I talked the moral principles of further punishment after a not guilty verdict. We prevailed by the skin of our teeth, and they were back in the air the next week. I couldn't believe it when, after all of that, Ingelido asked Scott and me to come over to his house for a drink. I went— just because. Benson even offered me one of his favorite cigars. I took it just to see what kind of crap he smoked and it was horrible. I took a couple of puffs and threw it away.

Ryan was so anxious to get rid of me that early the next morning, without me even having to ask, we had one of the plush little Sabreliners to take us back to Takhli. While we fretted around base operations awaiting takeoff, I got a call from General Lindley. His message was that Ryan says to get out of town. I thanked him politely and said that I had already received that message from his boss. Moments later I received a call from the officer running personnel for Thirteenth. He had been advised to tell me that General Ryan wanted me to leave. I repeated my acknowledgment. The first thing that greeted me when I stepped off the aircraft at Takhli was a message to get out of town. I needed no further urging.

I got my administrative noncoms together and sent them scurrying to get airline reservations for me out of Bangkok, to gather my records and papers, and to get my luggage packed. By midafternoon we had a C-47 to take me to Bangkok early the next morning, where I could catch a Pan Am flight to Tokyo, spend the day buying some gifts for the family, then fly on to Honolulu to join AJ and the kids. As I was finishing loading my suitcases I got a call from Scott, who had received a call from some sergeant in Lindley's office. The sergeant had said that there would be a C-47 going through Takhli the next morning, and that he was to order me to board it and ride on the steaming hot, twelve-hour carrier run that stopped at every base between Takhli and Saigon. The sergeant further informed Scott that upon arrival in Saigon I was to sit in the smelly MATS terminal on a wooden bench until 4:00 A.M., when I could catch a ride in the back end of a C-141 cargo aircraft going back to Hawaii. I told Scott that I did not care for that plan, so he called Udorn for Lindley, but could get no higher than a Colonel Berger, Lindley's newly arrived deputy. When he explained that I had made other arrangements, Berger said that such a complex problem was above his decision-making level, and since the general had told Scott to put me on that gooney bird, Scott must order me to be on it.

I rode that crate all the next day and dragged into Saigon about eight that evening. I sat in that dump until four in the morning when the flight finally left for Hawaii. Every time I started getting bitter, I thought how much more fortunate I was than many others who had risked all to do the job properly over Hanoi. Hundreds of them had been shot down by the enemy, and those who had lived were in hell on earth. I had been shot down by our own people, but I was on my way to freedom.

I had fought the system for my guys and won, but the system and I had little further use for each other. I stayed on long enough to go back to Washington and request a hearing by the Board for the Correction of Military Records. Getting the hearing arranged was a time-consuming process and I fretted over the delay. I felt no further obligation to the system that chose to scorn my contributions. I had paid my dues, led more than my share, and I wanted out. I filled out all my retirement papers, except for the date and the signature, which would come as soon as the review board acted. Then I scrounged a flight to Nellis Air Force Base, where my old friend John Black was running the flying business. He got me a Thud to do with as I wished for a day and I put the time to good use. I got in three good rides to the gunnery range and I about tore my guts out doing everything that the Thud could do. Then I returned to Washington to await the appeal decision.

Historically, only Congress has had the power to set aside the verdict of military courts. But as the size of the military establishment had increased, Congress had delegated that power to the secretary of defense and in turn to each of the service secretaries. Thus my hearing was before a board of the highest-ranking civilian members of the office of the secretary of the air force. They threw the court's judgment out and expunged it from the records. I found it interesting that in the entire history of the United States flying forces, only one other officer had ever had a general court-martial set aside and voided. His name was Billy Mitchell.

INDEX